W9-COS-558

Capitalism in Contention examines the ideas of British business leaders on political, economic and social issues since 1960. Utilising unexplored records, extensive interviews and biographical, narrative and conceptual approaches, it sheds new light on the Wilson, Heath and Thatcher periods from business points of view, on the 'mixed economy' and the 'New Right', the peak business bodies, and business-government relationships. Although the business ideas were often muffled or secreted, they made distinctive contributions to both public policy and thinking about 'capitalism'. Elite business opinion was largely divided into three ideological tendencies, 'revisionism'. 'liberationism' and 'reconstructionism'. These saw business respectively as adaptive partner in a pluralist system, pivot and liberator of economy and society, and focus of social reconstruction, and their struggle for influence forms a central theme. This book will be of interest to students of politics, modern history and business, and to policy makers as well as concerned citizens.

Capitalism in contention

Capitalism in Contention

Business leaders and political economy in modern Britain

Jonathan Boswell

Von Hügel Institute, St Edmund's College, Cambridge

and

James Peters

CAMBRIDGE
UNIVERSITY PRESS

PUBLISHED BY THE PRESS SYNDICATE OF THE UNIVERSITY OF CAMBRIDGE
The Pitt Building, Trumpington Street, Cambridge CB2 1RP, United Kingdom

CAMBRIDGE UNIVERSITY PRESS
The Edinburgh Building, Cambridge CB2 2RU, United Kingdom
40 West 20th Street, New York, NY 10011–4211, USA
10 Stamford Road, Oakleigh, Melbourne 3166, Australia

© Jonathan Boswell and James Peters 1997

First published 1997

Printed in the United Kingdom at the University Press, Cambridge

Typeset in Plantin 10/12 pt

A catalogue record for this book is available from the British Library

Library of Congress cataloguing in publication data

Boswell, Jonathan
    Capitalism in contention/Jonathan Boswell and James Peters.
        (p.   cm.
    Includes bibliographical references and index
    ISBN 0 521 58225 3 (hc). – ISBN 0 521 58804 9 (pbk.)
    1. Great Britain – Economic policy – 1945–   2. Great Britain – Economic
condition – 20th century.   3. Great Britain – Social policy.   4. Capitalism –
Great Britain – History – 20th century.   5. Mixed economy – Great Britain –
History – 20th century.   6. Business and politics – Great Britain – History –
20th century.   I. Peters, James.   II. Title
HC256.5.858   1997
338.941'009'045–dc21   97–8959   CIP

ISBN 0 521 58225 3 hardback
ISBN 0 521 58804 9 paperback

CP

Contents

Acknowledgements

This book grew out of a research project into 'The ideas of British business leaders on political economy and society since 1960', supported by the Leverhulme Trust. We express appreciation for the generous funding provided by the Trust between 1992 and 1995. We are also grateful to the then Master of St Edmund's College, Cambridge, Dr Richard Laws, and its Fellows, and to the Von Hügel Institute within the College, for sponsoring the project and providing material assistance.

Three organisations gave critical support to the archival work. The CBI were most helpful in relation to their important archives at the Modern Records Centre, University of Warwick, including records of their predecessor bodies, the FBI, BEC and NABM. The Institute of Management provided access to files of their predecessor, the BIM. The Institute of Directors similarly consented to examination of their records up to 1985–86. All three organisations were extremely co-operative and understanding over the use made of their records in this book, though of course we take full responsibility for the judgements expressed.

The following kindly gave permission to consult important archival or other unpublished materials: Sir Maurice Laing, Sir Stephen Brown, Sir Gerry Norman and Sir Michael Clapham (all in connection with CBI presidential papers for periods up to 1974); David and James Partridge (CBI presidential papers and speeches of Sir John Partridge); Peter Askonas (files relating to the Christian Association of Business Executives); Mark Boleat (papers relating to the Industrial Policy Group); Lady Brown and Angus Brown (personal papers of Lord Wilfred Brown); the Master and Fellows of Churchill College, Cambridge (Chandos papers); Rt Hon Aubrey Jones (Aubrey Jones papers, also at Churchill College); Sir Arthur Knight; Sir Donald MacDougall (extensive personal papers); the National Life Story Collection (City Lives); Sir Richard O' Brien; the Warden of St George's House, Windsor; Kenneth Adams (papers on relevant Consultations); and Lady (José) Villiers (papers of Sir Charles Villiers).

A large number of individuals agreed to be interviewed, sometimes more than once, for the study. These interviews, based on the previously examined 'record', were conducted by Jonathan Boswell and mostly took place in 1994–96. A list of those involved follows this preface. Their reminiscences, observations and comments contributed in many vital ways to the project as well as helping to make it enjoyable, and were deeply appreciated.

Among those who kindly provided relevant speech or published material were Lady (Edith) Chambers; Sir Reay Geddes; Lady (Sonja) MacFadzean; Giles Heron; Michael Ivens; Sir Maurice Laing; Sir Jeremy Morse; Sir Peter Parker; Denys Randolph; Lord (Nigel) Vinson; Lady (Constance) Weeks; John Whitehorn; and Sir Norman Wooding. We are also grateful to the following for assistance over sources or particular aspects at various times: Christopher Beauman; Edward Brech; George Bull; Gerald Frost; Stephen Frowen; Geoffrey Goodman; Edwin Green; Jack Hyde; David Jeremy; Michael Knight; Sir Geoffrey Owen; Alan Peters; Michael Phelan; John Staddon; Richard Storey and his staff at the Modern Records Centre, University of Warwick; and Alan Swinden.

Lucia Capogna and David Boswell came to our help over some computer problems. Stimulus came from discussions with friends in the History Faculty and elsewhere in Cambridge, contacts with the University of Leuven, and a seminar at the Judge Institute of Management Studies, Cambridge, in May 1995.

The writing of the book has benefited from conversations with many people. Thanks are due to George Bull, Sophie Boswell and Julia Gallagher for helpful comments on sections of the draft text. We express gratitude to Colin Crouch for generously commenting on a complete advanced draft at a time of great pressure. Throughout the project a special role was played by Frank McHugh, Director of the Von Hügel Institute. His comments and general assistance deserve our warm gratitude. Finally, we should like to thank Cambridge University Press for much academic and logistical support, and particularly our very helpful editor, John Haslam.

None of these organisations or people can be held accountable in any way for the book's argument and approach, let alone for any imperfections or errors, for all of which we take full responsibility.

JONATHAN BOSWELL
JAMES PETERS

Interview respondents

Kenneth Adams
Sir Campbell Adamson
Sir David Barran
Sir Terence Beckett
Lord (Henry) Benson
Sir Austen Bide
Barry Bracewell-Milnes
Sir Nigel Broackes
Sir Stephen Brown
Sir Adrian Cadbury
Lord Caldecote
Sir Fred Catherwood
Sir Michael Clapham
Roy Close
Sir Kenneth Corfield
Alan Davies
Edmund Dell
Sir Michael Edwardes
Lord Erroll
Lord Ezra
Sir Campbell Fraser
John Garnett
Sir Reay Geddes
Walter Goldsmith

George Goyder
Lord (John) Gregson
Lord Harris of High Cross
Jan Hildreth
Sir John Hoskyns
Michael Ivens
Sir Alex Jarratt
Rt Hon Aubrey Jones
Sir Arthur Knight
Lord (Hector) Laing
Sir Donald MacDougall
Grigor McClelland
Lord (Richard) Marsh
Sir Jeremy Morse
Sir Gerry Norman
Sir Richard O'Brien
Sir Peter Parker
Lord Plowden
Denys Randolph
Sir Peter Thompson
Lord (Nigel) Vinson
Sir Peter Walters
Lord Watkinson
John Whitehorn

Abbreviations

ABCC	Association of British Chambers of Commerce
AEA	Atomic Energy Authority
AEI	Amalgamated Electrical Engineering
AOI	Aims of Industry
ASI	Adam Smith Institute
BEC	British Employer's Confederation
BICC	British Insulated Callender Cable
BIM	British Institute of Management
BISF	British Iron and Steel Federation
BMC	British Motor Corporation
BP	British Petroleum
BR	British Rail
BSC	British Steel Corporation
CABE	Christian Association of Business Executives
CAC	Company Affairs Committee (CBI)
CBI	Confederation of British Industry
CBI PAC	CBI President's Committee
CBI SFC	CBI Smaller Firms Council
CE	Chief executive
CEPT	Committee for Economic Planning and Targets (FBI)
Ch. C.	Chamber of Commerce
CIR	Commission for Industrial Relations
Cl	Council
CPS	Centre for Policy Studies
cr.	Date of elevation to peerage
DEA	Department of Economic Affairs
DEP	Department of Employment and Productivity
DG	Director General
DTI	Department of Trade and Industry
EC	Executive Committee
EcC	Economic Committee
EcPolC	Economic Policy Committee

EDCs	Economic Development Committees (Little Neddies)
EEF	Engineering Employers' Federation
EIU	Economist Intelligence Unit
EPC	Employment Policy Committee (CBI)
ESC	Economic and Social Affairs Committee (BIM)
FBI	Federation of British Industry
FBI PAC	FBI President's Committee
FinPolC	Financial Policy Committee (CBI)
GPC	General Purposes Committee
HOL debs	House of Lords debates
IBE	Institute of Business Ethics
ICI	Imperial Chemical Industries
IEA	Institute of Economic Affairs
Imp. Grp	Imperial Group
Ind. Soc.	Industrial Society
IOD	Institute of Directors
IPG	Industrial Policy Group
IRC	Industrial Reorganisation Corporation
IWS	Industrial Welfare Society
LSAC	Labour and Social Affairs Committee (CBI)
MSC	Manpower Services Commission
MT	Management Today
NABM	National Association of British Manufacturers
NBPI	National Board for Prices and Incomes
NCB	National Coal Board
NEB	National Enterprise Board
NEDC	National Economic Development Council
NEDO	National Economic Development Organisation
NEDs	Non-executive directors
NIESR	National Institute for Economic and Social Research
PEC	Policy and Executive Committee (IOD)
PIP	Prices and Incomes Policy
PP	Presidential papers (FBI, CBI)
Pres.	President
Reg. Cls	Regional Councils (CBI)
RHA	Road Haulage Association
RPD	Reform of pay determination
RSA	Royal Society of Arts
RTB	Richard Thomas and Baldwins
SEC	Securities and Exchange Commission
SFC	Smaller Firms Council (CBI)
SGW	St George's House, Windsor

SMMT	Society of Motor Manufacturers and Traders
TGWU	Transport and General Workers' Union
TI	Tube Investments
TUC	Trades Union Congress

1   Business social ideas in the making

By the 1950s Britain could claim the longest record of experience of 'capitalism' in the Western world. Having largely pioneered the earlier mutations, she had now switched to the status of a 'mixed economy'. This could be regarded as an example either of the British 'genius for compromise' or of 'muddling through'. It could be greeted as a stepping stone to a more humane system, or by others deplored as semi-socialism or rampant statism. Britain's 'mixed economy' appeared to be well entrenched and aided by a broad political consensus. What no one could have predicted was that from about 1960 onwards further massive changes in the system would occur with accelerating speed. A situation which had been widely lamented as 'stagnant' or 'complacent' in the late 1950s would give way to extreme volatility, with Britain's political economy going through dramatic mutations.

The 1960s witnessed intensified efforts to make the 'mixed economy' work through 'planning', industrial strategy, diverse state interventions, prices and incomes policy. The post-war 'middle way' remained the inspiration for variations on a familiar theme. The 1970s, by contrast, would prove a decade of turmoil and disillusion. The 'middle way' appeared to crumble under the weight of stagflation, international pressures, political polarisation, industrial disputes. A bewildering series of 'U-turns' would emerge as successive governments switched from mild disengagement to an intensified *dirigisme* by 1972–74; then from left-wing experiments back to a war-weary centrism by 1977–79. Then came the biggest change. The 1980s brought the initiation of a purer 'market' model. 'Thatcherism' involved a decisive ending of efforts merely to revise or update the post-war settlement. Once again Britain became a cauldron of experiment, but this time for free market capitalism and the 'New Right.'

Throughout the period from the 1960s to the 1990s there was intensifying debate on Britain's lagging economic performance, while perennial controversy about the rights and wrongs of 'capitalism' as a socio-economic system persisted. Keynes and Beveridge had bequeathed

1

a concept of benign compromise, of a system still market-based but subtly co-ordinated to ensure high employment and greater security. Revisionist socialists such as Anthony Crosland thought such a system compatible with increased equality and expanding social services. According to some observers, the 'mixed economy' was the mode towards which advanced systems were converging, anyway. What mattered was to improve it, whether by increasing its 'public' elements (J. K. Galbraith), raising its moral standards (J. M. Clark), reforming its industrial relations (Henry Phelps Brown) or strengthening the ability of its key elements, government, civil service, business, labour, to co-operate intelligently, a field where Britain also appeared to be lagging (Andrew Shonfield).

Many others, however, rejected the 'mixed economy'. They included traditionalist socialists, a new wave of 'small is beautiful', 'green' or 'post-industrial' exponents, and, not least, believers in a purer 'market' model. To the latter the 'mixed economy' was at best a flabby, inefficient compromise, at worst a slippery path to central socialism or even 'serfdom'. By the 1980s and 1990s their views would be riding high. A more free market 'capitalism' appeared to be gaining global ascendancy.

The starting-point of this book can be simply stated. Neither the successive policy phases nor the controversies about 'capitalism' can be fully understood without reference to the roles and attitudes of the business class, in particular the top controllers of industry, distribution and finance, and the leaders of organised business. Just as business elites had played key roles earlier in the upsurge of innovation, trade and empire, and in the long and still continuing decline of British economic power, so they would become leading actors in the sagas of 'tripartism', industrial relations and a semi-negotiated economy, and later in those of monetarism, privatisation, deregulation and 'Thatcherism'. In discussions about economic performance and 'capitalism', too, their strengths or weaknesses would continue to hold centre stage. It had been thus during the earlier controversies about the 'capitalist' as hero or exploiter, the 'entrepreneur' as pioneer or source of decline, the corporate manager as rational planner or focus of anti-social power. Now competing theories would picture business interests as potential 'social partners', agents of spoliation or materialism, victims of state imposition, or catalysts of renaissance in revived competitive markets.

But despite the continuing importance of the business elites their ideas on public issues, political economy and society have received no specific attention. Their social opinions and concepts have been almost wholly neglected. No doubt, this reflects conventional theories of political economy and lack of cultural esteem as well as under-articulation. The limelight has nearly always been taken by politicians, media commentators or public affairs pundits. Our historical perceptions have similarly been dominated by memoirs, studies or stereotypes from non-business sources even when, as so often, sweeping models of 'business' itself have been employed. Even our thoughts about 'capitalism' have remained virtually untouched by the 'inside' views of the 'capitalists' themselves.

An articulate elite and its social ideas

This book grew out of a long-term study into the social ideas of business leaders since 1960. Our aim was to illuminate some dark corners and to contribute to both theory and policy thinking. Our main focus would be on the nature, sources and development of business *ideas*. Issues of business *influence* on policy or public opinion would be relevant to this but more tenuous and harder to discern, particularly for such a recent period. 'Business leaders' we defined as chairmen or chief executives of the largest enterprises, top people in the 'peak' representative business bodies, and national opinion leaders within other parts of the business community. 'Social ideas' would relate to economic performance, policy and organisation, and to politics, society, socio-ethical values.

We investigated a wide variety of sources, first in the public domain: memoirs, articles or published lectures, management journals, press reports, speeches in public forums, official statements by national business agencies. We undertook a pioneering examination of the internal records of the chief 'peak' organisations of business, relating to their main committees, governing bodies and leading people, and their discussions with government or other bodies (chiefly the Confederation of British Industry, its predecessor bodies, the British Institute of Management, and the Institute of Directors). In many cases interviews provided additional insights into people's underlying assumptions or visions, the sources of their ideas, their recollections of key incidents and personalities, and how things felt at the time.

Our work soon focussed on some 170 articulate business leaders: mostly company chiefs, who constituted about 25 per cent of the total number of heads of the largest enterprises during the period. However, our main concentration was on a core sample of 68 who made particularly substantial, varied and sustained contributions. Most of these, too, were heads of large concerns (rather less than 10 per cent of the total); some were leading officials of the peak business bodies; some achieved high profiles through sheer impact of personality and belief. Many were, or still are, familiar names, often because of their business prowess: many others deserve to be better known. The articulators generally were not necessarily representative of the whole business elite. The proportion with university backgrounds was probably rather above average; predictably, too, the numbers engaged in other forms of public activity. Financial interests were under-represented: so, more markedly, were small firms and founder-entrepreneurs. No doubt the articulate business leaders also stood out from their peers in more qualitative ways. In varying mixtures, their attributes of public concern, opinionatedness, political ambition or sheer eloquence would have been particularly marked. Their claim on our attention is as influences on business opinion, exponents of leading view-points, and contributors to both public policy thinking and social ideas.[1]

The articulate business leaders had come to public issues in diverse ways. Some confessed to lifelong interests in public affairs, economics or politics: for most such interests developed in mid- or late career. Influences going back to family, school or early formation were nearly always cited: childhood lessons about right and wrong, teachers or books, formative exposures to social conditions. Other contributory influences included corporate traditions or role models, overseas visits or postings, periods of work outside business, work in trade or industry bodies. Sometimes arrival in a leading role at the top of the CBI or another key organisation marked the entry point, occasionally a career move or sec-ondment into a semi-public role. For the large majority there was a dis-tinct widening of interests from pure business: often this signalled some perception of collective business imperatives, national crisis or social needs.

A choice had to be made in our approach to the material. Economists, sociologists or political theorists would tend to start out from familiar conceptual frameworks or models of business, as would historians influ-enced by their assumptions. However, we decided against organising the material along such lines. To do so might be unfair to the data we needed to uncover, particularly through unexplored archives. It might unfairly cramp the business voices in 'speaking for themselves'. It might also have the effect of prejudging business social ideas in certain ways, for example as fragmented, reactive or derivative. Instead, we thought it preferable to scour the ideas for distinctive patterns or trends. This would mean following through the views of particular individuals, groups or peak bodies over long periods. It would involve examination of under- or half-statements, looking beyond professions of pragmatic 'anti-dogma', teas-ing out value positions from imagery, metaphor, citation, personal narra-tive. There would, however, be no question of pure 'empiricism' since we had some central hypotheses as to categories, typologies or trends (see below).

Three highly influential stereotypes continue to overshadow this field. All of them draw strong support from mainstream economic theories of markets, competition and 'the firm'; also from interest group theory and classical liberal or pluralist ideas of politics. They underlie the scepticism we met among many academic colleagues as to the viability of this project. It is a striking feature that the stereotypes should be shared by people of widely varying ideological persuasion: by free market enthusiasts zealous to portray business in their own image as well as by 'anti-modern' disdainers of business, or by left-wing, 'green' or 'post-capitalist' critics.

First comes the common conception that business leaders are allergic to public policy thinking, uninterested in social ideas, or at least so absorbed in running the firm that they have little opportunity for anything else. Secondly, it is widely thought that business people's views on public affairs are likely to be mere reflections of corporate or commercial self-interest, or, in some versions, 'profit maximising', 'special interest lobbying', 'class interest' or 'pursuits of power.' On these grounds some would see them as impertinent or intrusive, an abuse of economic power, an arrogation of tasks appropriate only to elected or constitutional authorities. Third comes the related view that any pattern of business ideas is likely to be homogeneous, perhaps even a single 'business ideology', and predictable in content.[2]

Our inclination was to question all three stereotypes. The thesis of economic obsession or public uninterest might be undermined if a significant minority of business leaders were found to have made serious, sustained contributions to civic discussion. The theories of 'self interest' appeared to us as reductionist and likely to be empirically sterile, perhaps even circular, given their initial definitions or preconceptions. Our view was that while corporate, class or managerial interests would often conflict with those of other groups or with public interests, such conflicts were not inevitable. This was not to see business leaders or their representative bodies as necessarily idealistic or altruistic. Rather, it was a question of trying to do justice to the complexity of human motivations: the intellectual or aesthetic attractions of larger ideas, the lure of public affairs, the desire for honours and repute, perhaps the phenomenon of 'shifting involvements' from private to public concerns at points in individuals' life cycles.[3] There was also a possibility that large representative organisations of business might be able to transcend crude sectionalism to some degree, through 'encompassing' a wide range of interests.[4] As for the stereotype of a convergent, predictable business 'ideology', this we viewed as the most suspect of all, even though we were aware that to pursue a contrary hypothesis, of multiple, competing business ideologies, would entail some risks.

How far would the business social ideas be *distinctive*? On the one hand, they were unlikely to be purely derivative, taken 'off the peg', or selected from the offerings of economists, politicians or social theorists. This would discount the role of relevant social concepts within the business community; also the likely influence of people's working experience. The opposite thesis, of complete autonomy, would be equally, if not more absurd. More plausible was the idea that 'imports' from outside, whether of isolated ideas or full-blown ideologies, would be 'processed' or 'treated' in various ways. For example, the business leaders might tone down or moderate doctrines perceived as 'unrealistic' in business terms or 'too extreme'. They might make distinctive additions to the 'imports', applying them to business systems and cultures in greater depth, perhaps emphasising a continued or changed role for business in relation to future or ideal states.

Could the business social ideas meet demanding requirements of *content or substance*, as a condition for qualifying as 'ideology'? In this respect they would need to cover interpretations of business's place in the economy and its relationships with other interests, government and society. Such understandings would be part-historical, part-contemporary, part-predictive. They would include some sort of model of Britain's economic predicament, its historic sources, current attributes and possible remedies. Included would be concepts of virtue, the 'good life', the 'good society'; varying degrees of priority to the most widely discussed social values in civic debate (change *versus* continuity, freedom, democracy, equality, justice, community, solidarity, prosperity); relative preferences in political economy as between competition, direction and co-operation. There would be prescriptions for desirable change, notions of ideal states; also ideas for methods and instruments. On certain definitions of 'ideology', the presence of 'core conceptions', integrating a whole pattern, could be viewed as a further test.[5]

Finally, the notion of 'ideology' also includes the issue of *conflict*. Differences would be unavoidable in ways of interpreting or predicting the world, in weighting social values, in prescribing ideals or changes. But how far would contrasting *patterns* emerge, and how actually or potentially *conflictual* would these be? We were sceptical about previous classifications of business social ideas. Indeed, the list of typologies we saw as inadequate was a long one. It included a vague polarity of 'progressive' *versus* 'conservative' or 'cosmopolitan' *versus* 'parochial'; a too-selective picking out of categories like 'humanist' or 'corporate liberal'; a purely sectoral-economic or reductionist contrast of 'City' *versus* 'Industry' or between industries. Still less satisfactory would be an extrapolation of conventional economic/political labels such as 'free market' or 'mixed economy', let alone 'right', 'left' or 'centre'. Though doubtless borrowing heavily from such ideas, business would be likely to form its own constellations.

Ideas of management, the firm and 'business ethics'

Ideas about management, particularly as propounded by outside theorists, appeared unlikely to prove a fertile source of social ideas for business leaders. The reason for this is simple. 'Management' as a subject essentially related to the organisation or, in business, the firm: it nearly always avoided issues of political economy and society. It tended to treat wider political, economic and social factors as 'givens', background elements or, in some versions, 'constraints'; not as issues for business debate or managerial choice. Any wider impacts from this quarter would tend to be allied with larger currents of thought, for example of progressivism, positivism or technocracy. Thus the positivist, 'end of ideology' mood of the 1950s encouraged the idea that scientific research and rational discussion would yield rich returns for consensus-seeking, techniques of conflict-resolution, quantified models. It also encouraged notions of a 'practical', 'sensible', united front of business opinion, divorced from ideology. Of course, there were some explicit connections which will be watched for in this study. In particular, thought about relations with employees typically drew on social ideas with potentially wider implications relating, for example to 'authority', 'consent', 'manipulation' or 'participation'.[6] In the main, however, the character of ideas about management, as pursued in books, business schools or management studies, would remain essentially self-contained and detached from macro-issues.

A more direct source might be basic conceptions of business and the firm as expressed by business leaders. Such conceptions, we found, fell into three main categories. A first, small category focussed on the individual business leader as unique architect, prime mover or solo operator. Here was a primarily self-referential pattern of thinking, business activity being viewed essentially as a projection or extension of a single, potent individual: Charles Clore, Jim Slater, James Goldsmith, Tiny Rowland provide examples.[7]

A second, more prevalent conception, the technical-economic one, limited itself to the familiar, interlinked processes of product development, manufacturing, internal organisation, finance, and marketing. This, of course, came near to defining the bare essentials of corporate viability, the rudiments of survival and progress for any firm. Its rubrics of competition, profit and control were inescapable. Thus it was nearly always forcibly present somewhere within the outlook of a business leader. But for this second group the technical-economic conception was sufficient and satisfying, an adequate definition of 'business' and 'the firm'. Whether the emphasis was multi-functional (Leslie Lazell), or 'the excitement of trading' (Jack Cohen), or 'adroitness' and 'strategy' (Nigel Broackes), the keynote was corporate dedication and autonomy. On its own this conception would not generate wider economic, political or social interests: indeed, it might militate against them.[8]

A third conception of the firm put people or groups, relationships or human factors at the centre of business activity. Economic roles, though included, were regarded as inadequate on their own. Conventional issues of production, marketing, finance and organisation were accorded respect but not primacy, with profit viewed as no more than an essential instrument or mechanism. Occasionally, such a view centred on ideas of managerial social leadership with paternalist overtones: an eloquent exponent was Frederick Hooper. Sometimes, as with Ernest Bader, the stress was on management-worker unity or employee management and ownership, with overtones of syndicalism. More typical was an emphasis on plural relationships or 'social responsibilities' for the firm, involving employees, management, shareholders, suppliers, consumers, 'the community', sometimes described as 'stakeholders'. This became an increasingly familiar rubric. Its implications for wider social thinking, however, were far from clear cut. Its proponents expressed widely varying economic, political or macro-social viewpoints. Indeed, many avoided public declaration of wider views altogether, sticking closely to a micro-interpretation.[9]

One area of discussion developed during the period which at first sight might be thought promising: 'business ethics'. This concentrated on the conduct or behaviour of managers and firms, the nature of humane, sensitive interactions inside and outside the firm, and how these could be improved, often focussing on what decision makers saw as ethical problems in running the business, as well as discussion by interested theorists. The occasional joint declaration and a trickle of articles or speeches resulted; company codes in some cases; flurries of interest within the peak organisations. A *Code of Business Ethics*, published by the Christian Association of Business Executives in 1973, proclaimed the firm as 'a community of persons'. Senior people engaged in private conclaves in cloistered, prestigious surroundings at St George's House, Windsor. Typical subjects would include responsibilities to employees over redundancy; high pressure salesmanship and 'truth in advertising'; bribery; conflicts of responsibility for the firm in reconciling different interests and for the individual, for example as between family, personal integrity and career or company pressures.[10]

To pursue 'business ethics' meant rejecting narrowly technical-economic ideas about management. Invoking concepts of value or virtue familiar in the Christian, Greek or Hebraic traditions, the subject particularly attracted some religiously minded business leaders (though others preferred their ethics labelled as 'standards'). Where 'business ethics' parted company with traditional social ethics, however, including mainstream Christian social thinking, was in a resolutely micro-focus. Its concept of moral agency was restricted to firm, manager or entrepreneur within immediate contexts of market and hierarchy. Wider issues of competition, direction or co-operation were avoided, let alone of 'freedom', 'justice' or 'solidarity' in society, politics, the economy. What mattered was good conduct within existing structures.

How far this reflected individualistic assumptions, implicit conservative bias or desires to avoid controversy is a complex issue. One result was neglect of wider ways of encouraging 'good' business behaviour, for example through changes in corporate accountability, the media or social monitoring. Another was neglect of the long-established politics of the peak business organisations, notably in relation to taxation of companies or high earners or collective political influence. Not least was a distance both from public policy issues where business was highly active during the period and from the overarching issues of business's positioning in society. Though the sophistication of much discussion of 'business ethics' would advance, such features of parochialism persisted.

Dawning controversies in the late 1950s

We turn to the wider economic, political and social context in the period just before 1960. What grounds are there to expect an increase in social articulacy by business leaders at this time? Was the context such as to stimulate deeper questioning?

The 1950s had not seen major interventions by business in public debate. This contrasted with the often acrimonious exchanges which had occurred under the 1945 Labour government, featuring both implacably 'anti-socialist' business voices and those who sought a *modus vivendi* with that government. The return of the Conservatives presaged a more relaxed atmosphere: the expected withdrawal from *dirigisme* would allow business to carry out its functions more effectively in an environment where the UK's economic difficulties were seen as surmountable. The disengagement heralded by 'Conservative freedom' was broadly welcomed, and a sympathetic understanding with the new government, partially mirroring that of the Labour government and the unions, was expected to develop. By the end of the decade these hopes were disappointed, and an atmosphere of bewilderment and resentment permeated government-business relations.

Business social ideas through the 1950s were comparatively unsophisticated, and this was not unrelated to fragmentation among the main national bodies. For small firms there were the National Association of British Manufacturers (NABM) and the Chambers of Commerce; for economic and trade issues there was the Federation of British Industries (FBI), and for labour relations the British Employers' Confederation (BEC). This discouraged an overall strategy or outlook: with divided responsibilities it would prove difficult to develop coherent viewpoints. Organisations representing businessmen as individuals might have helped to overcome such weaknesses, but these lacked the financial and intellectual resources to stimulate new thinking. Perhaps most important were the Institute of Directors (IOD), which identified with traditional 'free enterprise' values, and the newer and more diffuse British Institute of Management (BIM), which many observers expected to take an important future role in business public policy. Bodies like the Industrial Welfare Society and the Industrial Co-Partnership Association included leading business figures concerned with industrial relations issues, but they were weak given the practical monopoly enjoyed by the BEC on these issues at a higher political level. Relations between the organisations were often jealous and suspicious, lacking the coordination to impress a case on non-business audiences. In addition, much of the services sector lacked strong representation, while financial institutions and the City, though influential, were characterised by aloof specialisation, reticence and secrecy, and a lack of forums.

Through most of the 1950s the forces of conservatism in British business remained deeply entrenched. An obvious example was the highly defensive outbursts from introverted small firm organisations and industry-level associations. Their support was less for the free market as a general economic instrument, more for restoring the power of the business sector simply by weakening the state and the trade unions. Such an outlook could embrace defences of protectionism, restrictive practices (perhaps in collusion with the unions), subsidies and aid for certain industries, and dismay at overly-enthusiastic competition policy. Revealingly, the NABM, the main small firm lobby, insisted that 'excessive zeal to encourage competition can well be as harmful as the wish to create state monopolies, which destroy it'.[11] This mind-set was still affected by the defensiveness of the 1930s, with limited expectations of how business itself could drive change. Similar forces of conservatism or cartelism were strongly evident in the City.

Another type of business conservatism was more flexible in mood. It complemented the rather relaxed, aloof attitude to economic problems of some more patrician members of the government. It did not quite coincide with the 'Keynesian settlement' but was as dismissive of austere economic medicine as it was of utopian interventionism. Whilst arguing for further concessions to business, it did not believe that British industry had seriously malfunctioned since the war. Rather, economic progress had maintained political equilibrium without widespread *dirigisme* or changes to the internal hierarchies of business. Expansion had maintained profits, satisfied the workforce and sterilised 1940s-style 'socialism'. Hence calls from business for radical institutional change in any direction were thought inappropriate. Perhaps the most articulate spokesman of this strand of thought was Lord Chandos, the former cabinet minister and chairman of Associated Electrical Industries (AEI). Although considered as 'the representative of the City wing of the Conservative party *par excellence*' and a stalwart of the IOD, Chandos was no straightforward free marketeer. His speeches revealed a blend of industrial paternalism, advocacy of major tax cuts and a relaxed attitude to inflation: he also preferred the 'statesmanship' of large firms on issues like price leadership to a potentially destabilising competition policy.[12] Such views, which were probably not uncommon in more successful larger firms, were whiggishly reformist, incrementalist but essentially self-contained.

Despite all this, by the late 1950s various challenges to complacency were at work. First, there was a wave of criticism of effete and self-serving institutions which, it was argued, were hindering the transition to a more 'modern' society. The Conservative political elite, the civil service, closed and class-ridden financial institutions, and to some extent trade unions, were thought wanting by critics assailing a complacent mood of malaise and decline. Industry, with the exception of retrograde small family firms, usually escaped the brunt of this critique. Indeed, some of the leading 'modernising' tracts of the period, such as Shonfield's *British Economic Policy since the War* (1958) and Shanks' *The Stagnant Society* (1961), argued that industry had been short-changed by economic policies geared to national prestige and political equilibrium at all costs rather than a commitment to economic growth and change. Hence there was a feeling that business could avoid being bundled up in the fashionable critiques of the 'Establishment' if it could show intellectual openness and a degree of political leadership.

Divisions between various types of 'conservatives' and 'reformers' were opening up in the field of industrial relations. Despite the atmosphere of calm and reason engendered by the Ministry of Labour in the early 1950s, severe strains were appearing later in the decade. The whole question of industrial relations would be opened to wider public scrutiny, some of it unwelcome to business. The number of unofficial strikes rose inexorably through the 1950s, the consequence, it seemed, both of weak-ening central trade union control and narrow attitudes among many employers. Inadequate labour productivity seemed to be the key problem for all shades of business opinion. To militant businessmen influential in the employers' associations, which still carried out the main functions of collective bargaining, the pusillanimous attitude of the government during major strikes, when the Ministry of Labour had failed to support 'employer resistance', suggested that employers' associations should go it alone. The Engineering Employers Federation's (EEF) failure to defeat the engineers' strike in 1956–57, the last of 'a series of humiliations', caused a rethink of attitude towards the unions. For some the situation demanded legal restrictions on the trade unions to halt unofficial strikes. Others called for a more open-minded effort from the associations to rebuild bridges with trade union leaderships, with better human relations policies and more formal, inclusive bargaining within firms.[13]

Conflicting approaches came out more fully in private, as at the 1958 conference of the BEC, which discussed a wide range of employment issues. Some were benignly conservative, others belligerent, with a few groping for something more 'progressive.' Given the lack of encourage-ment by government and of suitable arenas for debate with the trade unions, positions beyond the purely complacent or adversarial would evolve slowly. Yet new openings would be aided by the growing interest of economists and politicians in the dangers of cost inflation, the tentative remedies being outlined by the Cohen council (established in 1958) and the arrival of a new TUC leader, George Woodcock, known to be sym-pathetic to incomes policy. Within business more committed policies on 'human relations' were being urged by the Industrial Welfare Society and the Duke of Edinburgh's Conference, as well as practised to some degree by leading firms like ICI or Unilever.[14]

There was unease in some business circles about long-standing nega-tive stereotypes of business. A number of criticisms centred on both behaviour and culture, suggesting insufficient meritocracy or coordin-ation. Private business was criticised as introspective, socially exclusive or unintellectual. These failures had led to deeper economic deficiencies: the neglect of management education, poor labour relations, the weak grasp of marketing and export strategies. Although these criticisms were often levelled indiscriminately, many in business circles increasingly recognised this 'warts and all' picture.

All the more so because of a growing awareness of the UK's lagging position internationally. American productivity, admired for years, looked unbeatable. The apparent achievement of high growth, high investment economies by the Soviet sector seemed to leave business embarrassed by advocates of central planning. Perhaps most damaging was the increasing realisation of West European acceleration past the UK by the late 1950s. Statistical comparisons on economic performance were showing the UK falling behind in growth, investment and productivity. The formation of the EEC in 1957 stimulated some business leaders into thinking more constructively about how the UK could participate without suffering a breakdown in competitiveness. Hard choices about the economic future now seemed unavoidable.

Not least, there was a growing disappointment within business about the government's attitude to economic management. The Conservatives had come to office committed to strengthening demand management policies, whilst at the same time remaining determined to defend the position of sterling. Such a stance, when also encompassing support for private consumption and tax cutting at inappropriate periods of the economic cycle, had led to damaging 'stop-go' policies. For some the main failure of these policies was their discouragement of industrial investment by deflationary 'brakes'. For others the failure lay in the implicit acceptance of an inflationary environment which failed to provide sufficiently invigorating conditions for businesses to compete and export, until matters had got out of hand.

Economists argued endlessly about such questions in the 1950s: for business leaders 'stop-go' was important in revealing how little a supposedly pro-business Conservative government took note of their views. There was dismay at the choice of instruments used to engineer economic 'stops': purchase tax changes, hire purchase restrictions, credit rationing by banks to industry, even using investment incentives as economic regulators. While these measures hit private industrial investment particularly, public expenditure appeared to be treated leniently. Disappointment at the failure to radically reduce the state's share of national income grew accordingly. These frustrations and confusions were accentuated by the limited formal dialogues which now existed between government and business organisations. The wartime tripartist structures had withered: the National Joint Advisory Council and the Economic Planning Board remained but were low key affairs. For committed tripartists like Norman Kipping, DG of the FBI, this 'drawing apart of the government from the FBI' was deeply frustrating, but a quick reversal of the situation seemed unlikely.[15]

At one stage it appeared that significant sections of business opinion would adopt right-wing, free market policies. Some influential economists had pressed the case for more restrictive demand policies which emphasised price stability and gave the key regulating role to monetary control. Including Lionel Robbins, Dennis Robertson and Frank Paish, this school of thought argued for disinflation, tolerating slightly higher unemployment and forcing industry to seek out export markets.[16] 'Compensation' for higher interest rates would come through reduced taxation, together with tax reform and strict limits on public expenditure. During Peter Thorneycroft's Chancellorship (1957–58) this viewpoint seemed to be advancing. His tougher monetary policies won support from sections of the FBI, whose annual reports had been blaming high public expenditure for several years, finding striking commendation in the Federation's *Britain's Economic Problems and Policies* (1957) and its evidence to the Radcliffe Commission on the monetary system in 1958. Similar themes were sounded by bank chairmen during the period. The FBI spoke of inflation eroding the 'psychological capital of the habits of work and enterprise with which the present generation of business men grew up' and called for a major change in attitude to macro-economic management. However, following the defeat of the Thorneycroft measures within government, business support receded and enthusiasm for a strict monetary policy was dampened by the recession of 1958.[17]

The failure of a free market attack to materialise also owed something to the weak linkages between business free marketeers and sympathetic economists. The latter tended to restrict themselves to narrowly macro-economic approaches, while positive, well researched policies were lacking on the business side. Perhaps Richard Powell of the IOD was accurate in his criticism that market militants were still fighting the battles of the 1940s: 'Industry's case has usually been negative: anti-nationalisation . . . rather than pro-enterprise'.[18] But the IOD itself was guilty of this charge in the 1950s. Something more direct and abrupt than the subtle betrayals of contemporary Conservatism would eventually be needed to dislodge its own largely backward looking stance through this period and beyond.

By 1960, after facing its second 'stop' phase in five years, business had become deeply disillusioned with the superimposition of the electoral cycle over the economic one. Each time the impression of an inherently unstable economy gained force as the oscillations grew more marked. Poor economic forecasting by the Treasury was blamed, particularly as little effort was made to consult private industry in the process (the FBI had set up its own industrial trends survey in the late-1950s). Worse still was the complacency of the government, seemingly more attuned to the short-term aspirations of consumers and unable to produce an overall strategy to improve national competitiveness. The situation was not helped by the rapid turnover of chancellors. Tax reform, mooted by the Conservatives when first elected, had been replaced by an apparently arbitrary manipulation of fiscal levers irrespective of industry's needs. With the possibility of 'free market' methods of economic management receding, but with the traditional sterling regime still intact, business had seen enough and understood enough by 1960 to begin asking the hard questions. The need to boost investment, win export markets and control cost inflation would require searching self-examinations.

Parallelism, primacy or transformation?

To many thoughtful business leaders around 1960 it seemed that Britain's position was slipping, that government did not understand how to reverse this, and that business itself would somehow have to intervene more directly to redefine the frameworks for policy. Reflective business opinion was also anxious about the widespread critiques being directed at market or managerial failures. These seemed to call for active responses, reaching out to wider audiences. Opportunity and necessity both pointed to reviving the public voice of business. But in the process business would be bound to disagree. In industrial relations, divisions were opening up between hawkish employers who wanted to strike back, conservatives ready for piecemeal appeasement in the interests of a quiet life, and reformist seekers after a redrawn national settlement with the unions. In macro-economic policy differences were opening up over protection versus competition, intervention versus *laissez-faire*, expansion versus restriction. Reappraisal, anxiety, rebuttal, self-criticism, let alone any emergent new prescriptions, all would tend to undermine consensus.

As we started to investigate the developments in opinion a marked parting of the ways with conventional economic assumptions about business became apparent. Our expectation was that as the processes of questioning gathered force, competing *social* concepts of the overall role of business would come to the surface. Our reasoning here can be simply stated. In business as elsewhere, it is social value presuppositions that provide the foundations for thought. Only when some basic pattern of ideas has formed at this level, however rudimentary, can notions of the economy or economic policy start to take shape. Social assumptions or preferences will tend to condition economic viewpoints, not the reverse. And they are bound to have at their core some view of the existing or preferred relationship between business and the rest of society. But given the contrasts in people's backgrounds and temperaments and in the surrounding institutions, perceptions of the interaction are likely to differ, and, still more, preferences as to the nature of a better or an ideal relationship between business and society.

At this point we believe it is useful to employ 'ideal-types' or sharply defined conceptual categories as an aid to evaluation and analysis. Such 'ideal-types' do not claim to represent with historical precision the ideas people actually express. Indeed, their deliberately intense or extremist form mean that such a perfect fit would be surprising. However, while they do not describe reality, their pure, crystalline character, indeed their very polarity, usefully help to illuminate it.

We envisaged three ideal-types for the business-society relationship, each focussing primarily on a preferred positioning or re-positioning for business *vis-à-vis* other economic and social entities. Our expectation was that historical observation would uncover real-life currents or tendencies of thinking approximating to the ideal-types; that these tendencies could be usefully analysed and compared in the light of the latter; and that collectively the tendencies would take centre stage in business thinking about public issues, largely defining the content of 'business ideologies'.

The ideal-types can be outlined quite simply at this stage. According to the first, the desirable position for business is as a leading actor alongside, and co-operator with, surrounding economic and social forces. For the second, the ideal is for business to be social pivot, prime initiator and tone-setter, subject only to (a tightly conceived) government. For the third ideal-type business should be an extension of a strengthened, reconstituted society. All three claim an important place for business. All three, indeed, take an elevated view of its actual or potential role. But that role is pictured very differently, whether as co-partner, primary force, or tributary of social values. At stake, essentially, are rival concepts of parallelism, hegemony or joint transformation.

A few introductory words are appropriate for each ideal-type and its related historical tendency. The parallelist ideal-type, first, has a pluralist, 'mixed' vision of political economy. It envisages a series of balances: between diverse sectional interests; between plural economic objectives; between different types of economic co-ordination (competition, state control, voluntary co-operation). It invests heavily in positive sum ideas and discounts notions of fundamental conflicts between interests. An advancement for business is desired but not such as to diminish other major forces, even in the short-run. The economic and political constraints are regarded as malleable, with room for everyone to register gains. Such gentle magic is to be worked by a careful balancing of national macro-economic objectives, though with a primary emphasis on the pursuit of economic growth. Good relationships between sectional interests are necessary to this end, including national-level mutual restraints and organised negotiation and co-operation. Insofar as major reforms are required, these will be achieved primarily through education, persuasion, example, conversion. The tendency of thought associated with this ideal-type, as it develops historically from the 1960s onwards, is relatively optimistic, gradualist, incrementalist, voluntarist. We will call it 'revisionism'.

The hegemonic ideal-type is very different. It makes the greatest demands for the role of business. The core notion is of business leadership in society by virtue of its incomparable contribution to both wealth creation and liberty. Business enterprise in a large, diffuse sense is to be predominating. Its capacities as prime motor of the economic prosperity on which other social values depend requires no less; so even more does its indispensable role for creativity, initiative and freedom. Freedom, indeed, is the overarching value. But the ideal is far from necessarily being a defence or rationalisation of existing business behaviour or ideas. Conservative and anti-competitive forces in business are reprobated. There is dislike of undue compromise with government intervention or other social pressures. Pursuits of merely immediate advantages for business, stances of negotiation, bargaining or consensus-seeking, are viewed as supine, diversionary and harmful to performance. The concept is of the full potential of business energies released and stimulated for the social good, through the operation of a free market economy, with a minimum of state control and a maximum of resources in private, not public hands. This ideal-type will find its historical counterpart in an influential tendency in business which we will term 'liberationism.'

The transformational ideal-type is more concerned with 'society' than the others, and it is also the most radical. Calling in aid a more elaborate social architecture, it seeks a ranking within which business would find a useful, esteemed place but a subordinate one. The business basics of devolved economic initiative, markets, private property and managerial co-ordination of the enterprise are accepted, indeed prized. But business structures and cultures are to be recast so as to play their part within a larger organism, itself much improved: they are to be socially embedded or integrated. The major changes envisaged for both business and society are to promote an overarching social ethic, one giving paramountcy to values of democracy, justice and social unity. These values are regarded as essential for the 'good life' in both society and business. As long as they are lacking, business will be deformed: it is also likely to under-perform economically. Society, too, will be fundamentally flawed, not least in its capacity to contain or civilise business. Only through greater democratic participation, reduced inequality and social unification can business find its place as an offshoot of a healthy society. Historically, this ideal-type is likely to have a smaller influence on business than the others. We call the associated tendency of thought 'reconstructionism'.

We did not expect every business leader to conform even loosely to this three-fold classification. Some would be 'independents', standing aside from all three tendencies and expressing fragmented views. Such individuals could be aiming at special personal influence over government in the tradition of Lord Beaverbrook. They could be successful freewheeling entrepreneurs with policy ideas of no settled, coherent or consistent character which they would seek to communicate directly to the public, perhaps flamboyantly. Their public articulacy could be opportunistic and geared overwhelmingly to corporate interests. But it could also express genuine intellectual doubt or a stance of deliberate eclecticism.

We doubted, however, whether the independents would form more than a small minority of the socially articulate business leaders. Our expectation was that the tendencies of revisionism and liberationism, and to a lesser extent reconstructionism, would be found to influence a large majority of individuals. We also expected them to exercise a strong influence on the peak national organisations of business, and to shape most of the ideological conflicts. Social thinking would bear the marks of ideals for business conceived either horizontally (alongside others in society), or vertically (over and above them), or redrawn concentrically (as a subcircle within a larger circle). Whatever their relative strengths or weaknesses in particular phases, the basic ideas for repositioning business to society – whether as parallel joint force, enfranchised saviour and liberator, or tributary of a new society – would never be far from centre stage.

Examination of social ideas or views on public issues involves paying a price. It means concentrating on business leaders who formed a minority in their class (albeit an interesting and significant one), and for most of whom public interests represented only a small proportion of their total activity or career. Their predominantly business contributions, let alone their whole life stories, are not features of this study. Nor does it offer a rounded examination of the leading national organisations of business, although much will be said about them, based on new material. There is, too, a further aspect of selectivity. A focus on what people wrote and said about public issues, even in private or semi-private places, emphasises 'public' aspects of their attitudes and characters, whether of ambition, attention-seeking, desire for repute, idealism, conscience or public spirit. Rather less to the fore, perhaps, will be such things as private deals, log-rolling within public affairs, party contributions, the provision of favours, honours or special advantages. Similarly, elements of internal politics, office intrigue or personal loves and hates within the business organisations do not receive their due.

Yet even apparently abstract ideas are still a vortex for complex human emotions and experiences. Ideas about society and political economy cannot fail to reflect interplays between shared, collective understandings, unique individual choices and situations of sheer pressure. Hence the story that follows is not just about the general direction of ideas. We have to pay attention to the intricate details of belief that mark one person off from another, the richly varying sources of belief in people's backgrounds, the mutations of belief within the bodies that so often focussed discussion, and the idiosyncrasies of expression of belief. Contingency, accident and chance, as ever, loomed large. Social ideas characteristically developed under the stimulus of controversies in public policy, often under stress. However long established the predispositions, and however structured their underlying forms, the focus of crisis, emergency or external pressure was typically needed to activate, test or catalyse them.

Finally, a word on the structure of the book. Three chapters are mainly conceptual, describing and analysing the ideological tendencies. Five are historical, concentrating on the testing of ideas through successive phases of public affairs. We were tempted to group the conceptual chapters together at the start, and then proceed to the chronology equally *en bloc*. But though preferred by social scientists, such a procedure would do less than justice to the varying prominence or relevance of different ideologies in particular periods. Better for the ideologies to appear closer to the events which tended to 'bring them out': less 'tidy', perhaps, but truer to their history. Chapter 2 addresses the ideology of revisionism as emergent in the early 1960s. Chapter 3 examines the relationships between business opinion and the Labour governments of 1964–70 when revisionism was greatly tested. Chapter 4 moves back to ideology, this time to liberationism since this tendency was struggling to express itself up to the early 1970s. Chapter 5 deals with the Heath period 1970–74 when revisionism faced further trials and the sense of national crisis deepened. As more radical solutions to the UK predicament were being increasingly considered, this is the cue for introducing the third tendency, reconstructionism, in chapter 6. What follows is a story of fuller testing in the period 1974–79 (chapter 7) and under early 'Thatcherism' (chapter 8). A tentative picture of business opinion in the late 1980s and early 1990s is presented in chapter 9. Finally, chapter 10 offers an evaluation of business social ideas and ideologies in the period, their prospects, and their relevance to thinking about both public policy and 'capitalism'.

2 An adapted, moderated capitalism: the anatomy of revisionism

'We need an evolution of the competitive system, not a revolution into any other form of economic society' – 'Competitive enterprise' rather than 'free enterprise' – Not 'socialism' and not 'the old dogma where market forces reign supreme and where excessive demand is followed by recession and under-employment of all resources, labour and capital alike' – 'A marked improvement in top level industrial relations ... mutual education'; a reconciliation of increased profits with 'an Incomes Policy that is truly an Incomes Policy and not just a Wages Policy, and is seen to be broadly fair to both management and employees alike'.

Maurice Laing[1]

Social presuppositions

In 1960 leading circles in British business were restive, discontented, casting about for new remedies. But the situation was not yet fraught enough to bring the radical ideas of liberation or transformation onto centre stage. Instead, the rethinking most likely to impact initially would be of the adaptive, partner-oriented kind, relatively moderate, seeking major changes but gradually and persuasively.

Such ideas are non-utopian. They identify progress with a rebalancing of existing forces, a benign evolution. They imply change through education and consent, a convergence of increasingly enlightened minds and wills. The high value they accord to good relationships with other interests implies purposive consorting: a pursuit of organised inter-group relationships at national level, a degree of articulated consensus-seeking which we shall label 'mutualism'.[2] In Britain in 1960 this would have as its most obvious aim an avoidance of industrial dispute, indeed of class war. A more positive objective would be co-operation over productivity, investment and rationalisation, industrially and nationally as well as inside the firm, in the cause of economic growth. Moreover, an expanding, fully employed economy presented an even more complex test for mutualism. The danger of inflation seemed to point to some organised restraint over pay, prices, dividends or profits as imperative.

This viewpoint differs from narrow concepts of business 'self-interests' linked to 'profit maximising'. More especially does it differ from a simple concept of economic 'lobbying' as the indefinite pursuit of economic gains or power from government or outside forces, subject only to external 'constraints'. Instead, the concept is of a business advantage sufficiently collective and long-term to approximate largely to the general good. Deliberate processes of filtering or refining business interests are emphasised, as are major elements of 'encompassingness' or overlaps with public interests. From this sweeping implications arise for political economy. Government should not restrict itself to macro-economic levers but should pursue mediating or harmonising roles *vis-à-vis* sectional interests. Far from standing aloof or only relying on competition or regulation as co-ordinators, it should stand in a continuous relationship of consultation or negotiation with those interests. Correspondingly, a high degree of sectional interest organisation is implied, with business, labour and the rest concentrated in a few principal organisations or covered by representative intermediate institutions as a prerequisite for purposive mutualism at national levels. This comes close to 'corporatism', at least in its pluralist or 'liberal' forms.[3] But not completely; for the element of compulsion which would be needed for the intermediate organs to be both monopolistic and imbued with virtual constitutionality and legal or semi-legal powers is ruled out by a voluntarist, educative concept of self-reform.

Linked with all this are pluralist ideas about economic policy and organisation. By 'pluralism' is meant not so much a 'mixed economy' with diverse ownership forms (private, public, voluntary sector etc.), more a diversity of national economic objectives. There is acceptance of macro-economic eclecticism, a preparedness to juggle or balance pursuits of growth, anti-inflation, high employment, the balance of payments. Among these, however, one objective stands out, namely economic growth. Optimism, positive sum thinking and mutualism all gather round the lodestar of economic expansion. 'Anti-deflation' becomes if not a founding principle at least a derived article of faith. But diversity is also accepted for the economic system's co-ordinating methods, its necessary 'impurity'.[4] Markets and competition are still regarded as primary but the exclusivity of 'market dogma' is rejected. State intervention and consensus-seeking among sectional interests are also accorded an important place, albeit with wariness towards *dirigisme* and more enthusiasm for social co-operation, with the implication of a key and perhaps growing role for what is sometimes called a 'negotiated economy'.[5] The biasses towards pluralism, optimism and incrementalism emerge yet again on the techniques of macro-economic management. They appear in a recognition of the unavoidability of diverse policy instruments (fiscal, monetary, exchange rate, regional policy, incomes policy etc.), and an interest in 'fine tuning' the economy.

The use of the term 'revisionism' for this set of ideas requires some explanation. A parallel is implied with the efforts of (mostly West European) social democrats or moderate socialists, starting in the late nineteenth century, to revise the central formulas of Marxism with regard to class, state, ownership and revolution.[6] The analogy is, of course, far from exact. Marxism represented a more rigid ideological legacy for European socialists than did the ideals of market capitalism for the business revisionists. The controversies surrounding business revisionism were to be less blatant or extreme than those dividing traditional Marxists from moderate social democrats. Indeed, they would often be secreted from the public view. However, in both cases there was a sense that a homogeneous body of inherited doctrine or 'dogma' badly needed major overhaul, though not complete replacement. The purists of capitalism would find the ensuing compromises distasteful, smacking of emasculation or betrayal, much as the old guard Marxists had regarded the practices of parliamentary socialists or Fabian reformists.

For business revisionists, as for social democrats, there would be a larger than anticipated departure from the original *corpus*, and an extensive incorporation of other traditions of thinking. They would face many unpredicted and dramatic consequences. It would be in the nature of their aims so to combine with external pressures as to draw them, often despite their gradualism and caution, towards complex political entanglements, high-risk strategies and deep, largely uncharted waters.

People and influences

None of the leading revisionist initiators of the early 1960s was a household name. Their contemporary profiles were lower than those of business leaders who were pundits on public issues (like Chandos) or characterful, colourful entrepreneurs (like Clore, Butlin or Jack Cohen of Tesco). They were less in the public eye than trade union leaders who strode across major industries or exercised political muscle in the Labour movement. Few received much attention from the media; those who did soon returned to more typical situations of semi-private power. None of them projected a revisionist book to the public (though a few successors would attempt this), and only one wrote a personal testament. Beaver, Kipping, Geddes, Maurice Laing, Plowden, Pollock, Runge, Shone, Weeks...Who recognised these names at the time? Who *now* remembers them?[7]

Their philosophical lineage was equally elusive. The business revisionists were not able to appeal to any coherent intellectual or ideological
inspiration. No clear legacy of familiar ideas was available to them. No
giant thinker or magisterial *summa* had marked out the 'one true way'. A
synoptic focus could be drawn neither from social theory, nor political
writing, nor mainline political economy. A revisionist theory of advanced
capitalism was lacking, at least on a sweeping or accessible scale, though
of course some familiar intellectual currents were facilitative. The most
formidable of these was 'Keynesianism', with its apparent squaring of the
circle between market forces and a framework of greater stability, expansion and employment. The idea of a managed, depression-free brand of
capitalism was an important part of the legacy absorbed by these men, in
the main indirectly. Yet for all its policy significance and wide influence,
Keynesianism contained no vision for business institutions. These it still
viewed in neo-classical fashion basically as reactive-competitive mechanisms, albeit within a better managed framework of market forces or push-
button controls. Neither Keynes nor 'Keynesianism' offered a coherent or
usable vision of the good society, an ethical model.[8]

Other currents contributed to a revisionist suspicion of 'market dogma'
while putting even less of an alternative in its place. This applied, for
example, to the anti-industrial revolution brand of social history with its
sympathy for the long wave reaction towards social protection. Similarly,
leading interpretations of Britain's century-old economic decline might
differ from orthodox market economics while remaining purely explanatory or diagnostic. 'Institutionalists' would chastise conventional economic theory for its blindness to the realities of large corporations, the
'managerial revolution', social costs and benefits, imperfect competition
or market power; chipping away at the market paradigm but coming
nowhere near to replacing it. But then, a full replacement might not anyway be sought. The revisionists were not immune from the social science
positivism and ethical reductionism of the time. By the 1950s a widespread intellectual tendency was downgrading 'big ideas' of *any* kind,
rejecting 'dogmas' whether from right or left, preaching 'value freedom',
even predicting an 'end of ideology'.

Nor were these gaps made up by major writers closer to business.
Britain lacked a Jean Monnet, the businessman turned economic diplomat, public servant and 'planner', who became a persuasive exponent of
a negotiated, 'concerted' supplement to market economics.[9] Perhaps the
most widely read business pundit of the 1950s and 1960s, Peter Drucker,
exhorted an upbeat blend of managerial professionalism and corporate
'social responsibility' which offered little for the UK political economy.
Within British business a few precursors of revisionism – notably Alfred

Mond's sketch of a humanised, tripartist capitalism in 1928 – had had no more than a marginal influence.[10]

However, although these conceptual weaknesses were to prove significant in the longer-term, other influences had been at work. Shortfalls in explicit philosophical or theoretical inspiration would be problematic in wider ways, but for members of the business elite alternative sources were probably more powerful in building up a revisionist ethos. Even where strong intellectual interests existed, a greater debt appears to have been owed, at least directly, to occupational or experiential factors, people, events or ideas related to one's career, or various forms of social, civic or political exposure. Deep convictions were at work, linked with dispositions, commitments and experiences going a long way back.

One factor was managerialism in large industrial companies.[11] Virtually all the leading revisionists of the early 1960s had such experience. Correspondingly, some parts of business were under-represented by these men. None was a self-made entrepreneur. Small business activity hardly featured. Also under-represented were finance and banking and, more markedly, services and distribution. With respect to managerial functions, earlier phases in industrial relations or corporate economic planning were more frequent than usual (though by the 1960s largely subsumed by chief executive or top strategic roles). Such biasses would prove significant, particularly the industry concentration and the under-representations of small firm entrepreneur-ship and the City. On their own, though, they were hardly sharp differentiators and are unlikely to have been pivotal in nurturing revisionist inclinations as compared with some other factors.

One of these was experience *outside* business, particularly in public employment. Purely private sector careers were rare amongst the revisionist initiators. A few had crossed back and forth between private business and public service several times over. Hugh Beaver, leading elder statesman of the revisionists, had worked successively in the Indian Civil Service, Guinness, the home civil service during World War II, and again in brewing, with polymathic public activities added by the 1950s. Norman Kipping, another key revisionist, had moved from engineering works management, through the civil service, to the FBI. Edwin Plowden, an important background figure, had started by selling raw materials before a brilliant civil service career, followed in turn by chieftaincies in the Atomic Energy Authority and Tube Investments. George Pollock of the BEC had migrated to organised business from the law, Robert Shone of the British Iron and Steel Federation from academia. However, diversification into public or intermediary roles from an original or continued business base was more usual.

A more intriguing factor requires examination. This relates to previous involvements in public policy thinking or in national-level interactions, either (a) from within the public sector or (b) through peak business bodies, or even, at different times, both together. With regard to (a), no less than five of the revisionists already singled out had been through long periods of intensive work on government-business relations and public policy issues during World War II. They had worked at the Ministries of Works, Aircraft Production or, more often, Supply, or in the early post-war years in economic planning.[12] This experience seems to have left strong marks.[13] With regard to (b), most of the same group had been significantly involved along the same frontiers as office holders or senior contributors in peak business organisations in the late 1940s or the 1950s, mainly the FBI, to a lesser degree the BEC. Leading roles in national industrial relations or in the part-publicly supervised iron and steel industry were also relevant.[14] Moreover, these shared experiences had engendered significant contacts and friendships, even something of a club ambiance, between many of these men.

The revisionists' extensive involvements with the FBI require some immediate comment. These would increase after the FBI joined with the BEC and other bodies to form the CBI in 1965. Several issues arise over the interplay between ideas, people and organisation. What were the interactions between peak business roles or connections, and revisionist thought as it took off from 1960 onwards? How far would the organisations encourage revisionism or revisionism take over the organisations, and to what extent would they conflict?

For both sides there were *pros* and *cons*. First, workaday involvements with Whitehall, government and public policy seem to have influenced some people inside the FBI/CBI towards revisionism, at least vaguely. One could participate for reasons of self-fulfilment, status or the advancement of one's company or industry yet still have one's sectionalism tempered by pluralist, mutualist or politically adaptive ideas. Secondly, an FBI/CBI anchorage was invaluable to some with already established revisionist inclinations. Its top counsels provided access to government: particularly welcome where, in Kipping's words, 'the virus disease' of being 'at the centre' had been caught earlier ('once its fascinations have been experienced, men find it difficult to be out of it, not knowing what is going on').[15] There were, too, chances for leadership, national status or KBEs. Thirdly, the revisionist primacy which developed meant that a few business leaders with different inclinations could be partially or temporarily enlisted nationally to its colours, as occurred with several CBI presidents. And fourthly, revisionist ideas helped to provide the organisations with a degree of intellectual continuity and coherence, also with a general aura of statesmanship or public concern.[16]

It is easy to see an interactive, partly chicken-and-egg relationship between these factors in explanatory terms, even to suspect a benign symbiosis between ideology and organisation. Yet there were also dark shadows, even discords. For one thing the overlap was never complete: revisionist leadership of the FBI or CBI was always qualified, while conversely, though to a lesser extent, revisionism would appear in other places.[17] Nor would the linkage be conflict or even trauma-free. On the one hand, committed revisionists presiding over top FBI/CBI counsels would feel distaste for compromises with what they saw as narrowly parochial or conservative viewpoints. On the other hand, non-revisionists would accumulate an increasing litany of complaints against power concentrations, too much compliance towards government or public opinion, neglect of immediate business interests or, sometimes, disturbingly reformist projects. As long as the CBI's national representativeness remained uncontested, broadly for the first half of our period, the revisionists' primacy there would tempt both them and many outsiders towards an impression of some quasi-ideological monopoly of business. Yet their unrepresentativeness of smaller firms, new entrepreneurs and the City would tend to deflate such assumptions in the medium to longer-term. And, by the 1970s, a dangerous gap would open up between the CBI anchorage and some crucial revisionist policy pursuits.

Moderate business enhancement

No one propounded this theme more clearly than the arch-civil servant of industry, Norman Kipping, who had spent long years between the FBI headquarters in Tothill Street and the corridors of Whitehall. 'I always resented the FBI being dismissed as a pressure group which connotes narrow-minded, selfish ends', Kipping wrote in 1972. The term 'interest group', he thought, would better reflect a form of representation devoted to 'promotion' rather than 'defence' and showing 'an awareness of political realities and national needs'. Industry 'is still only part of the body politic'. Its peak representatives should seek consultation with government or negotiation', with 'room for concession and compromise on both sides'. This meant advocating 'acceptable solutions to problems' and, significantly, 'the probability of involvement': 'those who call for participation in decision making become parties to the decisions they accept'. This normative concept, with its inevitable accompaniment of 'insider' winks, nudges and secret diplomacy, of which Kipping was an acknowledged *maestro*, the revisionists would broadly follow.[18]

Kipping's viewpoint prescriptively elevated business conduct to a statesmanlike balancing akin to government's. 'Maximising profits' was already a misnomer for the practice of the better firms. Rather, they sought 'to hold the balance between different interests', as on a larger scale did the state. Thus, business's collective institutions also should avoid short-term maximising and join in the promotion of national purposes. This standpoint had little time for non-joiners, sectionalists or militants. Firms opting out of 'broad issues of national policy' had a 'narrow-minded and selfish outlook' which 'sooner or later discredits them'. Trade bodies could be 'selfishly inward-looking and inexpert' in public policy representations, meriting marginalisation by government. Even more distasteful were ill-organised sectionalism (sometimes 'little better than a rabble') and the extremism of 'backwoodsmen', 'wild men' or 'cries of anguish and bellicose tub-thumping opposition' within the FBI itself.[19]

At the start of our period such moderation could seem realistic as well as 'responsible.' Revisionists would resist temptations to mount a lamenting jeremiad or a sweeping case for fiscal action on behalf of business. If British society accorded a low status to industry, the remedies would surely be long-term, through education, culture or corporate behaviour. Insofar as national economic performance was lagging, revisionists accepted wider explanations than mere 'anti-government'. It seemed simplistic to focus too much on arguments to the effect that the UK was 'over-taxed', 'over-governed' or prodigally welfare-prone relative to other countries. Of course, a lower public ratio to GNP was hoped for and, partly in deference to the business grass roots, repeatedly exhorted. But revisionists would follow the Kipping concept of downplaying macro-fiscal militancy ('what was the good of asking for the moon'?) as well as sectoral log-rolling ('best left to the trades'). Aids to business would need arguing on 'non-doctrinaire', functionalist grounds. The case for lower income taxation should be aware of sensitivities over concessions to the high paid versus lower income groups. Certain issues were less clear in the late 1950s or early 1960s than appeared to be the case later, notably the disincentive effects of taxation on entrepreneurs, top earners or potential investors. There were also grey areas over the extent to which the quantity and quality of capital investment, a widely agreed failing, would respond to easier borrowing or fiscal inducements, as compared with other factors.[20]

To focus primarily on company orientated stimuli to investment either through specific tax reliefs or lower corporate taxation in general; to seek both to lighten estate duty burdens on small family firms and to encourage investment indirectly through fiscal sweeteners for savings; to look for openings to shift the incidence of taxation, mainly from direct to indirect taxes; and to add moderately expressed appeals for lower income or capital taxation and lower public expenditure in general terms and usually at the margin; all within a penumbra of national responsibility and macro-economic advice – these would be the classic ingredients of FBI/CBI budget representations under revisionist leadership.[21]

Thoughts of massive public sector invasion did not feature. Of course, Labour Party plans for further public ownership would be robustly opposed. 'Anti-nationalisation' remained a bedrock issue. But where nationalisation became inevitable, efforts would quickly turn to detailed parliamentary amendment, as with iron and steel. Once nationalisation was in place, arguments would arise particularly over commercial operation or diversification *versus* tighter constraints. In the 1960s the revisionists would be influenced by the nationalised industries' new financial and political clout and the high status of some of their leaders, as also by notions of overlapping interests, managerial improvement and the avoidance of further destabilising changes. Privatisation would be exhorted only vaguely or marginally e.g. for local authority building. CBI revisionists would welcome nationalised industry participation in the interests of 'a concerted industrial view on a large range of management matters'. Even in the throes of bitter protests over iron and steel, criticisms of the existing nationalised industries would be downplayed.[22]

A similar moderation extended to changes in the public and welfare services. Evidence to the Fulton Committee would suggest 'similar attitudes and skills to those required for business management' for 'parts of the civil service', but this related to generic rather than commercial or competitive understandings of 'management' (for example, advocating operational research).[23] The largely revisionist CBI policies of the 1960s and 1970s would include no proposals for privatising or commercialising the main social services, large public spending cuts on pensions, social security or education, or charges for schools or hospitals. It was thought wise to be vague over more 'selectivity' or to focus on things like loans for higher education, toll roads, reduced transport subsidies or increased council house rents. Generalised swipes at manning levels in public administration were part of the ritual, coupled with relative gentleness towards capital spending on the infrastructure.[24]

As we shall see, both social moderation and the caution over fiscal improvement would infuriate the free marketeers in business, creating battle-lines at one level after another, whether inside the FBI/CBI itself or within other organisations. Nothing illustrated more clearly the gradualism, mutualism and would-be holism of the revisionists.

Economic pluralism and the turn to growth

This next main plank in the revisionist platform first emerged clearly at an
FBI conference at Brighton in December 1960. The conference's topic
was 'The Next Five Years': few could have predicted that it would help to
demarcate business opinion for the next twenty years or more. It was a
typically urbane affair. The line-up of forces between the discussion
groups took place quietly. In Group 1 (National Fiscal and Monetary
Policy) there were virtually no revisionist-inclined industrialists but no
less than five top bankers, four trade association officials, and five free
market economists, including the discussion leader, Arthur Shenfield, the
FBI economic director. Weightier free marketeers of business such as
Paul Chambers were not involved (see chapter 4). Group 3 (Economic
Growth in Britain) was dominated by proto-revisionists: Hugh Beaver
(chairman), Hugh Weeks (discussion leader), Geddes, Pollock, Shone, a
number of business economists from planning-orientated large companies, and two leading Keynesians, W. B. Reddaway and C. T. Saunders.[25]

Major differences emerged. Group 1 sounded orthodox marketist
notes on price stability and monetary policy, along with familiar pleas for
major cuts in taxes and public spending, while being apparently resigned
to 'stop go' ('industry must learn to live with irregular changes of interest
rates') and offering no fresh thinking. Group 3 went much wider. It
emphasised acceptance of full employment as a fact of life; economy-wide
forward assessments for five-year periods; a fiscal policy aimed at increasing both capital investment and efficiency; and a primacy for economic
expansion: 'growth comes first and all else can follow'.[26]

For revisionists this anointing of 'growth' as *primus inter pares* in economic policy would have major advantages. It placed in the forefront,
more than Group 1's apparently boxed-in alternative, the dynamic role of
business drive and expertise (alongside appropriate government and
trade union responses) in achieving modernisation. It would lead to a
considerable diversification of policy thinking. It would combine echoes
of the civic spirit of the 1940s with a vision of modern rationality,
portraying growth as an intellectual or attitudinal problem calling for
non-partisan co-operation. Indeed, it was the epitome of progressivism,
consensus-seeking and positive sum thinking, squaring the circle of business and managerial enhancement with the familiar national pursuits of
private consumption and improved public services. 'Growth', in the
hands of the revisionists, was at once the means of therapeutic change
and a guarantor of post-war continuity: everything would change in order
to remain the same.

The business revisionists were not alone in making this shift.

Condemnations of deflationary monetarism, Treasury conservatism and effete managements were growing. Ideas were being more widely canvassed for managing a steadier growth in demand, an upward concerting of business investment, and a breaking down of business and labour restrictive practices and effete or conservative managements.[27] However, no group apart from the business revisionists was capable of acting in the same way as private intermediaries, brokers between grass roots business discontents and macro-policy intellectual debate, or enlisters eventually of a key constituency of support. With the government still wavering, economists characteristically at odds and the City overwhelmingly associated with monetarist orthodoxy, endorsement by the FBI leaders lent much credibility to the growth orientation. Since the 1950's, with some qualifications, FBI policy had come close to the restrictionist views of the free market economists and politicians. Brighton Group 3 and its aftermath brought a genuine mutation, however, recognised as such by both revisionists and their critics.[28]

A few individuals appear to have largely manouevred the change. Hugh Weeks, chairman of the FBI economic committee, had organised a dining group of businessmen and economists to discuss growth in early 1960. A quiet business intellectual with a laid-back, questioning, deceptively pragmatic style, Weeks was a persuasive behind-the-scenes figure.[29] Reay Geddes of Dunlop, from a family background of *haute politique* and an imposing public speaker, had made a seminal speech in February calling for higher growth and an institutional process to instil a national 'sense of purpose' looking five or ten years ahead.[30] In a class by himself, the elder statesman and business progressive, Hugh Beaver, was prepared to challenge publicly an over-cautious speech at Brighton by the Chancellor, Heathcoat Amory, and to pull his weight as a prestigious ex-President of the FBI.[31] The current President in 1959–60, Lord (William) McFadzean, in public terms primarily a national export champion, was less interested in revisionist ideas. As for Kipping, an impresario operator, his was probably the main hand behind Group 3's membership and the sidelining of Shenfield, an open private sceptic.[32]

Through much of 1961 an FBI committee pushed ahead under Beaver, including Weeks and Geddes, Leslie Rowan of Vickers, an ex-Treasury mandarin, and Maurice Laing from the construction industry, vying with each other over the breadth of their explanations of Britain's economic problems and consulting with key people from 'pathfinder industries.'[33] The growth emphasis increasingly took centre place in the FBI Grand Council through 1961, helped by the absence of weighty critics there at this time, Kipping's adroit management, and a more amenable President, Ernest Harrison. As the squeeze of 1960 led to further attrition for business *via* HP controls, credit restrictions and increases in profits tax, increased anger about 'stop-go' made more attractive the would-be smoothing or stabilising emphasis of the policy.

The turnaround had some distinctly ragged edges. Ways of tackling likely balance of payments crises were not examined (though here the revisionists were not alone).[34] Policy towards the EEC, where the FBI had done useful pioneering work in the late 1950s, was neglected. Advocacy of EEC membership would be pursued from a more independent vantage point by the revisionist-inclined Lord Plowden.[35] Competition policy, always a divisive issue, received little attention. Discussion of tax policy went further but with meagre results. More sophisticated investment stimuli, cherished by Weeks, the substitution of a general sales tax or VAT for purchase tax, and the idea of a payroll tax to encourage labour saving, perhaps in place of profits tax and specially advocated by Shone, all ran into the vortex of conflicting business interests which tended to surround FBI tax policy. While revisionists could defeat liberationist critics and successfully keep to fiscal moderation (see above), they could not pull off ideas for wholesale substitution or greater selectivity.[36] However, these problems were minor compared with confusions over the ideologically fraught area of 'planning'.

Here the revisionists were clearer about what they were against than what they were for. Predictably, they opposed the dirigisme of production targets, raw material allocation or physical controls, or the use of government purchasing power, discriminatory subsidies, taxes or bank credit to reinforce plan compliance at the level of the firm. Their attitude to French planning, only cursorily examined, was correspondingly selective. Even enthusiasts for an 'indicative' approach through the NEDC would fear a trojan horse towards 'a full planned economy' under a Labour government.[37] The view of 'planning' as a collective psychological device to gear up private sector investment plans found only limited support. If these stances were fairly clear, ambiguity clouded some other definitions, especially those geared towards the waverers. An example was the analogy with business planning robustly expressed in Harrison's message to FBI members in late 1961: 'Since all of us plan in our own businesses I see no reason why we should be afraid of the word.' The relatively greater controllability of some key variables in business, though exaggerated by managerial fashion at this time, made the simple parallel with the UK economy a misleading one. Moreover, revisionists were not alone in viewing 'planning' as an instrument for almost any desideratum; for example, 'to remove restrictive practices' or 'to increase competition' in a quasi-free market mode attributed to the 'Rueff element' in French planning, a rationale at one time even attracting a liberationist critic such as Shenfield.[38]

Some welcomed 'planning' as a means to revive socio-economic unity or civic spirit. Thus, Geddes' invocation of individual effort dignified 'because it's part of something [national] that matters more', or Kipping's praise of the French model as 'the consciousness of a common purpose' or 'the agreed character of the plan'.[39] Most important, however, 'planning' was conceived as (1) a conduit for a (revisionist-led) 'industry' to influence government, and (2) a pathway towards greater stability and non-partisan centrism in macro-economic policy. For revisionists (1) and (2) virtually equated. The policies which organised industry would advocate, under their aegis, would be precisely those to help both industry itself and the public interest by simultaneously reducing business uncertainty, excessive economic expectations and destabilising changes resulting from the electoral cycle. Sub-texts would be to pool or improve economic forecasts, equalise demand forecasts in highly interdependent sectors, or attune public expenditure plans more closely to private sector views. Essentially, it was the idea of a process towards both stronger industrial influence and a smoothed, largely de-politicised policy trend favouring steady growth which most inspired not only the early revisionists but also their CBI successors. These concepts could be attached to the elastic term 'planning' while the fashion for it lasted, but when 'planning' was demoted, the concepts survived.

Concerted mutual restraint: prices and incomes

Among the long-term implications of the growth emphasis (commitments to NEDC and NEDO, industrial policy, regional policy, a core emphasis on industrial investment etc.), none was to be more problematic for the revisionists than prices and incomes policy. This would also pose far and away the severest test of their social mutualism. The goal of joint restraint over incomes and prices could not be adopted by business revisionists (or by government and unions) until alternative economic strategies had proved fruitless or become the objects of even greater dread. Nor would a sustainable prices and incomes policy be feasible in the absence of major institutional and cultural changes which were particularly daunting in 1960s and 1970s Britain.

To elicit business (or trade union) co-operation in an obvious crisis would not be too difficult for a time. There were precedents in the FBI's history for quite successful short bursts of concerted 'voluntary-ism' over dividends, profits or prices (just as there were for wages in the TUCs). These fell into a British tradition of fire-fighting, blood and guts or 'Dunkirk spirit', to which businessmen were ready enough to conform. But not only would such short, sharp spasms fall far short of a continued, properly supported policy. They would tend to make the latter more difficult. Their very success would depend on *ad hocery*, a psychology of emergency, a threat of balance of payments disaster, even the assurance of temporariness. Frustrations and rebellions would soon ensue, with popular discontents exploitable by the party out of power. Thus the pursuit of a longer-term system would be undermined. It would be left to the small radical-reconstructionist tendency of business opinion, from a less engaged position, to emphasise that such a system would require a more measured build-up and more sweeping changes in business as well as trade unionism, culture and politics (chapter 6). For revisionists, awkwardly straddling a long-term reformist vision with collaboration with current governmental expedients *and* business representative roles, the short *versus* long-term problem would bring repeated troubles.

During the 1950s concerted national mutualism had languished. Indeed, many entrenched obstacles to it had worsened. Formal tripartism had become truncated. Conservative governments, impelled by desires both for 'decontrol' and *rapport* with the unions, had started out with policies of 'deliberate appeasement' of labour, with inflationary results. Later they had switched fitfully to a reverse bias, attempting a largely one-sided incomes policy weakly balanced, if at all, by other forms of restraint.[40] The trade unions were fragmented and generally conservative, with the TUC going through a trough of weak leadership. On the employers' side, the FBI/BEC split hardly helped. The BEC's internal problems we will come to shortly. When more deep-seated features of British labour, business and politics are added to this mixture, the contrast with countries which were successfully developing forms of system-wide mutual restraint could hardly have been more marked.

For business the biggest obstacle was not intellectual resistance to (increasingly plausible) 'cost push' theories of inflation. Nor was it even anxiety as to whether a national wages policy could be made to 'stick', given such factors as earnings drift or grassroots militancy. It lay above all in the field of reciprocity. Given that business would be expected to contribute, should or could the policy apply to profits, dividends, prices, or non-wage incomes? Each of these seemed to threaten a hornet's nest, whether the policy was voluntary or enforced. Curbs on profits would tend to damage investment while removing a key pressure for efficiency. Dividend restraint might be easier and would aid internally funded investment, but at a cost to the turnround of profits for investment through the capital market. Price restraint, though more directly anti-inflationary and visible to the public as a more obvious *quid pro quo*, could weaken competition. It would seem even harder to operate than wage restraint, given the vast heterogeneity of products and services, the multiplicity of prices, import dependences and other factors. In each case anxieties arose over bureaucracy, a slide towards indefinite continuance or a drift to coercion even with voluntary policies. Higher taxation of top earnings or capital gains might be viewed as a more precise concession to equity and better suited to a long-term policy. But here immediate anti-inflation would be less well served and much powerful business opinion would be up in arms.

How the idea of a prices and incomes policy came to be accepted by leading revisionists is a fascinating story. But there are really two stories, not just one. The first is top-down, largely familiar, featuring large collect-ivities and reluctant movements, with business leaders eventually yield-ing, it seems, only to outside pressures. The economy took time to mutate back to threats of over-heating; Whitehall opinion moved slowly; the TUC were suspicious; officially, the peak business organisations were resistant. NEDC's formation helped indirectly. Progress quickened in 1963, with government commitments now firmer under Reginald Maudling, wage inflation a growing anxiety, and a full prices and incomes policy more widely aired in the quality press. Then came a Labour govern-ment, stronger pressure and higher hopes of trade union co-operation by late 1964.[41] In understanding revisionism, however, the other story, so far largely buried, is more significant. It involves an advance party of business leaders inside the peak bodies, and a marked revival of mutualist ideas which helped to pave the way.

First, a few networks were quietly building up between business and trade union leaders on more neutral or convergent ground, notably the Duke of Edinburgh's Study Conference and the Industrial Welfare Society. The IWS was promoting advanced ideas of management-labour convergence or reciprocity. The burgeoning industrial relations and per-sonnel professions were developing a class of experts in entente-building with the unions, while a few firms like ICI were indirectly nurturing revisionist attitudes through their advanced labour relations practices. These influences had already left a mark on some prominent revisionists, notably Maurice Laing and Peter Runge, as well as on a number of their upcoming successors of the late 1960s and the 1970s.[42]

Secondly, a slow clearing of major road blocks at the BEC. This organ-isation's dominance by cosy complacency or union-bashing militancy was mentioned in chapter 1. The BEC's structure made it harder than in the FBI to establish a progressivist leadership based on a strong central executive and office-bearers from the vanguard corporate elite. Its director-general since 1955, George Pollock, had quickly shown mutualist inclina-tions but, in the main, had had to bide his time.[43] However, a posse of top industrialists had already mounted a partially effective challenge to a highly conservative leadership in the BEC's most important constituent body, the Engineering Employers' Federation (EEF).[44] A belief was growing that trade union power would need more subtle handling, through multilateral, negotiated policy changes. In 1960 the BEC's own heights were taken over by a *troika* of relatively 'progressive' industrialists who would reinforce Pollock's gradual reformism: Lord McCorquodale from the printing industry as president; John Hunter, an influential shipbuilder, as senior vice-president; and Maurice Laing as junior vice-president.[45]

Industrial relations sophisticates from firms like ICI were enlisted to counter the backwoodsmen. Official support was given to legislation and compulsory levies for industrial training, to overrule free riding 'poachers'. Advances were made towards the TUC. The rhetoric became more mutualist.[46] Overall, the change was less than the FBI's parallel move towards growth. For example, government proposals for greater security of employment and severance pay met with bitter resistance, particularly from marginal employers, and the 'progressives' repeatedly had to compromise in the face of angry opposition.[47] Also, the BEC's official support for incomes policy still lacked a reciprocal element. However, the idea of reciprocity was gaining some closet adherents in relation to non-wage incomes and dividends, at least from 1961 onwards.[48]

Thirdly, late 1963 brought a convergence between Pollock and Hunter from the BEC and the FBI top group, where Kipping, Beaver and Weeks also appear as closet reciprocalists from some way back.[49] By winter 1963 the five men were concertedly pushing for concessions behind the scenes: 'there was a need to demonstrate good will' and a stiff price would be 'worth paying for wage discipline'. In secret top-level talks only Archibald Forbes appears to have opposed on principle.[50] Arthur Cockfield, an independent (business) member of the NEDC, privately advocated a sliding scale for increased taxation of higher aggregate profits as a *quid pro quo* for three-year pay deals. The relative merits of this scheme and a straight price policy caused (sometimes fierce) argument before the latter won. By early 1964 a breakthrough came as the employer representatives jointly suggested a price review body to Maudling, to investigate and comment on controversial price increases, subject to a national deal on wages: a harbinger of the Prices and Incomes Board to be set up in 1965. This proposal soon foundered in the face of TUC opposition to the policy at this juncture and fears of conservative obstruction in both the BEC and the FBI.[51]

A peak of public advocacy had still to come. Peter Runge, FBI president 1964–65, a magnetic, mercurial figure who took up revisionist ideas with an infectious, slightly boyish enthusiasm, threw his weight publicly behind a price as well as incomes policy, alongside profits shown to be 'earned by efficiency': 'With a policy of full employment, the abandonment of which is not acceptable on political or on social grounds, restraint on prices and incomes can no longer be imposed by the workings of a free market. Inflation must be fought with more modern methods than laissez-faire.'[52] By 1965 Maurice Laing, as president of the new CBI, would preach the fullest rationale so far. Laing, who had been 'appalled' early in his career by 'inhuman' casual labour conditions in parts of his own industry, and 'appalled' again in the late 1950s and early 1960s by 'reactionary attitudes' within the BEC, was a deep-dyed mutualist. An enthusiast for fairly advanced ideas in industrial relations from both experience and religious belief, Laing stood at the morally earnest end of the revisionist spectrum. A complex chain of reasoning emerged: from 'the infeasibility of free enterprise in absolute terms', 'the duty to ... avoid the great periodic depressions of the past' and 'the vicious circle of "stop go"', through already established monetary and fiscal 'corrections' of 'unacceptable tendencies', to the need 'to interfere yet again at another point in the free market system' in the shape of a (voluntary) prices and incomes policy.[53]

The outline of a vision and commitment had been established from which there would be no substantive retreat for many years, despite political changes and mutations in CBI regimes. But the policy's vicissitudes and its strains and stresses for the revisionists would be highly fraught.

Education and persuasion as pathways to reform

We return finally to an important unifying strand with a wider social philosophy lurking behind it, half-acknowledged but pervasive. Here the revisionists show their kinship with a long line of optimistic, gradualist reformers in the past: Whigs, Fabians, turn-of-the-century American Progressives, US 'corporate liberals'. With these they share a high confidence in the extendibility of knowledge and reason to bear enlightened fruit. Most of their desiderata, it is thought, can be achieved through increasing awareness and stiffened will power leading to unified results. There is an overarching faith in the potential of education, persuasion and self improvement in securing beneficial change.

The liberal values contributing to this are mostly taken for granted or the subject of ritual tribute, as when Kipping says 'government by consent is more civilised than compulsion and control'.[54] To a large extent, of course, sheer dread of alternative methods leaves no option. A massive increase in competitive market forces: major denationalisation: rigorous monetarism: a purgative deflation: centralised control: massive new legislation – if all of these are ruled out, what significant instruments for change remain *except* education and persuasion? A more immediate political factor also counts. Much of business does not want change on the lines the revisionists advocate; or rather, mostly it wants change but in its own time and in its own way. Therefore, to get reformist policies adopted the means of implementation have to be prescribed as gentle or non-invasive. The elastic terminologies of 'voluntarism', 'self-government' or 'free consent' have to be stretched still further or even enlisted contradictorily. The theme of education and persuasion, working on supposedly independent units, appears as soothingly consensual, qualifying autonomy while seemingly protecting it.

The scope envisaged for these methods is almost as great as the revisionists' lists of desired changes are long. At one level their potential is seen as system-wide. Long-term 'possibilities and expectations' should be subjects for national discussion. As the 1960 Brighton conference Group 3 earnestly put it, 'the more public discussion and understanding of these issues the better.' The NEDC should '*preach* the need for real wages' (authors' italics), and 'ultimately only public education will aid the problem of wages and prices'. The 'education' imputed to management trade union dialogue becomes a further argument for the NEDC. Laing gives it an ethical slant: 'a mutual education' or 'mutual recognition of difficulties' is 'in itself of considerable value.'[55] However, it is on education and persuasion in the cause of 'a positive policy directed to altering business attitudes and methods' that revisionists have the most to say. The 1960s brought an explosion of training courses, business schools and colleges, conferences and seminars, and corporate management memberships. This fashion, though, the revisionists project upwards from the micro-fields of management skills and techniques to the higher causes of capitalist reform: to investment, rationalisation and reorganisation; to nation-wide concertation and mutual restraint; to the reform of business representation; to a new accommodation with labour.

The framework is never conceptualised overall. Ideas of information, persuasion, recommendation, exhortation or even individual arm-twisting blend into each other. The would-be transmission agencies are more or less distant from the company boardrooms which are to form the main targets, connected through a loose chain sometimes running from trade bodies, usually through the FBI/CBI, to national levels and vaguely implying concepts of collective representation or tripartite moral commitment. And the influence on business thought and action is expected to range from the general to the highly specific.

Thus an initial hope is that NEDO/NEDC will be able to improve not only the data for business forecasting but also attitudes towards

'the institutional impediments to growth' and the quality of capital investment decisions. The EDCs or 'little Neddies' should foster 'enthusiasm',
make people more 'planning conscious' or persuade firms to co-operate
on industry-wide improvements.[56] But after the high tide of tripartism
and indicative planning recedes, the overall theme makes no retreat, it is
just that more reliance is placed on industry's own organisations. When
the director-general of the new CBI, John Davies, exhorts 'conscious
effort on incomes policy' or the CBI Council states that 'manufacturers
should use restraint on prices', the assumption is of a certain deference
to their moral authority or political wisdom.[57] The CBI itself is expected
to be a major educational force not only towards government, trade
unions and public opinion, but also *vis-à-vis* its members. Revisionist
leaders of the FBI/CBI (John Davies, Campbell Adamson, Partridge,
and by the late 1970s, Watkinson and Methven) all aspire to a tutorial
role towards their grass roots, through speeches, publications, Central
Council debates, meetings, private correspondence, or discreet arm-
twisting of recalcitrants.

This philosophy presented obvious gaps. Prices and incomes policies
typically involved grey areas between *dirigisme*, business collectivism,
organised co-operation or 'free collective bargaining'. Yet though a classic-
liberal 'voluntarist' language could be equivocal or misleading, this was
still applied to schemes for restraint urged on under the threat of statute
or organised on collective lines by the CBI itself. Although revisionists
could accept the need for legislation in classic 'free rider' situations, for
example industrial training, they were loath to argue such cases on principle. On public intervention to end business restrictive practices in many
sectors, pro-activity would be lacking.[58] Moreover, the pursuit of a system
relying more on co-operation might itself require initially tough action to
get the necessary structures in place. Greater transparency in company
affairs in the interests of both market information and mutual education
would need increased statutory disclosure. Improved corporate governance and accountability might require statutory back-up. New methods
of public surveillance could draw on investigation, publication and public
opinion, still on essentially co-operativist lines, but these too would
require initial legislation, as with the Prices and Incomes Board. In such
areas again it would be left to a smaller group of outright business reconstructionists to advocate more radical changes (see chapter 6).

On two major fronts direct contradictions would appear. First, in the
field of industrial relations there was much understandable suspicion of
legal intervention. Yet while a limited case for statute would find growing
acceptance in relation to trade union archaisms or abuses, a matching
vigour was lacking on how to tackle neglectful or autocratic employers,

despite wide recognition that management's responsibility for industrial relations was greater than labour's.[59] Reliance would still be placed overwhelmingly on exhortation or persuasion (though some revisionists would later urge more reconstructionist ideas on employee participation). Second, criticism and prescription were strikingly at odds in relation to the system of collective business representation, trade associations, employers' organisations etc. Revisionists saw reform of this system as important for purposes of effective business involvement, education from above, complementarity to the TUC, and national mutualism. They deplored fragmentation and neanderthal parochialism in this field but, with their hands tied by voluntarist-educational-consensual doctrine, such irritation would prove almost wholly ineffective.[60]

For all its limitations, though, the 'educationalism' of the revisionists would show some solid virtues. Within the business community it struck the biggest blows against the narrow conservatism widely prevalent at the start of our period. Educative, optimistic, gradualist revisionism would show sustained ability to influence public policy as well as business opinion, in small steps, through varying regimes. As long as Britain's problems appeared amenable to reformism within an extended or refined post-war consensus, this tendency would enjoy optimum plausibility and high social recognition. But its 'educationalism' was not alone in this respect. Some of the palpable weaknesses in revisionism, even including the ideological inexplicitness and the lack of a central visionary model, could yield some counter-advantages, as we will see.

3 Co-operation or conflict? Business and the Labour government 1964–1970

During the period 1964–70 the business revisionism described in the last chapter faced its first crucial test. How far would it be able to work with a Labour government? Could co-operation with a left-centre regime help to promote the revisionists' objectives of 'enlightened' industry influence, steadier growth, tripartist mutual effort, and voluntaristic 'self-reform' by business? Some unwelcome compromises were predictable: a consummated marriage of both mind and heart would be too much to expect. It would not be unreasonable, however, at least to hope for a working entente, which would go beyond the merely *ad hoc* while avoiding rebellion from more militant parts of business. Indeed, the long-term feasibility of revisionist capitalism would to a considerable extent be determined by the creation of such a relationship.

The precedents from 1945–51 were not, in the main, encouraging. Although it is true that the predecessors of the revisionists had enjoyed certain successes with the Attlee governments, their relationships had sharply deteriorated by 1951, when industrial traditionalists seemed to be making the running. However, by 1964 the situation appeared more hopeful, or at least more open. The long period of Conservative rule had brought its own disappointments, particularly with 'stop-go'. Revisionist leadership, as we saw in the last chapter, had taken much of the initiative in recreating tripartism, with the hope of reducing industrial divisions and building a new compact within which 'enlightened' business priorities would prosper. Revisionist positions, it was strongly felt, had the important characteristic of dissociation from outdated party ideology, whether on right or left. It was a core assumption, therefore, that they would survive through changes in governmental regime. Moreover, the Labour Party of the early 1960s had itself gone through considerable changes, many of them, it would seem, helpful ones.

Other treatments of this period have concentrated overwhelmingly on leading political figures, social reforms, and still controversial issues of macro-economic performance and crisis. For us the focus is different. Our interest mainly lies in the public policy issues as tests, catalysts or yardsticks for top business opinion and ideology. The first part of this chapter considers the basic parameters and auguries for co-operation. How much scope existed for the revisionists, as the self-appointed vanguard of business, to co-operate with the Labour government in 1964 and through later phases? What categories of response emerged in practice from the revisionists, the national organisations they presided over and other business tendencies, and what deeper divisions did these reveal? We then focus on the three areas of policy which proved to be lightning conductors for all these issues: prices and incomes policy, economic expansion *versus* deflation, and industrial relations reform.

Labour and business revisionisms: the scope for convergence

A careful revisionist prospectus in 1964, if it had been conducted, might first have examined the ideas of Labour's own revisionists. It would have discovered that, since the early 1950s, older socialist stereotypes of private industry had been repeatedly criticised by revisionist circles in the Labour Party. It would have observed how explicit commitments had been made to the 'mixed economy', along with marked retreats from traditional, wholesale public ownership. Expanding, profitable firms were now regarded by revisionist socialists as a corollary of successful demand management. They were also viewed as more likely to instal 'progressive' human relations policies and to expand the power of professional salaried management at the expense of both the traditional entrepreneur and the rentier class. Indeed, some revisionists had gone further, perceiving a major shift in managerial psychology towards 'talk of service to the community', with profit, 'in place of being an end in itself ... an expedient': 'the habit of daily cooperation ... with members of other firms and government departments outweighs the crudely competitive instinct of the small businessman'. Anthony Crosland could optimistically conclude: 'the worship of individualism has given way to a positive cult of teamwork and group action'.[1]

Labour revisionists, their views reflected in party documents and the 1964 election manifesto, had come to favour tripartist dialogue, 'indicative planning', and a tax system designed to reward productive industry rather than dividends or financial manipulation. The price system would be heavily relied upon within a framework of broad strategic objectives, Keynesian demand management, and fiscal sticks and carrots. Nationalised industries would be made more competitive, an active competition policy would ensure more efficient markets. There was little in this to disturb business revisionists. Moreover, the proposals of most of the revisionist socialists stopped short at this point. They showed little interest in more radical reconstructionist ideas for a subjugation of City institutions, an enactment of company accountability to public interests, formal employee participation, or comprehensive corporatist structures for both business and labour, as in parts of Western Europe.[2]

Socialist revisionism, very much the work of intellectuals in the party, was not, of course, the only factor to be reckoned with. For business believers in a revised capitalism it would be as important to consider hard issues of *Realpolitik*. Not the least important was the fear that a Labour government would give preferential access and concessions to the TUC. On this front, however, a cautiously optimistic prognosis would seem justified by 1964. There was a deeply held desire to work with the trade unions nationally (see last chapter). There was a fair degree of confidence in most of the TUC's and the main unions' current leaders. Not least, there was the aspiration for a mutualist incomes policy, including reciprocal concessions by business: the hope that a Labour government, unlike the Conservatives, would be able to elicit trade union support for pay restraint, an attack on low productivity and restrictive practices, perhaps even a more understanding attitude towards corporate profitability.

Inevitably, much would depend on the willingness and ability of leading members of the new government to understand and communicate with business leaders. Here, perhaps, the plusses and minuses were more finely balanced. Mutual misconceptions still abounded. The revisionists' attitudes to Harold Wilson would lack warmth. Wilson's more popular qualities eluded them, his 'scientific revolution' rhetoric did not touch central chords for them, he was felt, largely correctly, not to enjoy formal consultation with business organisations. He was, though, credited with some realism about industry and abilities to persuade the unions to accept difficult truths, the reverse side of a suspected tactical 'trickiness' or unpredictability as arch-party conciliator. James Callaghan would not be a great success with the revisionists or business opinion generally. Some other leading ministers, notably Frank Cousins, Barbara Castle and Tony Benn, were suspected of being too reliant on small groups of doctrinaire academics. It was clear that the Labour Party's 'Clause 4' or dirigiste traditions were not silent inside the cabinet. The biggest fear, however, was that Labour would over-spend and over-tax. In fact, an otherwise disparate government did have as its unifying aims both a measure of egalitarian redistribution and a major increase in welfare expenditure.

Generally, the Labour leaders were regarded as remote from corporate management. Contacts during the opposition years had been meagre, often idiosyncratic, marred by distrust. This was the case even with Labour's leading revisionists. Gaitskell, Crosland, Jenkins, Healey, Jay,

Stewart: these men seemed to be, and to a large extent were, somewhat remote, donnish, their surveys of the private sector conducted at a distance, inclined to generalise from economic theory and still, despite their abandonment of old-fashioned ideological baggage, rather disdainful of business. The problem was mutual, however: even the 'progressive' business circles praised by socialist revisionists had taken little trouble to contact leading Labour figures in opposition. A major cultural gap, reflecting widely differing experiences, styles and habits, would see little diminution during the years of Labour rule.[3]

A partial exception eventually would be Roy Jenkins, viewed as a sympathetic and 'responsible' chancellor by CBI leaders in the late 1960s, though still socially distant from them. Their liking for Ray Gunter at the Ministry of Labour belonged to a different, more familiar genre of rapport with trade union 'moderates'. Their liaison with George Brown at the Department of Economic Affairs (DEA) would be in a class by itself. Bullying, canoodling and wheeler-dealing by turns, Brown would prove to be far the most charismatic, if often exasperating minister for industrialists, and the most sincerely interested in *them*. With him relationships would be colourful, sometimes explosive, yet often fruitful, Brown being trusted because his sympathy for a mixed economy was seen to come from gut understanding and enthusiasm rather than mere pragmatism or acquiescence.

The ability of a Labour government to avoid being blown off course by economic crisis remained the central question. If stark crisis could be kept at bay, the positives just mentioned would have time to show: a relational learning curve on both sides, tripartite consensus-building around a long-term prices and incomes policy, supply side policies for information-sharing, rationalisation and productivity, innovation and training, on which wide agreement existed. Such a scenario would still leave a Labour government facing conflicting pressures. It would still face tough dilemmas in reconciling both its welfare-redistributive aims and powerful electoral demands for 'more money in the pocket' with priorities for investment, exports and market confidence. In the absence of destabilisation and relapse into deflation, however, at least traumatic collisions between these pressures would be averted. A little more could be winnowed out for everyone. Revisionist business circles would still have much to play for. Although such an entente might in the longer-term risk resurgent militancies in both the Labour movement and business, it would have provided an exemplary pilot for future co-operation.

It is tempting to see business opinion simply as responsive to this scenario's dramatic unravelling. The story can all too familiarly be reduced to one of reflexes or ebbs and flows in business opinion in response to economic crisis. The period began with some optimism: two sets of shocks followed, the July measures of 1966, with the demoralising return to deflation, and the enforced devaluation in November 1967; then a longer phase of half-disillusioned realism or semi-healing set in until the 1970 election. Such a neat chronology of partial honeymoon, trauma and bruised confidence contains strong elements of truth. Yet the interpretation of the business mind as merely reactive to these vicissitudes is superficial and too reductive. It ignores the emergence of deeper forces. For the truth is that profound ideological cleavages were already building up by the time Labour came to power. During 1964–70 the deeper divisions within the business community would accentuate, though they were often to be secreted, disguised or suppressed. And repeatedly, it was the revisionists leading the peak business bodies who would be the lightning conductors.

Spectrum of personalities and opinions

Large elements of business stood apart from the beginning, adamant in their hostility to a Labour government. Here were hard-core Conservative supporters usually on the party's 'free enterprise' wing, veteran warriors of anti-nationalisation battles and many pragmatists who feared penal taxation, government interference or market instability. Here, too, was a new wave of adherents to free market models whose significance would increase. An important dividing-line marked off all these elements. Their antipathy would insulate them from the lures of official or semi-official tasks under the new regime, whether for themselves or their staff. A high profile example was Paul Chambers of I C I: many more had their heads below the parapet, particularly in the City, where distaste for Labour was characteristically intense. Lists of potential business recruits to nationalised industries, little Neddies or new public bodies like the National Board for Prices and Incomes (NBPI) and the Industrial Reorganisation Corporation (IRC) would quietly circulate around Whitehall. But these people's names did not figure or, if by chance they did, a would-be head hunter or nobbler would soon discover the mistake.[4] Over the next six years, these dissident elements would generally lie low (see next chapter).

This left widespread attitudes of ambition, opportunism, public service or sympathy on which the new government could draw, at least in the earlier stages. As always, the mixtures remain elusive. A complex combination would apply, for example, to Fred Catherwood, ex-managing director of British Aluminium, recruited by George Brown to be chief industrial adviser at the DEA. Catherwood's beliefs encompassed professional, scientific management and a mixed economy conceived in decidedly revisionist terms, though with a thick layer of government activism laid on top. An evangelical Christianity helped to inspire a quest for improved moral standards and business ethics. By 1964, disillusioned with the Conservatives, already in touch with Labour's industrial policy-makers and excited by the theme of dynamic modernisation, Catherwood was ready to develop into an assiduous constructor of little Neddies and a tireless propagandist for both indicative planning and incomes policy at the DEA.[5] But Catherwood's brand of managerial rapport with Labour's modernisation themes would find lesser echoes elsewhere. Later, some business leaders in unexpected quarters would confess to partial initial sympathies, for example James Goldsmith and David Young.[6]

Somewhat different were the long-standing Labour supporters from business who moved into official positions. Most senior was Wilfred Brown, unusual as both a tested chief executive and a veteran socialist, translated to the Lords as a minister of state at the Board of Trade. There, however, Brown's abilities and his reconstructionist ideas would often be frustrated. Austen Albu and Edmund Dell, both with middle manage-ment experience, became junior ministers with industrial portfolios; Richard O'Brien was elevated from industrial relations in the motor industry to the DEA; Grigor McClelland, a management theorist who had run a small retail chain, along with Frank Schon, a chemical manu-facturer, found himself catapulted into being a Labour counter-presence in the Industrial Reorganisation Corporation (IRC). Then there were a few leading independents, not Labour stalwarts, whom ministers would sometimes enlist for tactical counsel or stimulus, notably the philosophi-cal merchant banker Siegmund Warburg and the motor industry chief-tain, Donald Stokes. These, in turn, differed sharply from less respectable figures, like Joseph Kagan and Rudi Sternberg, who loomed on the margins of Harold Wilson's small circle of backroom cronies.[7]

In a class by himself was a leading exemplar of our category of 'inde-pendents' (see chapter 1), Frank Kearton. Kearton's brand of independ-ence would prove as unproductive to the revisionists as it was to be help-ful to Labour's new style of merchant bank-type interventionism at the IRC. He would take a high profile in supporting the government as 'more appreciative of business than many of its predecessors', slightly enjoying the distaste of many business colleagues for this stance. A gap existed, however, between a self-confessed 'balefulness' evident in Kearton's autocratic headship of Courtaulds, and a relative 'sweetness' felt by public opinion and the politicians he served. Although patriotic, public interest notions contributed to his IRC activism, even to his (corporately aggrandising) plans to rationalise the textile industry, it is hard to discern much, if any ideological coherence, let alone a thought-out design for capitalist-socialist reconciliation. Rather, Kearton was essentially a pragmatic, highly capable activist who identified with a limited range of Labour's more 'modernising' aims.[8]

Others moving into leading public roles were more ideological. The biggest 'catch' for the government was Aubrey Jones, a Conservative left-winger and ex-minister with strong industrial concerns. As chairman of the NBPI, Jones would pioneer a dynamic, if astringent effort at 'middle-way economics' with major implications for revisionism, in his case backed by passionate conviction, though less so for the business people he recruited as colleagues. Lord (Julian) Melchett, a youngish merchant banker, would take on the newly nationalised steel industry partly, it seems, from revisionist inclinations as well as public spirit and ambition. Ronald Grierson, another City figure, was to be a wild card choice as managing director of the IRC which, however, he soon exited to show his truer colours as an outspoken free marketeer. A better ideological fit at the IRC was another merchant banker, Charles Villiers: discontented with the City, keen to prove himself in public affairs, a man with wide social sympathies, his slightly old-fashioned mannerisms disguising proto-reconstructionist leanings.[9]

The fulcrum of business-government relationships, however, remained the peak organisations, the FBI and BEC, soon to be merged into the new CBI in 1965 (along with the small firm dominated NABM). Although a major undertaking, the transition to a single representative organisation was, in the end, smoothly engineered by revisionist stalwarts. The creation of the 'single voice' CBI was seen as a natural response to the demands of tripartism, a prelude to further rationalisation of business bodies, and a more effective means of marshalling forces to deal with a Labour government and the TUC.[10]

Between 1964 and 1966 the leading group in the FBI/CBI were still largely of the 'Brighton generation': Peter Runge, jovially embodying an initial entente with the Labour government; Norman Kipping, reliving a high collaborationism from much earlier times; Maurice Laing, staying just long enough to move from one nation moral enthusiasm (to 'put the community first') to a somewhat jaundiced view by summer 1966 (the initial goodwill 'has largely dissipated').[11] Laing's successors as CBI presidents, Stephen Brown (1966–68) and Gerry Norman (1968–70), were revisionists by adoption more than long-standing belief. Brown was intensely practical, avuncular, a capable consolidator. Though he had opposed 'reactionaries' when president of the EEF, he tended to take a cautious, more conservative line on industrial relations and politico-economic issues in the CBI. Norman, from De la Rue, with pro-EEC views and some NEDC experience, was something of a role model of the youngish, successful top manager. Also rather more conservative, with a bluff, attractive persona, he was more at ease with the grassroots than in Whitehall and became privately critical of the relationships pursued with Labour. Both men defensibly saw their role primarily as internal concilia-tors within the new organisation.[12]

However, the more influential figure was typically the director general, and John Davies (1965–69) was no exception.[13] Trained as an account-ant, Davies had been managing director of Shell-Mex. He was a mobile figure, fast-thinking, fluent, sometimes fiery-tempered. His style as direc-tor general was that of a new brand professional chief executive. Davies's social understanding was not marked: his experience had produced no closeness to shop-floor or trade union factors, or to heartsearchings about national industrial relations. The classic ingredients of 1940s civic effort and cross-sector experience were also missing, as were relevant intellec-tual influences, though he was to be a quick learner. Support for tripart-ism and active industrial policy and his backroom manoeuvres against the Industrial Policy Group (see next chapter) showed no retreat from re-visionism, though he was not one of its deeper thinkers. His commercial orientation was an asset. Something of a technocrat and mercurial in style, Davies could seem hard to pin down. However, three abiding passions clearly emerge. A keen linguist and Francophile, Davies was pro-EEC. Zealous for rationalisation and 'modern management techniques', he found himself shocked, for example, by the 'chaos' of business organ-isation and representation in the UK. Perhaps most important, by common consent, simple political ambition would eventually propel him from the CBI (some thought, prematurely) into a third, albeit less successful, career in party politics and government.

The structure of power in the CBI would limit the practical influence of the nascent liberationists, although they were to be vocal from the floor in the unwieldy new Council. The size of this body, nevertheless, tended to make it easier to control. The revisionist primacy was likely to be main-tained also by the strong membership concentration on manufacturing rather than finance and the City, and it increased when (after some mis-givings) the nationalised industries were admitted. Small firms at this stage did not have separate representation. Under the strategic direction of John Davies, the policy making process would be largely in the hands of two veteran revisionists, Hugh Weeks, still chairman of the Economic Policy Committee (see last chapter), and Kenneth Allen, chairman of the Labour and Social Affairs Committee. With some exceptions, the staff at Tothill Street were enthusiastic about implementing the relevant strate-gies. All that remains to be said about the revisionist ascendancy over peak business representation during this period is that as yet no other national body could compete either organisationally or ideologically (see next chapter). Internally that ascendancy would be often challenged, sometimes qualified, but never seriously in doubt.

The greatest prize? Prices and incomes policy

As explained in the last chapter, prices and incomes policy was an acid test for an adapted, co-operative form of capitalism. No issue would put revisionists more on trial with their own constituents, nor would focus more sharply their relationships with the Labour government. Stripped to its essentials and applying some hindsight, the problem was simple. There was no single 'prices and incomes policy', but rather two projects with very different aims, time scales and implications. One project would be 'long-term', aimed at reforming pay bargaining cultures and systems, building up mutualism between labour and business, and agreeing norms for pay, prices or other variables in relation to productivity and economic prospects. It would be non-*dirigiste*, using methods of investigation, persuasion, education, accountability, and pressures from public opinion (though these would probably need strong institutional back-up, more so than revisionists usually acknowledged). Its role in short-term economic management would be limited, pending a build-up such as successfully achieved by some overseas systems. The other and much less inviting project would involve statutory control, along with back-up sanctions. It would represent a fire-fighting, emergency response to immediate economic crisis.

The problem for the revisionists was going to be that while they aspired warmly, if usually vaguely, to the first, ideal-type project, it was the second, bleaker one that would soon become central, to the detriment both of the former and of their own and wider business relationships with the government. While their business constituents might be got to agree to the ideal-type prospectus without undue difficulty once both the new government and the TUC were behind it, the emergency version would bring great strains. Revisionist leaders, even more their grass roots, would resent its *dirigisme*. They would suspect (not necessarily correctly) that, under a Labour government, it would bear down more on prices than on pay. Even this might be bearable in the face of acknowledged national crisis, at least for a time, and to avoid the even worse alternative of draconian deflation. Justified, too, if it could prepare the way for the longer-term goal. But the latter assumption was flawed. More likely would be pent-up reactions once the controls were taken off. In the event, too, there would be the further result that new institutions which had been set up to operate the first type of policy would suffer from later stampeding into the second, and that the Wilson government would lose direction after an exhausting and eventually unpopular, albeit partially successful, emergency phase.

As the last chapter showed, the goal of mutual restraint in the interests of anti-inflation and steady growth had become central for believers in an adapted capitalism. A turning point had come with the FBI and BEC top circles' acceptance, by early 1964, of reciprocity in the form of price 'investigation' and 'restraint' (though some preferred measures on dividends or aggregate profits): a sacrifice considered worthwhile for the sake of trade union collaboration and pay moderation. Opposition within the FBI and the BEC, and the TUC's stand-off from the Conservatives, had led to the idea being shelved. Now came hopes that the new government would push it forward, aided by allies in the TUC, particularly George Woodcock, with organised business joining the compact provided there was sympathy for their difficulties. The revisionists, indeed, were ready for major moves not just on prices. Maurice Laing, again in the vanguard, was quick to urge a broad-based compact including other incomes besides wages, and wider benefits to employees.

For a time things went quite well. Leading revisionists were encouraged by George Brown's go-getting thrust, not only in eliciting quick signature from the TUC to a Statement of Intent as a prelude to prices and incomes legislation, but also in making cordial (if stampeding) advances to themselves. The Statement, signed in December 1964 by Government, TUC and the main business organisations, was voluntarist and productivity-oriented. Its main emphasis was on boosting efficiency to allow money incomes to grow in line with productivity. The attitude towards business appeared to be constructive: restrictive practices were roundly condemned, and the main onus for restraining wages was placed on the unions. At the FBI Council Runge and Kipping won acceptance by stressing these positives, citing fears of wage inflation, and appealing to idealism as well as *realpolitik*, with Runge opining that 'a good many [managers] would be roused to action by it'.[14]

The early phases avoided serious storms. In spring 1965 came the creation of the NBPI, headed by Aubrey Jones, to investigate difficult price and wage claims. This body would have a tripartist make-up and a strong productivity orientation. Revisionist leaders welcomed it and got it through.[15] Initially, it was hoped to give a more active role to both the CBI and TUC by allowing them to exercise moral suasion on affected constituents before a referral. This would have complemented the Board's essentially educative rather than policing role (as it turned out, this aspiration was soon left behind by events). After wage pressures failed to decline through 1965, the government legislated in late 1965 for early warnings on price and wage increases, but though the CBI had not wanted this, still there was little discontent.[16]

The turning-point came in July 1966. Even before, evidence had gathered of stagnating growth and over-shooting wage increases, and the government's general economic policies were running into major difficulties. It was the deeply disappointing 'July measures', with their resort to deflation and statutory control, and the symbolic resignation of George Brown, which initiated a new and more stormy phase. The return to 'stop-go' and the ensuing phases of 'freeze' and 'severe restraint' dealt severe blows to morale. CBI revisionists had supported price and dividend restraint on assumptions of non-*dirigisme* and expansionism, both of which were now in disarray. Criticism from the CBI Council to price control became frequent, endangering the revisionists' overall strategy in dealing with the government.[17] The price freeze was felt to be particularly onerous, especially as the government's tax changes were thought, if exaggeratedly, to be hindering profitability (see below). Although much of its reformist work on costs, productivity and pay systems continued, using methods of investigation, evaluation and public pressure which gained respect, the NBPI became loaded with unwelcome, semi-draconian functions, and hence stigmatised. Thus had the emergency version of prices and incomes policy taken over.

This version would evoke a different calibre of revisionist support. It was now a case of grim acquiescence, acceptance that some alternatives could be even worse, considerations of overseas confidence, winnowing out marginal concessions through lobbying. The sense of high common endeavour receded. Price control would be accepted, in a more grudging way, for purely 'political reasons'.[18] Incomes policy by *fiat* would be seen, rather dismally, as a corollary of deflation in necessary, moderate doses. A morose sense grew of something transitory, second or even third best, unfortunately necessary yet also politically unsustainable for the government. The revisionist leadership flirted with other counter-inflationary ideas. Some of these reverted to the ideal-type but fragmentedly, notably tighter national parameters for productivity bargaining and, more controversially, trade union reform (see below).[19] Others edged, mostly in private, towards a mild proto-monetarism, with rather more deflation and unemployment reluctantly accepted as the price.[20] The CBI still supported prices and incomes policy but in lower gear. After devaluation in late 1967, and the end of both freeze and severe restraint, the leadership would still urge members towards voluntary price restraint, along with productivity and export effort, its stance dutifully patriotic and 'responsible' yet somehow lacking in spirit.[21]

It should be said that the prospects for a return to the ideal-type project appeared hardly encouraging. Existing instruments which could be used for it, particularly the NBPI, were under a cloud. Only minorities of social democrats or left-leaning Tories, economists and commentators, clearly favoured it. Trade union militancy, TUC stand-off, Labour Party opposition, official Conservative uninterest by this time, all were negative factors even before business's own disillusions were considered. The difficulties would be further exemplified by the government's plan for a Commission of Industry and Manpower in 1970, to amalgamate the Monopolies Commission and the NBPI, strongly opposed by the CBI as offering too much on the side of price control while abandoning a realistic incomes policy.[22]

The chances of long-term voluntary agreement seemed remote. For the CBI revisionists alone to have stood out for such a thing would have required a large dose of commitment, and much intellectual effort to back it up. Overseas models would have to be researched, resources diverted from other pursuits, wider currents of thinking drawn on, a manifesto-type vision adopted. This was still a viable proposition between 1966 and 1969. A major revisionist effort could have redesigned the long-term policy, but there was little sign of enthusiasm from the leadership: the efforts of Davies, Brown, Norman and the rest were now devoted to the narrower aims of damage limitation. Not until a new phase of leadership had been installed after 1969 did some of the earlier boldness on this issue return.

The vicissitudes of planning and growth

As indicated in the last chapter, revisionists' views on 'planning' were secondary. They feared a 'trojan horse' for 1940s-type *dirigisme*, even a drift to French-style selectivity. Their commitment was to a channel for (a) information-sharing and consultation, (b) a stronger say for industry, (c) supply side policies to sustain Keynesian demand management, and (d) 'indicative' signals towards a steadier and (slightly) higher growth rate. Not a path to 'breakthrough' nor a centre-piece of macro-management. It is unsurprising, then, that Labour's sweeping idea for a National Plan was received without enthusiasm. Even in autumn 1964 the FBI's main economic committee was reappraising 'planning', and it was widely felt that existing NEDC growth targets had been too optimistic. A conference in January 1965 showed some cooling of the 'growth first' mentality of Brighton 1960.[23] Thus, the draft National Plan's vaunting targetry and would-be paradigm quality, voluntarist though it was, met with private scepticism, and it took all George Brown's threats and blandishments (including a comic opera hot pursuit to Sunningdale) to get the business leaders' consent. In the event, the Plan proved largely anodyne and, after July 1966, inoperable. What mattered more to the revisionists were the concomitants, and here it was the inter-related issues of 'consultation' and fiscal change that soon loomed larger.[24]

In private, considerable doubts were expressed about the feasibility of the Plan's growth targets. On the other hand, it was seen to have some promise in stimulating greater activity through EDCs and related policies on manpower and training. Publicly, the revisionist leaders praised its educative role as a benefit to productivity-consciousness. The business representative bodies enjoined co-operation and (though still privately sceptical) accepted the 3.8 per cent growth target for 1964–70.[25] Companies' ideas on their own future growth, composited by trade associations, provided the groundwork for DEA macro-projections: it was never on the cards that this would be refused (though extreme liberationists flirted with non-co-operation). However, discussion on the realism of firms' objectives was not given high priority by the DEA as it hustled to produce the Plan, intended to be a centre piece in the general election. The CBI view that preparation had been rushed, leading to the NEDC business members initially refusing to sign, was privately shared by TUC officials.[26]

With the collapse of the National Plan in summer 1966, many CBI figures, notably Weeks, argued for a more modest version based on a mixture of independent forecasts, avoiding single-figure targets, with implementation of micro-measures largely in the hands of the EDCs. They further relegated the idea of a psychological boost to industry *via* aggregate targets, restating the belief in a core of joint industry-level activities, as against the direction-from-above of the DEA. The stress was on productivity gains, rejecting the more expansionary projections of meeting 'productive potential', as argued by the NEDO.[27]

For revisionists, though, a more abiding aim was a stronger voice for 'industry' as represented by their own brand of 'progressive' leadership. From this point of view the Labour regime would demonstrate some major advances on its predecessors but also major derelictions. Its warm support for the CBI's formation was appreciated. The government was initially considered to have a closer interest in industrial issues than the Conservatives, its very activism expected to give rise to more intensive consultation. High points of interaction were achieved with George Brown, on a narrower front with Ray Gunter, in the earlier stages.[28] On the other hand, Brown's decision to downgrade the NEDO and put new EDCs under DEA control conflicted with the revisionist view of the autonomy of the NEDC from government. Although Brown himself was trusted, it was felt the DEA had sufficient power to implement *dirigiste* policies under a left-wing minister. In early 1966 the CBI proposed a more independent NEDC. The overtaking of the DEA by a more interventionist MinTech under the less sympathetic Tony Benn provoked the CBI into one of its most outspoken attacks of the period, on the Industrial Expansion Act 1968, with its plan for industrial subsidies regardless of consultation processes and less than careful as to the usual profitability criteria.[29]

But these were minor issues compared with dismay over the government's fiscal changes. Every one of its leading new tax/subsidy measures – Corporation Tax, Selective Employment Tax, expanded development grants, the shift from depreciation allowances to investment grants – provoked a sharp critique. Some of these measures involved a suspect discretionary element. A common feature, it was felt, had been unexpectedness and lack of careful preparation and consultation. Overall, the impression was that Labour still underestimated the importance of higher corporate profits in a successful mixed economy, and that the total burden of corporate taxation was being increased.[30]

CBI economic thinking in 1967–70 tended to edge away slightly from expansionist, Keynesian positions. Some thought not nearly enough: the free marketeer Arthur Shenfield, a section within the economic committee and, as always, a number of eloquent City or small firm voices on Council. A few staff papers broached issues like money supply targeting: a return was even mooted to the pre-Brighton principles of 1957.[31] At the other end of the CBI spectrum some maintained a bolder, more 'social' revisionism, whose voice began to be heard again after 1969 (see chapter 5). The mainstream tendency was to show cautious sympathy for more modest demand management strategies. Veteran revisionists like Weeks still baulked at wholesale deflation and unemployment, rejecting 'Paishite' policies. But, partly reflecting the retreat of incomes policy, partly gloom about general prospects and, by the late 1960s, EEC entry conditions, they judged that lower demand pressures and a slightly higher margin of unemployment would be necessary to stimulate competitiveness.[32] A further approach, favoured by John Davies, was to increase activities addressed to micro-economic improvement, through industrial policy, the EDCs, and education of CBI members. The emphasis on information-sharing, education and persuasion for 'self-reform', an important feature of revisionism, was maintained and expanded.[33]

The CBI leadership kept up the Kipping tradition of 'responsible' budget representations. Despite sweeping attacks on government 'profligacy', particularly by Norman, appeals for reduced public expenditure were still moderate, differing in both extent and tone from the Institute of

Directors and the Industrial Policy Group (see next chapter).[34] In fact, during Roy Jenkins' tenure at the Treasury, with its sympathetic, 'responsible' aim of restraining public spending and shifting resources to exports and investment, the fiscal policy gap with the government was tending to lessen. The CBI wanted more to be done along these lines. As to what should actually be cut, however, they remained coyly unspecific. For this the reasons ranged from public relations, through tactical fears of offending some members and disagreements among themselves, to the argument that specific priorities were the government's role, not business's.[35] Despite these ambiguities, a constructive core persisted, becoming increasingly clearly a hallmark of the new organisation: the appeal, year in, year out, for greater industrial investment. Much practice was being developed in this task, though it would call for a tenacious, often harder slog through later phases.

The limits of voluntarism: the reform of industrial relations

To develop industrial relations policies would be a particularly delicate task for the new CBI, inheritor as it was of such an extreme diversity of industrial relations practices and attitudes in its constituent parts. The new organisation incorporated a legacy of stark contrasts from the old BEC, between penny-pinching and welfare-rich companies, the large and the small, the despotic, paternalist or sophisticated, along with a byzantine system of representative bodies, ranging from the separatist engineering and shipbuilding federations to a long tail of often outdated and insular-minded lesser units.[36] Various organisational compromises with this system had been tactically necessary in putting the CBI together.

Not all the revisionist leaders were deeply experienced or involved in industrial relations issues: men like Runge and Laing (or, later, John Partridge, Campbell Adamson, Lord Watkinson) much more than Davies and Norman, Plowden or Benson. The field was one where an 'enlightened', welfare-ist leadership, close to 'progressive', profitable companies, the Industrial Society or like-minded trade unionists and academics, could easily run ahead of much conservative grassroots opinion within the CBI. However, government and public opinion as well as revisionist would soon produce pressures for an active policy, particularly in relation to the work of the Donovan inquiry between 1965 and 1968.

The potential resources for such a policy were considerable. It could draw on the tested practices of vanguard firms like ICI or, more recently, Esso and the NCB: boardroom priority for human and industrial relations, a developed personnel function, schemes for employee welfare, joint consultation, plant or company councils. It could examine overseas models like those of West Germany or Sweden. Ideas circulating in the Industrial Society could be drawn on, for example for reducing top managerial 'perks' or secrecy or status divisions between 'staff' and 'labour'.[37] Reforms widely discussed at this time could be urged on the trade union movement, towards a rationalisation of unions and a stronger TUC, and away from restrictive practices and archaic attitudes. A parallel priority, as many revisionists were well aware, would be rationalisation of the employers' own organisation and representation. Pressing issues arose as to existing or new legislation on, for example, trade union immunities or unofficial strikes. But then, in equity, there would be a case for strong pressures to be applied also on companies with poor human and industrial relations practices. For it was widely agreed that the main responsibility in this field tended to lie with management.[38]

Awkward issues arose for revisionists. In view of their preferences for gradualism and mild reform, how much change in industrial relations practices and institutions did they really want? How far could change come about through their favoured methods of education, persuasion and example, without at least some legislation? The policy dilemmas here would be acute. Insofar as wide reforms were proposed, let alone some statutory back-up envisaged, how could this be reconciled with 'voluntarism', a CBI consensus, the objections of powerful business traditionalists? And what implications would arise for relationships with the trade unions, given not only the revisionist aims for mutualism and a tripartite incomes policy but the fact that the trade union movement was also, in the main, deeply conservative?

In practice, the CBI regime of the late 1960s would make only tenuous progress on industrial relations policy: it would take a new leading group from 1969–70 onwards at least to aim higher. Nor would external developments favour such progress. Towards the end of the period an unpredicted snarl-up would arise between the Labour government and the trade unions. The earlier revisionist scenario, which had invested much hope in a constructive rapport between the two, in the interests at once of incomes policy, trade union reform and industrial peace, would unravel, and business-government relationships would also suffer.

The first main test was the CBI's initial evidence to Donovan. Its preparation was left to the Labour and Social Affairs Committee (LSAC), a group dominated by representatives of the industrial/employer bodies inherited from the BEC. Initially at least, the LSAC did not favour a one-sidedly hawkish view on legislation exclusively to discipline the trade unions.[39] To avoid such a 'reactionary' approach was considered vital by revisionists, given their aims for tripartism, pay policy and rapport with the government. Hard-liners on trade union law had been marginalised. For the LSAC to promote constructive proposals on other fronts was, however, another matter. Its composition was unlikely to encourage much reformism or even competence on intra-company industrial relations or personnel practices, still less to favour rationalisation of employers' associations. Rather, its main interest lay in formal collective bargaining policies: a professional concentration shared, it should be said, with the industrial relations academics who would strongly influence the Donovan Commission itself, albeit with a different slant.[40] No strong counter-concerns were evident at the top, either from the presidents after Laing or, more significantly, from the director-general. An inquiry into the key issue of 'worker participation' did not start until after the final evidence to Donovan had been given, and the formation of a new committee largely of personnel experts, the Employment Policy Committee (EPC), did not take place until 1969. The LSAC's own initial proposals received little discussion in the CBI and were agreed by the Council without demurral.[41]

The first written evidence to Donovan showed much caution over employer failings, described in vague terms and stressing gradualist, 'voluntarist' improvements; also over trade union reforms. The main focus was on formal collective bargaining processes. New 'voluntary' procedures were envisaged to better allow the union leaderships to control unruly members. Voluntary registration of unions was proposed (in order to preserve immunities enjoyed since 1906), overseen by a new strengthened registrar (probably a major public figure agreed by both employers and unions). The registrar would advise and caution on unions' internal procedures in order to reduce the frequency of unofficial and unconstitutional strikes.[42] Persistent failure by a union to enforce its own procedures against recalcitrants would mean deregistration and liability for civil damages. Resort to the courts, as argued by both the EEF and the Conservatives, was ruled out.[43] The idea of a registrar would continue as a centre piece until the 1971 Industrial Relations Act. These proposals did not advocate 'top-down', inclusive business-labour institutions on Scandinavian lines: understandably, in view of current trends towards decentralised or plant bargaining processes, often related to productivity deals. More seriously, they fell short in the areas of managerial responsibility and intra-company practices, and reform of employers' associations. Indeed, they offered little in the way of *quid pro quos* by employers even in terms of exhortation to self-reform, let alone comparable public registrar-type surveillance. Yet their relative moderation on trade union law did not satisfy more hawkish business opinion inside or outside the CBI.[44]

Events soon conspired to push the LSAC towards a tougher line on trade union law, though still without comparable moves on issues of employer responsibility and organisation. Unofficial strikes seemed to be spreading. Increasingly, the grass roots growled about tougher measures, as did the EEF, more sophisticatedly, while the Conservative opposition and the press were moving in the same direction, even, it soon appeared, leading members of the government. As a result, when evidence was resubmitted in late 1967, the CBI had moved some way towards the EEF, both in accepting the prosecution of individuals who carried out unofficial actions, and in agreeing the arguments against LEPAS 'weigh[ed] less heavily'.[45] Negative noises were also made about reform of pay bargaining, the extension of collective bargaining and white-collar unionism, with opposition thrown in to the idea of worker directors, but again without alternatives.

The Donovan Commission Report itself disappointed keen reformers: its gradualist, 'voluntarist' proposals for case-by-case investigation of trade union and employer defects through a new Commission for Industrial Relations (CIR) appeared to miss many important targets.[46] Predictably, the CBI fully supported the CIR while finding the Report unsatisfactory in other ways. It was felt to be weak *vis-à-vis* the unions. In a more technical sense, its assumption that plant-level bargaining could be institutionalised was considered naive in the absence of measures for improving intermediary bargaining at industry levels. None the less, the idea of an employers' counter-offensive would be ruled out by the majority. Gloom about shop-floor militancy made the CBI wary of direct intervention and it equally conspired to discourage positive alternatives. A degree of implicit collusion with trade union conservatism was apparent, in line with Samuel Beer's theory of UK sectional interests locked into 'pluralistic stagnation'.[47]

As the debate on union power split the Labour Party and helped to energise the opposition, the CBI was reduced to commenting from the wings. Barbara Castle's *In Place of Strife* was supported on ideas for conciliation pauses and inter-union disputes, but the CBI leadership took a low profile and, like other interested parties, was not much taken into the confidences of Castle or Wilson. As TUC opposition grew, the CBI leadership warned the government that no union legislation should proceed and, when the government decided against legislation, seemed relieved that extreme confrontation had been avoided. These experiences, though, had confirmed a belief from most of the membership that some form of legislation was inevitable in the future.[48]

An opportunity for all-round reform had been missed. Revisionism had not fulfilled its promise in this important field. The CBI had been mainly reactive, one-sided and hardly very innovative. The government seemed to be falling between all the·stools in its relationships with the trade unions. After drawing heavily on their goodwill through the pay 'freeze' and 'severe restraint', the unions would be alienated by *In Place of Strife*, in some ways, it could be argued, misdirectedly; then had their conservatism and power placated, with free collective bargaining restored and the chances of a long-term incomes policy put back. It was a curiously ironic fade-out for revisionist hopes of an entente with the Labour government.

Final comments

During this period the arguments for and against co-operation with the Labour government assumed an almost ritual consistency within parts of the business community. Certain underlying logics of confrontation or collaboration appeared, which were to recur repeatedly in the '70s, particularly under Labour but also with the Heath government in 1972–74. Such ritual exchanges were particularly marked in private, in the Council of the CBI, where two sets of rhetorics tended to become standard. They were mainly conducted in the 'non-ideological' language of strategy or tactics even though important differences of ideological belief were reflected.

Critics from the floor would urge that the CBI should 'take a stand', 'make a collective resistance', 'not have anything to do' with this or that government measure, 'not be governed by threats'. The leadership would be criticised for being 'too ready to co-operate', 'carried too readily in the slip stream of the government's economic policy', with 'too much going on behind the scenes.' To seek concessions or safeguards from government, for example on steel nationalisation or prices, indeed to be drawn into consultation with them, would risk the impression of accepting these ideas or even 'becoming an agent of Government policy.' 'Non-co-operation' should be threatened unless 'conditions' were met.[49]

The case for co-operation, as expressed by leading moderates or revisionists, equally developed familiar qualities through its various mutations. At one end of the spectrum were moral or patriotic appeals: 'pulling together', 'faith in the British people', 'a responsible contribution', 'the CBI must help'. Then came defensive patriotism or 'national emergency' criteria: a degree of co-operation was needed to reassure foreign opinion and avert dangers to sterling. Occasionally, the disadvantages would be cited of criticising the party in power, appearing to take a party political stance or disregarding public opinion. Much would be made of Kipping-style arguments for staying at the centre in order to gain moderate concessions. Increasingly dominant was the bottom line argument that, unwelcome though they were, measures like early warning of price increases or the voluntary pay and price 'freeze' were, none the less, preferable, or 'the lesser evil', to compulsion or legislation.[50]

Even now, after all these years, the potential scope for co-operation appears controversial. In practice, the relationship had proved less stressful than many on both sides had feared, not so much riven by doctrinal discord as hassled and irritated. By 1970 the worst stereotypes had given way to a wary respect at least between the main revisionist leaders of organised industry and most of the Labour ministers involved in economic and industrial affairs (though these gains would be set back in the mid-1970s). A benign interpretation would suggest that a constructive working relationship could well have developed but for faults in economic sophistication and political psychology. The problem, according to this view, lay in the government's early economic judgements particularly over sterling and devaluation, overseas commitments and corporate taxation, their grandiose promises and the expectations they aroused: all of which, once mixed with some City and market over-reactions, led to the successive unravellings over deflation, incomes policy and industrial relations. The view would be that, barring these mistakes, Labour's policy stances by the 1960s provided few obstacles that could not have been ironed out over time, subject also to steady revisionist adaptability on the business side.

An obvious objection is that an entente would still have been vulnerable to counter-reactions, perhaps even in the short-run, whether from shop-floor militancy, left-wing influences in the Labour Party, or conservative and liberationist opposition within business, not to mention a Conservative Party jealous of its traditional majority hold on business opinion. Other more sombre interpretations also claim attention. One is that a genuine rapprochement was unfeasible within the ambit of ideas offered by business revisionists and reformist social democrats at this time. According to this view, such a rapprochement would have been artificial or elitist, a 'corporatism' without roots, lacking appropriate changes from the ground up, not only in firms, markets and trade unions but also in politics, culture and social values. For it to work, a fundamental redrawing of boundaries would have been needed. The reconstructionist tendency of business opinion, close to this viewpoint, will be examined later (see chapter 6). But according to a rival and even more astringent interpretation, the very idea of a rapprochement was essentially misconceived, indeed yet another sign of Britain's long slide to decline or disaster. It is to this ideology, with its explosive potential for the whole post-war settlement, that we now turn.

4 Liberationist capitalism in the wilderness 1960–1975

> Businessmen would have more confidence ... if they could operate under the certainties of the rule of law rather than the uncertainties created by delegated legislation, exhortation, pressure and directives ... The best guarantee of a healthy economy would be ... for government to confine itself to ensuring that the economy is intensely competitive ... and leave everything else to the forces of the market. Leslie Lazell
>
> I want to see Britain so galvanised by the necessity to survive ... competition as to achieve a rebirth of national morale. George Bolton[1]

Liberationist capitalism was in many ways the most sharply drawn and uncompromising business ideology. Its assumptions about the role of business in society and the workings of the economy left little ground for either political compromise or social balancing. Although the defence of 'free enterprise' had been a major pillar of an earlier business conservatism, liberationists challenged the complacency of introspective business leaders as much as they disdained the 'appeasement' of the revisionists. Business in an overall sense was to be adversarial, expansionist, ultimately predominating, but this would first require the reintroduction of a competitive environment not seen in the UK for most of the twentieth century.

Underlying the arguments of the liberationists was a sense of business having lost its previously dominant role in society through an odious mixture of managerial incompetence, political corruption and cultural neglect. The mid-twentieth century recession of UK business had run in exact parallel to the extension of the state's functions of economic management. Business had been shackled, markets manipulated, enterprise disdained. These weaknesses, although primarily associated with 'socialist' government and politicised trade unions, also reflected a longer-lasting malaise. Business itself was held to have lost sight of its true functions of enterprise, risk-taking and productivity, preferring the temporary advantages of protected markets and shop-floor peace. Business organisations, both peak bodies and trade associations, were wrongly nurturing a belief in economic benefit won by political negotiation or macro-economic trade-offs. Even worse for liberationists was the easy way in which, as it appeared to them, revisionists had abandoned the notion of business leadership within society through its incomparable contribution to both wealth creation and liberty.

Liberationism was a minority position amongst articulate business opinion in this period. Efforts to push it into the mainstream organisations as a basis for policy fell foul of major obstacles, as we will show. This factor, fully recognised by the liberationists themselves, contributed to a sense of the superior insight available to those virtuously detached from the centre of affairs with all its compromises and temptations. Hence, their prescriptions were much more doctrinal, irreverent, goading. In the eyes of its proponents, liberationism was 'anti-Establishment'; it offered business's only true line of defence against encroachment and its opportunity to fight back. Liberationists would challenge the elitism of the revisionist leadership, and speak for businesses marginalised by the prevailing channels of debate.

Liberationism was a fundamentalist outlook, intent on returning to an idealised earlier settlement where business operated within the normative constraints of a free market economy, not compromised by competing ideals, especially not from within business. The implied fundamental break with post-war experience justifies their liberationist nomenclature. However, the notion of relentlessly proselytising and defending an irreducible ideological core undoubtedly applies. For them the ideas associated with revisionism were subversive excrescences and the ensuing compromises far too costly. Though their free market evangelism rarely compared to that from non-business or more theoretical sources, indeed had some significant differences with these, their motives for speaking out could lead them to a semi-religious fervour.

Liberationism tended to oversimplify and it could also appear introspective. Compared to revisionism and reconstructionism, the breadth of its conceptions of polity and economy was not great. It was less concerned with the ideas of non-business groups and viewed opposing ideologies as monolithic and adversarial. Its spokesmen did not generally share the same conceptions of political constraint or winning an immediately achievable advantage. Consequently, during the 1960s and early 1970s it was rarely in a position to influence government directly or to mobilise opinion on its behalf within the peak business organisations.

This distance from other groups and ideas had its advantages. Liberationists admitted to strong *a priori* convictions about the workings of the economy. Assumptions about the priority of rules over discretionary management in economic policy, the difficulty of explaining, let alone manipulating, macro-economic aggregates for preconceived ends, and a corresponding belief that the sources of both economic stability and creativity were to be found at the micro-economic level: these were basic convictions, confirmed rather than discovered through corporate experience. So strong was their hold that many of the policies revisionists viewed as unavoidable for business simply were unavailable to liberationists. Indeed, although there was a reluctance to indulge in utopian competitive models in the manner of some economic theorists, there was an equally strong refusal to admit to interventionist 'exceptions' generated by the 'mixed' economy. A refusal to follow precepts of 'economic man' and perfect competition in their public rhetoric made for apparent similarities to revisionism. But a refusal to accept that rivalrous economic motivations required political modification maintained the distinction.

Communicating the message: the liberationist voice

The liberationists' message was conditioned by the method of its communication: this is to state the obvious. In the early 1960s it was already clear that the revisionists had gained the upper hand in the key representative organisations. Liberationism was not able to sustain a full-fledged debate within these organisations or even to operate a coherent opposition standpoint. Moderate liberationists could not prevent their leaderships committing them officially to support 'mixed economy' compromises, tripartism and incomes policy. This, in turn, affected the fundamentalists' self-image. Their viewpoints would increasingly be broadcast in speeches to business and non-business sources, often deliberately aiming for press attention by provocative statements.

Paul Chambers, chairman of ICI in the 1960s, was particularly outspoken, offering a running critique in the press columns of practically all aspects of revisionism in this period. A self-confident, occasionally aggressive polemicist, Chambers was a rare business leader admired by free marketeers in the Institute of Economic Affairs (IEA), never 'flinching' when accepting the consequences of their proposals, but treated more warily within the business community. Many of his acerbic assaults on Labour (which were to lead to equally caustic rejoinders from James Callaghan in 1967; see below), were notable for their insistence and uncompromising stance. As he proudly told an IEA audience: 'I am not a typical industrialist'.[2] Chambers was an asset to liberationism because he represented one of the largest manufacturing firms with a traditionally 'progressive' image yet was able to use his position to criticise 'planning' and the unions in a manner which attracted much attention. However, even as independent a figure as he was constrained by corporate considerations and by I C I collegial conventions not to break its consensus on industrial relations policies.

A reputation for outspoken independence and distance from organisational constraints marked out a number of other leading liberationists. They were able to exploit the need of the press for 'pundits' who could offer personal comments on key economic and business issues. This helped several major figures to gain attention: George Bolton, a banker and expert on international economic relations; Leslie Lazell, a key figure in the emergence of Beechams as an international pharmaceuticals firm, a skilled 'technocrat', whose apparent diffidence disguised passionately held free market views; and Halford Reddish, a self-consciously old-fashioned defender of free enterprise.[3] In later years, liberationist views were also heard in the House of Lords from such figures as Frank Taylor (Taylor Woodrow), Frank MacFadzean, Ray Brookes of G K N and Nigel Vinson.

Although it was felt by some free market economists and publicists that business support for their cause could be double-edged because of a weak grasp of the relevant theory, some liberationists published well-worked analyses in pamphlets and lectures. MacFadzean and Vinson were particularly involved with the 'New Right' pressure groups. Both were well acquainted with such ideas, and were able to put their case in attractive, accessible language, drawing on business experience. MacFadzean, a tough-minded Scot, nicknamed 'fearless Frank', chairman of 'Shell' and later of British Airways and Rolls Royce, argued a sober, well-documented case for the continuing relevance of entrepreneurialism even in the largest multinationals. He devoted considerable energy and acumen to rebutting J. K. Galbraith's prediction of the inevitable dominance of the 'mature' corporation, serviced by a large, functionally independent 'technostructure'. Instead, he related how Shell's board was forced to act entrepreneurially in the competitive energy sector and the risky world of oil production.[4]

Nigel Vinson, a successful small business man, argued the case from the other end of the spectrum, contending for the entrepreneurial talent of the small firm as the best pathway out of decline. He was also passionately committed to the wider ownership of property and capital, sympathetic to a greater employee involvement in the enterprise, and for a greater sense of popular engagement in the 'capitalist system'.[5] Others defended their convictions by showing how liberationist precepts had been confirmed in their corporate lives. Lazell's memoirs, *From Pills to Penicillin*, emphasised the gut realities of entrepreneurialism and the irrelevance of governmental associations in the success of Beechams. Others, such as Bolton and, later, Nicholas Goodison, published widely, explaining and defending the role of the City in the UK economy. Groups like the IEA and Aims of Industry (AOI) were also keen to draft in business leaders for publications which had a specific industry slant.

Links with sympathetic intellectual traditions set the liberationists apart from business conservatives of an earlier period. Earlier free enterprise campaigns were held to have been too narrow, negative or purely defensive, and often too secretive. Liberationists were invariably keen to banish the notion that they were social traditionalists, with close links to diehard Conservatism. As we shall see, the Institute of Directors (IOD) encountered problems precisely because of this image. This is not to deny that some sympathisers retained attributes of an older social elitism, including an unwillingness to engage in open debate. Many preferred a behind-the-scenes role as patrons or *eminences grises* for anti-socialist pressure groups. This was particularly the case within the IOD and with those involved with Aims of Industry such as John Reiss of Portland Cement, Ian Lyle of Tate and Lyle, Lord Rank, and Garfield Weston. Along with many City figures, such people did not court publicity, and did not have a deep intellectual engagement with free market ideas. They generally had closer political attachments to the Conservative right-wing. They represented a form of business intervention which had changed little from its Victorian precedents in the Liberty and Property Defence League or the Industrial Freedom League.

The platforms which the liberationists chose to speak from helped to differentiate their message from that of the revisionists. It was freed from the tactical considerations inevitably associated with peak organisation membership; it made for a bolder, manifesto-type statement; it could appeal directly to gut feeling of businesses excluded from the representational and corporate elites, whilst avoiding marginalisation because its spokesmen were prestigious figures within business. Some were to be called before statutory commissions because of the distinctive positions they adopted (for example, Halford Reddish before the Donovan Commission or, much later, John Clark of Plessey before the Aldington Committee).

The liberationist message, therefore, was highly individualised and relatively unconstrained by corporate or collective disciplines. The language was often pungent: Chambers, Lazell, Grierson and MacFadzean could be caustic critics especially of opposing business opinions. An air of frustrated and bemused disbelief frequently hangs about their statements. At the lower rhetorical level of the CBI and IOD councils, such convictions would be repeatedly voiced in an even more 'disgusted' manner. Liberationists would have damning things to say about the 'boy-scout enthusiasm' of their fellows for the fashionable economic nostrums of the time.[6] Repeatedly, they would resound a self-image as unique, righteous defenders of a true faith too often suppressed or surrendered.

Social visions: liberation, competition, predominance

Although the economic basis of liberationism was the benign working of free markets, the core social concepts were those of *liberation* and *competition*. Liberationists believed that business should have the dominant role in a restored free market economy. Entrepreneurs would contribute not only to material well-being but, through the display of their virtues and excellences, would restore public faith in business. Such leadership, far from leading to destructive social atomisation, would encourage workers to identify more closely with their enterprise, and to derive satisfactions (not simply material) from it. A number of liberationists saw the company as an oasis of good human relations; necessarily so in order to endure the rigours of competition. The guiding role of business would, however, require legitimation through whole-hearted acceptance of a thorough competitive regime. Hankerings after business privilege won through protection or restrictive practices had to be removed: in their acceptance of modernisation the liberationists stood with the revisionists.

Liberationists believed that the role of business in the economy was paramount; it alone provided the mechanisms of economic success. They were less sensitive to the complex interdependences of modern economies. What stood out for them was a notion of dynamic change to remove artificial obstacles to surging entrepreneurial energies. The almost intuitive understanding of economic forces enjoyed by business rendered negotiation and information-sharing with government and unions irrelevant. Hence their limited belief in bodies like NEDC (see below). Indeed, politics was seen as a trap for business, because politicians of all stripes were dedicated to maintaining a monopoly on the direction of change in society.

Since the outbreak of the Second World War *dirigiste* economic management had been preferred to the free play of competition. Artificial restraints on business had accumulated while trust in the entrepreneur had diminished. Business had succumbed or compromised in the main, relying on the predictable, though sadly under-achieving gains available through protected markets in an inflationary environment. The removal of this atmosphere was seen in uplifting, quasi-moralistic terms. Its abolition was even viewed as the clue to a rebirth of national morale, with a related revival in non-economic areas. The removal of restraint would allow inherent and abundant potentials for risk-taking, enterprise and creativity to spring forth. That these qualities were widely distributed was a key contention of liberationists. Like their allies among free market theorists, they felt that both growth and coordination would be best served by spontaneity.

In practice, liberation would come about largely through reduction of taxation, both corporate and individual. This would release the resources in a tangible way to allow entrepreneurs to create directly. Lord Brabazon of Tara maintained that the restraint of these latent powers through taxation was an appalling wastage of talent:

History shows repeated examples of peoples rising, monarchs being overthrown and governments swept away by the injustices of taxation. Yet political parties have sunk to such depths of craven fear over the next election results that not a thing is done . . . Imagination, enterprise and enthusiasm have made us the envy of other countries in the past . . . Today we are the same race, we still have all the drive and divine inspiration and initiative; but the Treasury thinks this is a terrible thing and stops it.[7]

The centrality of tax reductions became a distinguishing characteristic of the liberationists. In contrast with the revisionists, they repeatedly argued in both strategic and tactical terms that maximalist demands should be made on this front. They hoped thereby to build up a climate of business discontent and to shift the climate of public opinion. Even if the main benefits would redistribute at least initially to business, the eventual gains would be to the wider society, and hence no shame should be attached to such demands. As an IOD budget submission candidly declared in 1970; 'we should not be worrying about appearing "self-seeking" in calling for radical tax cuts'.[8]

Although similar views were expressed to revisionists on the need for more indirect taxation, and in reducing the role of corporate tax as an economic regulator, liberationists held a radically different view on the priority of tax reduction. They believed this would be of crucial importance in achieving at least three aims: to release resources to set up new businesses; to provide work incentives both for entrepreneurs and workers; and to inculcate a sense of popular involvement in capitalism. Liberationist maximalism reflected an unadorned belief in the dynamism of restoring funds to their true creators. Tax reform should be bold, transparent and unapologetic. Resulting economic inequalities were to be accepted as a necessary condition of business's new role in society, and indeed as reaffirming the inherent inequalities between individuals.

Fiscal neutrality had to be upheld (though perhaps not as unambiguously as by some free market economists). Special tax incentives for business were deprecated as favouring established interests sometimes to the point of potential corruption. The favourable tax treatment of retained earnings to boost corporate investment caused profound disagreements with revisionists because liberationists saw it as excessively 'managerialist', reducing the role of the capital market as a discovery process for new projects, especially for new businesses. Their tax proposals emerged as bold for the time (though less so in retrospect): abolition of surtax, top rate of income tax reduced to 50 per cent, ending differentiation between earned and investment income, severe reduction of capital taxes, especially on small companies. Importantly, all these measures were seen as part of a single package, and as politically highly charged in sharp contrast to revisionist incrementalism. As Paul Chambers put it 'there must be a revolution in the nation's tax system', and business must lead it.[9]

The liberation of business would end the economic stultification which had prevailed since the inter-war depression. Economic failure bred caution and lack of imagination; entrepreneurialism was denigrated, restrictive practices by both big corporations and unions had developed often with help from government. The liberationists viewed the whole economic environment as inimical to competition, a situation with which revisionist-type nostrums had colluded. Leslie Lazell believed that 'our environment has not been a truly competitive one for the whole of my business life' and that 'the only way ... to achieve efficiency, in a free society is to let the pressures of competition operate and to abolish all restrictive practices, whether of management or labour', replacing the 'cost-plus philosophy' which had predominated since the war. Frank MacFadzean recalled that his political instincts were awoken when he returned to the UK from Malaya in the late 1940s, and realised that the competitive challenge had already been lost: 'Instead of vigour, large sections [of industry] had sunk into lassitude, as they reeled under the development of government intervention, while their entrepreneurial function came to be usurped by individuals and institutions ill-equipped to perform them'.[10]

Such viewpoints strongly coloured liberationists understandings of the public sector. This was understood as a place of inherent conservatism, punctuated by indifferent resistance to pressure group activity and wrongly concerned with setting patterns which business would be cajoled to follow. Such concerns 'clashed head-on with the essentially disorderly thrust of capitalist enterprise'.[11] As suggested above, the 'mixing' of the mixed economy was for liberationists only a dilution or displacement of this function. British business could not debate from a position of strength with government to win concessions: any talk of the inevitability of public-private negotiation simply reflected the unwillingness to demand radical change. Dislike of operators on the borders of the mixed economy, who seemed excessively 'politicised and managerialist', was shown in mistrust of the nationalised industry chairmen. A major debate occurred within the IOD in the late 1960s about allowing them membership of the Institute, amidst accusations that they were not true business leaders. The public sector was compared unfavourably with the rough-edged, single-minded attitude of the true entrepreneur. As the IOD put it, 'An institution run by high-minded and unselfish men who are yet sheltered from the outside world can get into a worse state than any conducted by those interested in making a fortune by any means, but circumscribed by the legal framework and the pressure of rival forces'.[12]

The revisionists' flirtation with 'planning' revived fears of the illusion that modern corporations flourished through technical managerial competence rather than entrepreneurial drive. Ronald Grierson, from his experience at the IRC, warned that 'large, semi-institutionalised businesses' were undermining the case for free enterprise from within. He bewailed the 'feverish search for consensus' which characterised UK business in the 1960s as a genuine failure of nerve. He felt this reflected a deeper sense that 'competition is not man's natural instinct', a viewpoint fully shared by many businessmen who preferred the 'safe anchorage of the corporate state'.[13]

Diminishing opportunities for entrepreneurial talent were thought to have bad consequences for the whole of society: the loss of personal initiative and independence; enforced conformity; even increased social conflict as efficiency stagnated. In such circumstances the revival of entrepreneurship acquired a wider legitimacy; as one writer argued: 'enterprise is a sufficiently important social force to need no economic justification'.[14] Liberationists welcomed the hard challenges of competition as character-former, a pathway to a wider meritocracy, showing tangible evidence of the individual or firm's worth, in contrast to the indefinite, skewed or even corrupting results of political engagement. In a revealing phrase, Grierson associated it with 'Old Testament severity, heavy with wrath and punishment' against a mixed economy of 'New Testament ... sweetness, compassion and light'.[15] This could imply a certain self-satisfied conviction that business opponents lacked a similar experience of the sheer hard work of building up an enterprise (and a good proportion of liberationists were themselves founder-entrepreneurs).

A revival of the competitive economy would require new public attitudes to business. Whilst not requiring special privileges, it would need institutional and cultural protection from renewed non-business encroachments. Politicians would have to be suitably modest about their economic understandings; the unions would have to accept with equanimity a reduction in influence from the national political level to the plant. A radical break in political regime would have to occur, supported by a disillusioned public opinion. Yet liberationists were emphatically opposed to ideas of 'businessmen's government', as desired by some business leaders, as mistaking the true areas of business competence. As Grierson insisted: 'It is a contemporary fallacy that some natural identity exists between the responsibilities of government and those of business. This in turn leads to the belief that all will be well if only we had a government of businessmen'. A proper 'distance' from politics should be maintained: 'the business citizen, individual or corporate, is no different in status from any other citizen, and the relationship with the state should be governed by law and nothing else'.[16]

The social justification of business was correspondingly exclusive: 'The contribution to wealth-creation, to value-added, and therefore to profit . . . is the single greatest contribution (business) can make to society'.[17] Most liberationists, however, went much wider than this to include the nurture of vital social values. By contrast, their belief in the corrupting nature of public sector involvements remained strong. This partly reflected disillusioned or limited exposures to public sector roles. Some had held posts which reinforced a sense that the state's effectiveness was best conducted in narrow, specialised channels (Chambers in the Inland Revenue and the German post-war Control Commission, Bolton at the Bank of England). Others had frustrated or unhappy experiences of the public sector (MacFadzean at the Colonial Development Corporation, Grierson at the IRC, to some degree also Edwards at the Electricity Council). Generally, liberationists had lacked the exposure to integrative public sector careers during wartime or post-war, as experienced by leading revisionists: hence a sense of distance was set by the time they reached their peak positions.

The notion that business qualities were transferable to other sectors was undeveloped, perhaps partly as a result of these factors. There was an often stated belief in the need for a commercialised public sector, but rarely a conviction that entrepreneurial mentalities could be transferred into non-business roles. Although this reflected a sense of the exclusive excellences of business, it also revealed a modesty of ambition, itself the product of an under-conceptualisation of other sectors of society. Business liberationists in the 1960s and 1970s were not would-be colonisers of the public sector: even later they were less so than some free market ideologues and politicians. Moreover, they rarely attacked the tripartist involvements of business colleagues head-on: yet the distaste and occasional ridicule for revisionist efforts was never far below the surface. Underlying this was a normative conception of the state, traceable to wider classical liberal precepts, as detached and distant, committed to setting rules of the game for competition and not invested with powers to regulate business with 'non-economic' criteria or to constrain it within 'national' objectives. Preference for 'action not talk' and a professed contempt for 'talking shops' also reflected these tenets.[18] For liberationists it was a fundamental belief that state disengagement from business would have beneficial consequences for all, switching attention away from distributional conflicts and enabling production and creative innovation to flourish.

Ending the post-war settlement? Liberationist economic prescriptions

Liberationists believed that the market economy had been misunderstood by the post-war public, and that in this they had been encouraged by a mistaken body of economists and politicians. As Graham Hutton saw it, economics in the Keynesian ascendancy had been dominated by an unholy alliance of econometrics and 'economic moralism', which had usurped the 'economics of scarcity'. A consequence was the view of economic processes as discoverable through studying macro-economic variables, and hence amenable to a degree of central direction. This belief, allied with a left-wing moralism, had led to the claim that economic management could be subjected to political and moral objectives without losses to efficiency.[19]

Liberationist business leaders shared the general view of 'New Right' economic thinking that greater emphasis had to be given to micro-economic analysis in understanding problems of co-ordination and allocation as well as growth. This fitted in well with the individual contributions that business leaders could make to such an analysis, and they were often recruited specifically to demonstrate the relevance of such a micro-economic analytic approach.[20]

Liberationists showed less interest in neo-classical economic concepts. These, according to MacFadzean, were 'good pedagogues', but hardly featured in their rhetoric. Austrian economic analysis, with its insistence on economic 'subjectivism' and its interpretation of economic co-ordination as unpredictable and spontaneous, had a more obvious appeal, particularly in its central role for the entrepreneur. Few liberationists showed an explicit interest here, though Austrian ideas on the market processes of risk and uncertainty were promoted by Shenfield and MacFadzean. As the latter was to argue, contemporary political language had devalued the market order by 'use of such infantile phrases as 'taming the jungle' or, 'restoring order out of chaos', as if industry was 'simple and homogeneous'. In future, emphasis would have to be given to the 'unquantifiable' and 'intangible', which could by definition only be fully understood by those closest to the market.[21]

This conviction that individual perception and spontaneous coordination underlay the efficiency of market processes was shown variously in discussions of indicative planning, incomes policy, and investment psychology. These were issues where belief in the workings of markets was much more robust than the revisionists'. The underlying understanding appeared broadly to reflect methodological individualism (even if 'the individual' was a firm), and hence denied any major role for central economic coordination. This was to be clearly shown in the ridicule for introducing 'national interest' considerations into decision making.[22]

The appraisal of 'planning' particularly demonstrated these concerns of the liberationists. They were to take the claims of 'planning' enthusiasts more seriously than did revisionists, arguing that it was not only a device for 'creeping nationalisation' and for restriction of competition in favour of larger firms, but that it fundamentally misunderstood the nature of economic coordination. Both Chambers and MacFadzean made intensive critiques of indicative planning under Labour. They argued it represented an unhappy projection onto the macro-level of a narrow aspect of micro-economic analysis of industry: a mistaken assumption that corporate planning was of the same nature as central direction of the national economy. They pointed out, in contrast, both the uncertainties of real-world corporate planning and the deleterious effects of planning for competition. Planning efforts in the UK had seen the dangerous circular reasoning of asking firms to plan production according to politically inflated growth targets, which in turn led each firm to exaggerate its potential market share. With the projections of each firm in the industry leading to production targets in excess of the original plan, the targets of each would have to be reduced by central planners who would then inexorably encourage market-sharing: otherwise, there was the equal danger of over-production and macro-economic disequilibria. Chambers, for example, was adamant that no manipulation of language could make planning acceptable: he attacked as early as 1961, saying his objections were 'quite fundamental'.[23]

As to what should be done until the new dispensation had been introduced, however, the liberationists were less clear. Their thinking about macro-economic policy in the short to medium-term made few advances on the cautious framework of 1950s-style restrictionism. The reluctance to yield a paramount role to 'monetarism' and the muted response to it once it achieved greater recognition in the mid- to late-1950s forms a clear case of business 'filtering out' a concept regarded as 'too extreme' or 'unrealistic'. At the same time Keynesian ideas were downplayed but not abandoned: they remained of value as a last-resort economic remedy for recession. There was a desire to show that lessons of the 1930s had been learnt and that business, as much as other interests, had been a victim of excessive deflation.

Liberationists were more explicit in their calls for a redefinition of 'full employment' but, importantly, they did not suggest that it could be dropped from the economic rubric altogether. Though sceptical of 'politicised' aspects of Keynesianism, they followed their economist mentors, Lionel Robbins and Frank Paish, in putting their macro-economic case quite modestly and conservatively.[24] Little new thinking was done on the question of exchange rates or control of interest rates until 'monetarism' had been firmly established in public discourses. Liberationists preached the long-term benefits of disinflation, but with much less zeal and analysis than with their pursuit of micro-economic issues and the latter's long-term potential for overall economic advance. As a result of all this, their immediate macro-economic stance in the 1960s could easily appear simplistic or inadequate, bringing disapproval particularly from CBI revisionists more directly in touch with the constraints of short-term economic policy.

Monetary policy was still to be given a larger role because it reduced the discretionary powers of the state, whose relationship with the economy it made more transparent. As an earlier FBI document had put it: 'We need the power and status of the State in the field of monetary management and control, but we must reduce its power and scope as a spender and direct participant in economic activity.' Correspondingly, fine-tuning was treated sceptically, partly because its failure led to an ever-ascending tax-take by the state, though relegated in importance rather than dismissed. Liberationists were keen to stress that a conservative financial policy, for all the necessary rectitude it provided, was on its own an inadequate response to national problems, and if over emphasised could weaken the free market case. As the business journal *Scope* put it, monetary policy was backed not 'as an absolute dogma, but in the framework of dynamic, competitive, successful, enterprising people and firms'. Paul Chambers, while contending that inflation was demand-led, with price stability a necessary aim, was careful to insist that private industry should not take the weight through interest rate control and that the true nature of the problem lay in budget deficits.[25]

New views of monetary policy had received some internal discussion within the CBI in the late 1960s but got nowhere.[26] The Industrial Policy Group failed to publicly back similar policies, so the muted support offered to the doctrine in the early 1980s by a number of liberationists becomes more explicable (see chapter 8). There are likely to be complex reasons for this, one being that liberationists, like other business leaders, tended to sheer off theories which seemed excessively one-tracked or 'mechanistic' in form.

Ambivalences and caution existed in other areas as well, particularly industrial policy and denationalisation. In both cases liberationists backed off from bold prescription or creative thinking. Although obviously antipathetic to the nationalised industries and viewing them as an important source of macro-economic instability, they were nevertheless sceptical about returning such industries to the private sector. In 1958 the IOD had concluded that denationalisation was 'an extremely difficult process' and could not suggest any immediate candidates for it; and the organisation's view did not change much for the following twenty years.[27] The absence of a thrust to recolonise industry by the private sector is another example of the business liberationists' caution compared to their allies among free market theorists or purists. But there were also organisational and political reasons for such mutedness, and it is to these that we now turn.

The gentlemanly capitalism of the Institute of Directors 1960–1973

The Institute of Directors was the best-known 'free enterprise' business organisation. Established in 1903, it had long pursued a dual function of making authoritative comments on the status and duties of company directors, and acting as a campaigning organisation not only on their behalf but for general business interests as it conceived them. Here its sympathies were clearly with 'free enterprise' Conservatism. Unlike the other main business organisations (except the BIM) the Institute had an individual membership, and consequently a narrower representational role. As a result it could concentrate on a few technical issues, such as company law and personal taxation, while at the same time ranging more freely over the political scene.

The IOD maintained close links with Conservative backbenchers and peers, where its influence can only be guessed at, and ex-cabinet ministers featured in its upper echelons. Lacking the prestigious rights of access to government of the FBI and BEC, the IOD was forced to concentrate on limited issues of taxation and company law, and any opportunity it had for major political action would be bound up with the concerns of the Conservative right-wing. Its elite was more attached to traditionalist Conservatism, concerned about business in the White Commonwealth, more socially traditionalist, more influenced by non-economic values of public service and social authority, sometimes couched in imperial or military language. The IOD was therefore rather different from the liberationism examined in this chapter, and its transition to this more modern, more economic form was to be a difficult process.

The IOD was for this period still largely dominated by the group which had re-established the organisation in the late 1940s. These men were imbued with traditionalist political values, at a certain social distance from most of their business membership. General Louis Spears, chairman of the Institute's Council 1951–1971, was a former soldier, diplomat and Conservative MP, an author on military topics, a strong personality with limited business experience as an active director.[28] Spears' political beliefs remained in the mind-set of late 1940s anti-socialism, strongly influenced by imperial and Cold War issues. Alongside him was Robert Renwick, a leading City stockbroker, who had been involved with Aims of Industry and funded the IEA. A former chairman of an electricity supply company, his anger over nationalisation in the 1940s had helped to make him a bitter anti-socialist. Essentially a behind-the-scenes figure, Renwick largely guaranteed the control of the post-war leading group until his death in 1973.

The most influential and colourful member of the triumvirate was the director-general, Richard Powell. A baronet and career soldier, he had worked with Renwick at British United Industrialists in the late 1940s and was drafted in to reinvigorate the Institute in 1951. He brought a debonair stylishness to the role, and as a 'great showman' he was an inspired recruiter and the dominant figure up to the mid-1970s. Powell held a somewhat romantic concept of a director's role, with a sense of social obligation and a distaste for crude go-getting. Defending free enterprise with a mixture of 'revivalist fervour' and 'engaging naïveté', he could appear as a slightly unwordly figure, who spoke for the old-fashioned, gentlemanly 'knight of free enterprise' rather than the upwardly mobile entrepreneur.[29] Indeed, the aura of Edwardian grandeur at the IOD's Belgravia HQ under Powell could disconcert even sympathisers.

Much of the public tone was given, however, by the presidents of the IOD, a largely honorific role held by senior industrialists who would, for example, give keynote addresses at the Annual Convention. Two of the most prominent were Lord Chandos and Paul Chambers. Power within the organisation was unsurprisingly hierarchical and even deferential: the symbolic politics of the IOD came through its Annual Convention, where invited speakers, mostly non-business, addressed a passive business audience. A Policy and Executive Committee (PEC) was responsible for strategy and important policy initiatives, which a larger Council would tend quietly to confirm. Businessmen involved at the peak of the organisation were normally from smaller corporate concerns than in the

FBI, often founder-entrepreneurs, and with a disproportionate recruitment from City institutions. Although claiming to speak for small, especially family firms, this sector did not yet have much direct representation in the top echelons.[30] Apart from a certain social distance from much of its membership, the IOD was also hampered by geographical distance. A significant minority of its membership was based in the old white Commonwealth, including Australia, Rhodesia and South Africa, and this factor could exert a strong influence on the leadership, sometimes with markedly right-wing overtones.[31]

To business outsiders the Institute was best-known for its work on personal taxation, and for producing a professional business journal, *The Director*. The journal, edited by George Bull, produced attractive articles on the wider business and political environment, putting business debates into a wider context and encouraging business leaders to speak through its 'business forums' and interviews on key issues of the day. The Institute was also proud of its Taxation Committee, acknowledged for its expertise on corporate and capital taxation issues, where radical proposals were emerging more clearly by 1970.[32] In other areas the Institute's capacities were severely limited. Its full-time staff was still tiny: research had been neglected, it lacked professional economists, and it was wary of offering running political commentaries to the press. In addition, the leadership cultivated an aloof image: political activism tended to be defensive; a cultural barrier to rebellion existed *vis-à-vis* Conservative governments. Hence the 1950s were spent largely in ideological slumbers. The changing climate in the FBI seems to have been missed: even the revival of 'planning' invoked scepticism rather than outright hostility.[33] There appears to have been some reluctance to sponsor either the more radical free market ideas being developed by the IEA or the vigorous campaigning style of AOI.

The election of the Labour government in 1964 seemed to give a fillip to the Institute, especially with the new CBI continuing to make overtures to an ideological enemy. To some extent the Institute became the beneficiary of the backwash of business resentment at high taxation and 'planning'. But although a 'fighting approach' to nationalisation had been adopted even before Labour had been elected, an alternative strategy to that being developed by the CBI was not forthcoming. Powell had an egregious plan to publicise discontent by arranging a mass march of 'bowler-hatted company directors' down Whitehall.[34] Although such public relations gaffes were avoided, the IOD was not successful in utilising the undoubted business discontent with the government by the late 1960s to relaunch itself. The one-day mobilisation of the Annual Convention, however uplifting for liberationist grass-roots, was not developed through a new programme of policies. Rejuvenation would require a new regime (see chapter 7).

Breaking out from revisionism? The Industrial Policy Group 1967–1974

The Industrial Policy Group (IPG) was the most formidable liberationist challenge to the revisionist ascendancy in this period. Unlike the IOD, it aimed to modernise and broaden the appeal of the free market message within the business community. Its novelty lay partly in a desire to go beyond the typical pressure group campaign to embrace the think-tank approach of publishing well-researched policy papers, with help from leading free market economists. It was also novel in recruiting most of its members from top-level manufacturing companies rather than the traditional mainstays of 'free enterprise', the City and small businesses. Moreover, its founders had the intention of recruiting not only known liberationists but also revisionists and the previously silent to convert them to a free market programme. The Group, which has been largely ignored by recent histories of the free market think-tanks, is therefore important because it promised a richer, more diverse debate within the business community, and might have provoked more interesting disputes on key issues in the early 1970s rather than the strange silences which in fact prevailed during the Heath administration.[35]

The IPG was the brainchild of two ideologues: Paul Chambers and Arthur Shenfield, the outspoken CBI Economic Director. Both were deeply concerned about the drift of business opinion under the Wilson government, particularly the 'appeasing' role of the CBI. They mooted the IPG as a body transmitting the 'business voice' on fundamental policies, with the CBI commenting on more immediate issues. Operating under the auspices of the CBI, which partly funded it, the IPG would be able to launch a determined assault on prevailing revisionist nostrums.[36] The formation of the Group had been widely reported, especially after James Callaghan had impugned its motives in strong language in the Commons. In the immediate aftermath of devaluation, when business was deeply disillusioned with the government's performance, its hopes of success seemed high. However, revisionists recruited into the IPG were equally concerned that its outspokenness should not hinder their aim to influence the government to more 'responsible' policies after devaluation. Their ideas differed from the liberationists' and they feared misrepresentation if 'big business' were to speak too controversially outside the normal channels. Internal tensions were therefore present from the start.

These tensions were played out in three phases. From formation in

October 1967 to the retirement of Chambers and Shenfield in summer 1969, there were often acrimonious debates between liberationist and revisionist members about the radicalism of the Group's proposed programme. The revisionists were sufficiently influential to ensure that the successor regime between 1969 and 1972, with more moderate liberationists, David Barran and Arnold Hall, as chairmen, and John Jewkes as Director, concentrated on proposals more likely to win consensus. Within the original ideological context of the Heath government this was viable, but after the government had made its 'U-turn' in 1972 and as the CBI increasingly moved to an advanced form of revisionism, deep disagreements opened up again on such issues as inflation, investment and the unions. There were no further publications and the Group quietly folded in 1974.

The IPG's public position can be traced from its ten published pamphlets, similar in tone and format to IEA monographs. Some papers were published only after intense debate and much correction; others reflected a broad consensus (examples of the former would be taxation and investment, of the latter monopolies and mergers policy). For liberationists the papers were intended to plot a path which could be fruitfully followed by bodies like the CBI, whilst revisionists aimed to moderate their content to such a degree that the latter's own policies could proceed regardless. A subsidiary aim was to rebut criticism of British business as monopolistic and addicted to restrictive practices; hence the overarching theme of the papers was 'competitiveness'.

The early papers had enjoyed the greatest input from committed liberationist members.[37] The tone was similar to the pre-Brighton FBI document *Britain's Economic Problems and Policies* in terms of scepticism of Keynesian economics, critiques of high public expenditure and taxation causing low growth, and the assumption that business should dissociate itself from middle ground political positions.[38] These views persisted even after substantial modifications by revisionist members. Thus one paper, *Britain's Economic Performance*, advocated consensual attitudes on productivity agreements, based 'on hammering out of workable arrangements ... between trade union representatives and industrial bodies', but deprecated the role of incomes policies and economic expansion as supports for the policy.[39]

Liberationist sentiments were more pronounced in the papers on taxation and public expenditure. There was a predictable call for a smaller, less active state, its diminution to be achieved by a major extension of private provision of public goods funded by deep tax cuts. Charging for certain health and education services would be introduced, a major extension of private pensions undertaken, accompanied by the means-testing of all benefits, with subsidies for public housing being severely curtailed. Such measures would 'favour experiment and innovation amongst providers' and educate the public on the debilitating effects of expecting tax payers and business to fund ever more public services. To achieve this major tax cuts, both personal and corporate, would be necessary, seeing an immediate cut of basic rate income tax to between 20–25 per cent, and with the ultimate aim of restoring pre-1939 tax levels.[40] Expenditure taxes would not be allowed to take up the slack, with fiscal neutrality the preferred course, special fiscal incentives for business investment being ruled out as inefficient and diversionary.[41]

Later papers concentrated on less divisive subjects like the SET and competition policy. However, the final published paper, *Economic Growth, Profits and Investment,* saw basic ideological differences re-emerge on the issues of corporate taxation and investment. The paper argued, in time-honoured liberationist fashion, that industrial investment was best stimulated through general cuts in corporate taxation, rather than the localised stimuli of investment incentives which, it was claimed, allowed governments to avoid more radical reforms. This was a provocative position, given the sensitivities of the Heath government on the issue. It went clean against official CBI policy, which welcomed incentives as a vital short-run support of company liquidity for investment. As a result, the CBI officially dissociated itself from the paper, making clear its sympathies were now bound up with revitalising the tripartist process rather than underwriting independent business positions.[42]

Although no further papers were produced, the energetic Jewkes continued to make provocative proposals on key economic issues. His proposed paper on inflation, drafted in the winter of 1973, aroused the greatest controversy with its support for monetarist positions. Business leaders responded in very different ways. Some, like Frank MacFadzean, showed a fair understanding of the new monetarist policies; others were attracted by gut political instinct. But as many members continued to uphold Keynesian/institutionalist positions on the issue it was clear that no agreement would be possible.[43] Similar fates befell papers on the unions and industrial policy: in such circumstances the disbandment of the Group was inevitable.

The IPG therefore appeared as a misconceived idea for both revisionists and liberationists. The causes of the failure are not hard to find, and they illuminate some of the deeper problems faced by liberationists in the pre-1979 period. Many of the weaknesses were personal: the more zealous members had little conception of how to persuade mainstream business opinion. The economist members, Shenfield and Jewkes, compounded political naïveté and lack of managerial feel with a rather suspicious attitude to the motives of business members. There was little political sense of how the CBI members could be successfully accommodated, and the recruitment of other key revisionists did not seem to cause great concern that policies would be diluted. The liberationist high command appeared to see the Group as a means of purifying business ideology of current heresies rather than best exploiting the available political situation.

Jewkes was not mistaken in seeing the CBI as deeply suspicious. The mistrust of John Davies and John Partridge and more particularly Campbell Adamson was overt, but once the Group had accepted CBI backing its position was inevitably constrained. When Partridge could insist that Chambers' desire for 'an aggressive position in defence of private enterprise' be replaced by papers based on 'facts and analysis' and Davies could go on stressing 'continuous discussion' with government, selective interventions and incomes policy, the incompatibility was clear.[44] Yet with a wide but largely passive membership (over forty company chairmen belonged at various times), it was difficult for the IPG to regroup without the revisionists. When members were encouraged to intervene as individuals in political debates, they invariably demurred.[45] This diffidence was shared by many liberationist sympathisers as well, still uncertain of the public reaction to business leaders speaking out as individuals rather than through organisations.

While published papers might tend towards the bland and uncontroversial, the degrees of diversity and disagreement within the IPG were often sharply conveyed through private exchanges. During the Chambers–Shenfield phase, liberationists would assert, for example, 'no flinching from denationalisation'; the NBPI as 'damaging to the proper conduct of economic affairs'; 'inevitably harmful consequences' from over, say 25 per cent of the national income being taken in tax; the possibility of a 'three-tier NHS'. Revisionists fought back vigorously. They criticised the 'obsession' about promoting free enterprise seen in Chambers and Shenfield, a 'quite disastrous' partisanship, and various proposals as 'quite antagonistic', 'petulant', 'unbalanced and unjust'. Reay Geddes, for example, felt 'there is enough recrimination without company chairmen indulging in it'.[46]

Later private exchanges were to be no less sharp. Jewkes would tell the Group that the Heath Government was 'one of the most amateur since the War'; MacFadzean would attack its 'gross political incompetence' and argue 'inflation is like a war and it cannot be solved by normal political means'; while other assertions would include more strikes as 'an acceptable price for cutting inflation', and 'dangers to liberal democracy' from managerial involvement in public policy and tripartism in a 'corporate state'.[47] But other members of the Group would make vigorous counter claims; for example, attributing inflation partly to government social policies, land speculation or inter-bank competition, implicating the social class system or 'past exploitation', and defending price controls and 'more stable [trade] unions'.[48] In some ways the divisions ended up sharper than in 1967. This was particularly the case as between the liberationists and a CBI leadership which was now more earnestly dedicated to social centrism and a new mixed economy settlement (see next chapter).

By the mid-1970s, therefore, liberationism had made an uncertain progress. Far from there being a long march through the business institutions as a prelude to political influence, liberationists remained somewhat marginal, independent figures with a poor organisational infrastructure. Their influence on other business leaders was consequently difficult to gauge. Their ideological opponents within business were still able to present liberationists as rather eccentric, political lightweights: an accusation sufficiently colourable, it seems, to convince many who otherwise doubted the positive value of the revisionists' own leadership. They faced genuine difficulties from current governmental orthodoxies, both Labour and Conservative. For free market ideologues outside business, however, liberationists presented different challenges. Although fellow travellers, their instincts to conceive and promote a radical, fundamentalist agenda of market reforms was seen as circumscribed both by the under-statedness of their ideas and a corresponding desire to appeal to as broad a base of business opinion as possible.

5 The peaks and precipices of revisionism 1969–1974

An obvious break point for conventional history is the return of a Conservative government in May 1970. But for business revisionism a more important change is the arrival of a new director general, Campbell Adamson, at the CBI in autumn 1969. Not that this event was at all colourful, or predicted as significant at the time. Campbell Adamson, the future impresario of advanced revisionism, the commandant of major business-political efforts up to the mid-1970s, would have seemed an unlikely candidate for such roles. He was a quiet, grave, rather school-masterly figure. Here, it might be thought, was a competent, non-ideological chief executive, a consolidator. Hints of the national civic figure would have been hard to find. It would have been still harder to tease out either the social vision which inspired the man or the essentially romantic, occasionally irritable zeal which would accompany its pursuit, alongside others with similar ideas.

The advanced revisionists and their ideas

The biggest influence on Campbell Adamson had been a twenty-year career in the steel industry within a single firm, Richard Thomas and Baldwins (RTB), much of it in works management and in South Wales. Economically, he had long contended with the problems of managerial traditionalism, outdated plant and fraught investment decisions within an ageing basic industry. Economic optimism, let alone managerial triumphalism, would not come easily after such an experience. Long years in a large organisation would encourage a more professional-managerial than entrepreneurial spirit. Ultimately more potent, however, were the lessons Campbell Adamson drew from the social side of industry. Shop floor contacts and works councils: the shock of seeing women workers exposed to bad working conditions: a relatively moderate brand of trade unionism: the derelict, communally close-knit environment of South Wales – these things were to leave the strongest marks.

This man would soon be propelled from relative obscurity towards the centre. Help and stimulus had come from Hugh Weeks in the latter's capacity as an outside director of RTB, and from Richard O'Brien, an industrial relations expert and early recruit as an Industrial Adviser into the DEA (see below). It was O'Brien who suggested Campbell Adamson's own move to the DEA as a seconded Industrial Adviser in 1967. Although that department was by now a dim shadow of its former self, it provided him with a welcome change of career as well as teaching him the ways of civil servants (whose skills he tended to admire), and exciting a fascination with pursuits of tripartism (through industrial policy and EDC work): a brief Whitehall experience which helped to convert his industrial convictions into a national frame.

Campbell Adamson shared the ideological understatedness shown even by other advanced revisionists of similar 'social' orientation. A shift from Davies's more economic emphasis was typically muted by a day-to-day focus on tactics and diplomacy. Adamson was to face problems at the CBI partly because he was better at motivating the HQ staff than the grassroots, partly because, in rather public school prefect fashion, he seemed to prefer collective responsibility to individual flair. He could seem buttoned-up, burdened or remote: his deep commitments were held inwards. However, three gut convictions were to provide a guiding thread. First, a sense of mission to project industry to the public as professional, responsible and humane, banishing the bad old image of exploitative capitalism. This 'high' view of business, the CBI and his own role was held so strongly that he could become intolerant, even unpredictably emotional, if he felt it threatened. Second was an instinctive and value-driven desire for social partnership, both corporate and national, between management and labour. Thirdly, his support for an incomes and prices policy reflected not only arguments about cost inflation and wage discipline but also a concern for 'fairness'. Adamson possessed a mildly egalitarian streak, a sympathy for the underdog, a dislike of financial speculation or unearned wealth. This did not displace a loyalty to the CBI's established economic policies, particularly on profits and investment where his experience ran deep. Nor did they compromise a careful political neutrality, whatever some later critics alleged. But the value preferences for social harmony, business responsibility and mutual discipline – and the distaste for swash-buckling capitalism – were ultimately more important to him.[1]

Some of these attributes were shared with the second key revisionist of this phase, John Partridge, CBI president 1970–72. Partridge had had a long career with Imperial Tobacco, rising mainly through marketing to be chairman and chief executive. A West countryman from a quite humble background, largely self-educated, Partridge's *persona* was impressive: striking, saturnine features, beautiful voice, an air both avuncular and dis-

tinguished. His charm and persuasiveness would repeatedly swing CBI
doubters into line: his wide reputation as an exceptional president would
persist. There were gaps in his understanding of both industrial relations
and economic issues but, though sometimes elusive, cloudy or rotund, he
had a penetrating, reflective mind, fine human relations skills, and a 'feel'
for big decisions.

Partridge had long been an expounder of corporate humanist concepts.
He had delivered many elegantly worded addresses to professional groups,
social workers, church congregations, and employees. At one level would
come a measured defence of profit as an economic instrument or social
'aid'; then a rubric of four-fold corporate responsibilities (to employees,
customers, community and shareholders, with the last tending to trail
behind the rest); and at the summit, a resounding ethic for economic life
which focussed above all on social interconnectedness. This, for Partridge,
had largely Christian roots: he was an active Anglican churchman. He had
expressed few (and usually conventional) views on wider themes; for
example anxieties about the effect of 'welfare' on 'personal responsibility'
or a desire for a 'lower tax, higher incentive economy' (though references
to Third World poverty were less predictable). The ethics of smoking
remained an awkward issue for him. Partridge's beliefs allowed an ample
role for the business leader as civic statesman and for a judicious view that
management-union-government relations 'won't get less, could well
enlarge': he had been a strong critic of extreme libertarian views within
the IPG (see last chapter). Instinctively a 'one nation' Tory, he had been
studiously 'non-political' as a big company chairman but would warm to
the Heath government's eventual move along this path. His socio-
economic ethic of 'interdependence' and 'lessening divisiveness in our
society' would accord well with national pursuits of partnership and
mutual restraint.

The fact that Partridge was less committed *a priori* to a prices and
incomes policy lent weight to his eventual espousal of it. His prestige
would win over many CBI waverers who could more easily see him as
'one of us', even down to some subtle voicing of their own doubts or dis-
tresses; and he would be crucial in rounding up consent to the Pricing
Initiative in 1971–2. His effective chairman/chief executive relationship
with Campbell Adamson was fortified by great warmth between the two
men. Partridge would provide avuncular support, at least, to concerns
over unemployment, corporate reform and employee participation, and
he would engage in some marked revisionist advocacy later as a retired
senior statesman.[2]

Partridge's successor, Michael Clapham (president 1972–74) was a
less commanding figure, though highly informed both socially and

economically. He came from a donnish background, being the son of Sir John Clapham, the economic historian. Later he would deprecate his early economic connections ('drinking tea with Marshall and brandy with Keynes', or mountain climbing with Pigou). An interest in economic ideas from Cambridge days was later reactivated through the NIESR council and would be reflected in a well-worked analytic defence of multinational enterprises. Clapham had spent twenty-five years in ICI, including industrial relations, commercial and international experience, having been personnel director, then commercial director of the (largely Midland-based) Metals Division, a main board director with international and European roles, and a deputy chairman. In 1970, having just missed the chairmanship, he was head hunted by Partridge to be his CBI deputy and successor. His rapport with Campbell Adamson would be less close. He would be the most 'intellectual' of CBI presidents, and the least 'entrepreneurial', often appearing less effective in action or diplomacy than either Partridge or, later, Watkinson. Of the CBI quartet under discussion, he was to become intellectually the most comprehensive expositor of advanced revisionism.[3]

Clapham's speeches could be puckish or sardonic, bracing, humorous, half-mocking. To a regional CBI audience in early 1973 he could say, 'I've been accused of approving, without your mandate, the Socialist policies of a Conservative government, but remain unrepentant.' He could refer to absurd suspicions of a Fascist-style corporate state, to dreams of 'an Arcady over which the effigies of Adam Smith and Gladstone preside, and in which the grinning skull of Karl Marx is never seen', or to the false seductions of 'loud public attitudes' which merely 'relieved emotions at too high a cost.' Such a donnish or 'debating' style would not always endear him to the grass roots. For a defender of the 'social benefits of capitalism', Clapham's range went wide. It included ideas for making the nationalised industries 'less governmental', an active view of the state ('to ensure competition, protect investors and consumers, safeguard the health and long term security of employees … protect the weak and curb the over-strong'), and a stress on social and public services as a primary reason for promoting growth.[4]

Clapham was trenchantly pro-mixed economy: the natural monopolies, at least, 'can reasonably be in public ownership', though not to have a vigorous private sector would be 'a disaster'. His ICI experience encouraged support of both structured employee participation and a European social policy. A critic of the early Heath government for 'not trying hard enough for a central position', he would applaud its later 'one nation' phase while also pinpointing its PR inadequacies, including privately to Heath himself. Clapham's advocacy of national partnership could have adventurous overtones; for example, an implication that since the CBI and the TUC together 'formed less than half the nation', they could hardly be '*the* social partners', or a suggestion that 'social justice, like legal justice, requires permanent institutions ... perhaps a standing Royal Commission' to determine pay in the public sector and advise on rewards more generally. Not always so effective in the battle for influence, he was to be one of the most disappointed revisionists when the renewed 'middle way' efforts of 1972–74 came unstuck.[5]

The last member of the CBI's quartet of key revisionists was Richard O'Brien, chairman of its powerful Employment Committee 1971–76. O'Brien had put down significant markers in his evidence to the Donovan Commission; for extended employee rights, a more disciplined TUC and CBI, and means of reconciling industrial and local bargaining with anti-inflation. Privately, he would be more impatient with the CBI right wing than the others. Invoking reconstructionist ideas of community and fairness-seeking (see next chapter), he sought various structural changes, if necessary to be backed by statute: rationalisation of both industry associations and trade unions, joint committees in all but the smallest firms, standing institutions for Swedish-style bipartism, public surveillance and consensus. O'Brien favoured 'a fairer distribution of rewards', with a functionalist view of 'rational inequality' to validate managerial differentials, and a permanent prices and incomes policy for 'a civilised social democracy based on affluence'. He was to be a constant source of ideas, usually to the left of Campbell Adamson and the rest, and able to draw on diverse talents in the top echelons of corporate industrial relations expertise.[6]

This was a formidable group even before taking into account other key insiders: Hugh Weeks, who continued as chairman of the Economic Policy Comittee up to 1972; the ex-mandarin turned senior industrialist, Alex Jarratt, his successor there 1972–74; the pan-senatorial figure of Lord Plowden; and, more loosely associated with the top group, the polymathic Lord Watkinson, chairman of the Company Affairs Committee from 1972.[7] The hegemony of this group owed much to ability. It was also a tribute to the exceptionally concentrated character of business national representation at this time. Not only was there no additional or contrary voice to the CBI's, possessing significant representativeness, political capacity or ideological force; the CBI itself was still fairly centralised and amenable to influence from its leading elite. Organised focusses for anti-platform feeling would be slow to emerge. In a wider sense, this was not a period for business leaders to enter public debate in a big way as individuals. The call to embattled advocacy was still muted: radicalisation and polarisation had still to come.

The political and economic context

The Conservative government of Edward Heath was to be deeply ambivalent for the advanced revisionists: for all its faults, largely congenial yet eventually, in large measure, a scene of tragedy. Its significance lay in confounding them first by mutations to the right, then to the left, while also sharing most of their reformist aims. The Heath government was to draw the CBI leading group into some long-cherished pursuits which were frustratingly elusive in the context of the time. To a large extent their fortunes became interchangeable with *its* fortunes. But not completely; for during these years the advanced revisionists also made some (much less recognised) reforming initiatives of their own. That these efforts largely unravelled as well owed much to the surrounding contagions. It also witnessed to inherent problems in revisionism which it was the peculiar character of this period to expose.

The Heath government's much debated U-turns (repeatedly the stuff of controversy in modern Conservatism) would put the advanced revisionists on their mettle in several ways. They would struggle through its initial biasses over disengagement, 'marketism' and industrial relations legislation; then through its moves, starting in 1971, towards interventionism, prices and incomes policies, increased social spending, and astringency towards business. It would be tempting to lament the extremism of both phases and indeed to see them as interlinked (though CBI revisionists would not be the only business observers to draw this connection or to view the complete seesaw as yet another example of dogmatic extremism in an adversarial political system).[8] But the advanced revisionists' ideas implied some sharper tests. How far would they seek to draw government policies back towards a 'middle way' through both phases? How effectively would they support the policies which were sympathetic? More difficult, how would they deal with the conflicts in their own position highlighted by these pursuits?

It may seem strange to claim that the political conjuncture of 1970–74 was, on balance, exceptionally favourable to revisionism. There are so many reasons to discount the period. The revisionists would see the government weakened by the early loss of Iain McLeod (potentially a better chancellor and a more effective bridge towards social Toryism); by a lack of ministerial strength industrially (both the politically disappointing John Davies and his less than heavyweight successors); and by Edward Heath's lack of public relations touch. Despite much admiration for him, a gulf would be created by Heath's style of irritated impatience with business and its complex decision making, notably over investment. Overshadowing this were the domestic and international crises. The period would bring a further collapse of the 'Phillips curve' hypothesis of a standard inverse relationship between inflation and unemployment as both went on getting worse; serious Treasury under-estimates of the growth of broad money supply, especially in banking and credit, helping towards the perverse property and take-over booms in 1973; and a violent overthrow of all known margins of error over the balance of payments through successive international crises between 1971 and 1974: in commodity prices, money movements, OPEC and oil, and the Middle East.[9]

To all this must be added an apparent downward drift on the labour relations front. This was not evident at the TUC, where the arch-conciliator Vic Feather would continue to box agilely for tripartite consensus, nor for the most part in the trade union leadership (though both Jack Jones and Hugh Scanlon were to prove harder to deal with than their predecessors). It was partly a case of reactive left-wing militancy towards the government's initial policies. More fundamentally, it related to tendencies towards fragmentation and confusion on the shop floor for which wide social factors and management itself, as well as the unions, could be held responsible. For the advanced revisionists, this was a Pandora's box. They accepted that the remedies would have to be complex and multilateral: a reform of pay bargaining systems, a permanent form of incomes restraint, an extension of good industrial relations practice, including employee participation, from a corporate minority to the generality of less progressive firms. As we will see, though, such ideas would conflict disturbingly with their commitments to both business representation and voluntarist 'self-reform'.[10]

Despite all this it can still be argued that the 1970–74 conjuncture provided the revisionists with their best chance so far (and considerably better than any since). Despite its initial right-wing and later *dirigiste* excesses and its persistent limitations, the Heath government had certain advantages for them. It was committed to the idea of an adapted private enterprise system. Both its consistency and its success over EEC entry would be a major bull factor. Its relative immunity from doctrine on the technical issues of public borrowing, money supply or interest rates (though not initially on the exchange rate) would make it a quick learner on many key issues as it backed away from some early simplicities (to the dismay of its free marketeers). Indeed, the government's (and more particularly Heath's) basic beliefs on economic policy were essentially congenial to the revisionists. Its stance was always broadly Keynesian, never really free marketist, still less deflationist or monetarist. Its deepest fear was of large-scale unemployment, bankruptcies and stymied growth. Its historic decision when unemployment threatened to become unbearable but still in the teeth of worsening inflation – to opt for both expansion *and* a prices and incomes policy – was in tune with the revisionists' own convictions.

Two further attributes of the government would be congenial to the advanced revisionists: its eventual turns towards both social mediation and business reform. On both they would be drawn to ascend certain high mountains or indeed to attempt some perilous climbs on their own initiative. Yet here again conflicts would loom up penetrating to the core of revisionism, as discussed in chapter 2. How could one combine such potentially conflicting sets of objectives as advocacy of all-round changes to business as well as labour and government (now espoused with greater intensity), pursuit of day-to-day civic co-operation, opposition to coercion, and the pursuit of hard advantages to business? To satisfy all four demands – as visionary reformers, co-operative citizens, voluntarists and sectional partisans – would always be an elusive task. But it would be the special character of the period to test this uneasy combination to the limit or beyond.

Business and Heath-ism Mark 1

The period began with problems over the new government's urge to ditch some of its predecessor's favoured institutions. Ironically, the revisionists would find themselves defending some of the Labour government's instruments. The CBI leading group favoured both a unified department of industry and a revised CIR. More controversially, Campbell Adamson and Partridge were prepared for the IRC to continue in diluted form, but in the event it was scrapped even though some previous discussions with the opposition had pointed to a conditional reprieve. The most sensitive issue was the NBPI. Despite its association with some discredited policies under Labour, the NBPI had developed a sophisticated function of appraising economic interests, trade unions and professions as well as business. As 'an investigative body . . . but without powers' (in the words of a CBI staff paper), it could have contributed over issues like restrictive practices, differentials, top people's remuneration, or norms for non-inflationary pay increases, as well as helping to save the government from some later frenetic institutional re-building over both prices and pay. However, the NBPI's unpopularity in both government and business circles was now such that any serious salvaging effort on its behalf would not have got far.[11]

The new chancellor Tony Barber's first two budgets generated bigger dilemmas. Concessions on company and personal taxation, and a switch to indirect taxation, had been expected. Anxieties over an accompanying switch from investment grants to tax allowances for investment were predictable and duly appeared. But a subtler challenge soon emerged. Would the direct benefits to business (or higher tax payers) be outweighed by the methods used to finance them and the attendant risks to inflation, social consensus or industrial relations? For the revisionists the familiar answer was to seek only moderate tax concessions while (more or less disingenuously) avoiding detail over the form any public spending cuts or welfare changes. But would this now be enough?

The autumn 1970 budget incorporated moves towards cuts, charges or increased selectivity in the welfare services, affecting school milk, council rents, NHS prescriptions, museums etc. It simultaneously heralded the income and corporation tax cuts and the switches to indirect taxes which were to feature in the budget of spring 1971. Previous ideas for a counterbalancing wealth tax had long been ditched by the Conservatives. Overall, the change from the post-war consensus was less than left wing attacks suggested. But the impression was of resolute, right-wing 'Selsdon man', and damages resulted for the RPI, pay demands and increases, and the sense of equity (with fears of one-sidedness exacerbated by a parallel rush towards 'anti-union' industrial relations legislation, see below). The revisionists could hardly criticise the welfare changes *per se*, having just recently reaffirmed their case both for cuts in current public spending and for a (vaguely defined) increase in welfare 'selectivity'. However, they did run true to form in restraining tax pleas for the most wealthy, e.g. over surtax (holding the CBI liberationists at bay), and in deploying investment-related rather than populist arguments for the latter. More innovatively, reflecting Campbell Adamson's new social emphasis along with mounting fears of social unrest and pay inflation, they moved to an emphasis on compensating measures 'to aid the poorest groups'.[12]

In January 1971 John Partridge, with Campbell Adamson at his elbow, explained the rationale to the CBI Council. Both men heralded a higher profile on 'fairness'. Since the CBI's (and the government's) tax and anti-inflation proposals were likely to benefit the better-off, they argued, these should be balanced by representations for higher tax thresholds and extended income support, aimed at helping 'those in the lower range of incomes who were most hit by the recent substantial increase in living costs' and 'the weak in society.' One industrialist, L. J. Tolley, agreed it was 'proper to show social concern in relation to the lower income groups'; others doubtless agreed with Partridge's case for 'expediency' as well as 'principle' here; no one seems to have demurred openly, though a few still wanted more stress on tax reductions (best to maximise these, it might seem, early in a Conservative government's life). In the event, the spring 1971 budget disappointed those who felt that the corporation tax changes did not compensate for the withdrawal of investment grants. But Adamson told Council he was 'in total, highly satisfied', and the official line was that 'the incentives arguments' had been nicely balanced with 'help to the poor.'[13]

On the macro-economic front, disconcertingly, real movements, indicators and sheer explanatory puzzles all seemed to be worsening. Doubts as to the desirable balance between moderate reflation and 'a neutral stance' reflected not only increased wrangling over cost-plus *versus* demand-pull theories of inflation but also sheer barometric difficulties in reading the trends (e.g. in output relative to productive potential). The CBI's perplexities here scarcely differed from the government's: what to do about 'a rapid rate of cost and price inflation against the background of slowly rising output and a high and increasing level of unemployment'? In one respect, though, the revisionists were clear. Despite only scant hopes that the trade unions would be able to 'deliver' in the teeth of bargaining fragmentation and shop-floor militancy, a voluntary incomes policy seemed, as ever, a lesser evil than deflation. This view was forcefully conveyed to the government from the start, particularly by Adamson. As usual there were dissenting voices in both the economic committee and Council: legislative changes affecting trade union power could check inflation even in the short-run; its actual 'elimination' should be the aim (implying a lower priority for growth and employment); monetary policy should be 'tightened'; the reciprocal disciplines on prices and profits attendant on an incomes policy would be unacceptable; a private sector incomes policy was 'not plausible in the present period'; an alternative (implying a supply-side mystique of liberated energies) might be more radical tax cuts.[14]

But the revisionists prevailed. An inclusive incomes policy remained the aim: fiscal and monetary policy alone would be inadequate. Contact was maintained with the TUC, with considerable rapport growing between Adamson and Feather. Meantime, support was given to the government's attempted toughness on public sector pay (local authority workers, NCB, electricity supply, Post Office), and CBI members were urged to resist excessive pay demands. Whatever else, severe deflation was ruled out. As Hugh Weeks put it in January 1971, deflationary measures, whether fiscal or monetary, would have only limited effects on wage demand levels 'unless carried to an extent which would be socially impossible'.[15]

More complex were the issues posed by the new government's industrial relations legislation. Encased in a long-refined legalistic bias, targeting trade union militancy as the principal (or at least most actionable) cause of both bad industrial relations and inflation, determined to outdo Labour's *In Place of Strife* and egged on by their right wing, the government pressed quickly ahead with its preconceived legislation, surprising the civil service at the lack of consultation, both within and outside Whitehall.[16] For the revisionist CBI leaders the problem was not just that much of the legislation appeared irrelevant, unworkable or damaging. Even if the new Industrial Relations Act (IRA) helped to rectify the 'imbalance of power' in the longer-term, would it not endanger both employer-worker relations and the chances of a voluntary incomes policy meantime? Was not the Act a prize case of political pendulum swinging, liable to produce a strong counter-reaction when Labour returned to power?[17] A further and less clearly recognised issue was one of equity. Given the advanced revisionists' recognition of the business-managerial defects in both industrial relations and economic performance, to support the legislation would be one-sided unless a comparable measure of radicalism were directed towards employers.

Outside the CBI, even praise for the Industrial Relations Bill would be less than full-blooded. The Industrial Society expressed a widespread view among industrial relations experts that fines and prison sentences were ill-judged and that the bill put pressure in the wrong place: 'unions don't employ their members and can have nothing like the influence on their behaviour that employers can'. Lord Robens feared a provocation to 'the swing to militancy' and saw threats to 'personal links' or 'give and take' from 'codification'. Calls for extensive amendment were to come from Maurice Laing and Lord Watkinson ('much of it is inoperable' and 'don't rub people's noses in it'), and later from A. W. Pearce of Esso among others.[18] Within the CBI a working party under Leonard Neal, moved to tougher positions than in the Donovan period but still put the main emphasis on a stronger Registrar 'to represent the community', a less binding Code of Practice, and voluntary methods. At the core was a fear that industrial relations would be damaged by putting the main onus of pursuing the unions onto employers. Following the Neal working party's report and a meeting of some thirty top industrialists, strong representations were made to Robert Carr for 'major changes' in the Bill. But little appears to have come of this so that Partridge was stung into expressing 'disappointment' privately to Carr. Publicly, though, the CBI's criticisms of the Bill and subsequently of the Act became understated.[19]

Campbell Adamson, for one, would probably have preferred a more vigorous line. As well as breaching the CBI's customary political caution, particularly towards a newly mandated government, this would have offended a significant portion of its members. Here was another case of the revisionists' representative role conflicting with their prognosis of the problems. None the less, to the extent that they appeared to go along with much of the IRA's legal targeting of unions and workers – at least in the absence of vigorous balancing proposals for managerial and business reform – their even-handedness was impaired. A sense of unease was left as much of the Act increasingly crumbled under the weight of its anomalies, facing legal absurdity, employer abstention or passive opposition, and effective trade union defiance.

Moving into higher gear: pro-active revisionism

During the early part of 1971 the leading group became increasingly frustrated. There was an apparent worsening in the economic situation and a risk of draconian deflation combined with social confrontation. Campbell Adamson, Partridge and their immediate circle believed that a renewed effort at consensus, tripartism and restraint over pay and prices was essential. But the government did not appear ready for this, let alone the unions. There was an increasing sense that the CBI should do something to break the log-jam, if necessary on its own. Given the reluctance of its potential partners, could it not take some sort of lead?

What followed was an unprecedented effort at do-it-yourself business collectivism, the CBI Price Initiative. The idea was to organise 'undertakings' by the 200 top companies to restrain their prices for twelve months: this in order (a) to assist anti-inflation (both directly and *via* tougher resistance to pay claims), (b) to make it easier for the government to reflate the economy and to avoid either a statutory prices and incomes policy or deflation; and, it soon emerged, (c) to facilitate pay restraint. This plan had precedents in earlier phases of FBI 'voluntaryism' and it owed much to the collaborative monitoring system for pay increases in big companies already built up by the CBI.[20] It is highly probable that soundings in government attended its inception. Campbell Adamson took the lead, but with John Partridge an early enthusiast and Hugh Weeks at least acquiescent as chairman of the economic committee. A quasi-military operation was mounted, including private discussions with government and informal meetings with top company chieftains, an increasing feature of the period. The probable early advantages were oversold. Only a few refused to sign the undertaking. Off stage, there were ideological rumblings. On Council, despite concerns over the *modus operandi* (e.g. for food, insurance, newspapers), and calls to include nationalised industry prices and to emphasise a trade union response, no objections on principle appear to have emerged, and a show of hands 'indicated widespread support.'[21]

Nothing could have demonstrated more clearly both the convictions of the leading group and their hold on CBI power. The Initiative soon generated a patriotic, almost war-time excitement in Tothill Street. It produced a sense that, while government might falter and the trade unions might fail, business was now making a dynamic contribution to national needs. Though this role of patriotic front-runner was to prove two-edged, its positive attributes dominated for quite a while. Through the rest of 1971 and much of 1972, mildly rising profits and tax reductions helped to facilitate price restraint except for a few. The desire not to rock the boat was fortified by a genuine slow-down in price increases, mounting jitters over international factors, and renewed anxieties over wage inflation following damaging disputes in the docks, railways and coal. Also important were continued hopes of an echoing response from the trade unions, Partridge's charisma and the appeal to behave as 'responsible citizens'.[22]

From summer 1971 to summer 1972 was the revisionists' finest hour. Favourable responses were forthcoming from government, within the CBI there was little overt dissent, press and public comment was benign. Informal tripartism was reviving and Campbell Adamson had ample cover for his participation in a private dialogue with Frank Figgures of the NEDO, Vic Feather of the TUC, and Sir William Armstrong. A *modus vivendi* with the nationalised industries was developing inside the CBI: wider arguments over their economic role had been softened by a stress both on generic managerialism and on stable frontiers between the private and public sectors. Adamson was able to pursue his high profile concerns over unemployment, putting arguments about wasted human resources and 'social aspects', neglected infrastructure and 'the total costs to the community' in both committees and Council. CBI proposals for training, infrastructure projects, building grants and regional priorities very much reflected his views.[23] The CBI's fiscal stance in early 1972 repeated the familiar blend of tempered pleas for investment-orientated reductions in Corporation Tax and suggestions for the lower income groups, within a moderately expansionist macro-economic package. Overall, the hegemony of socially flavoured revisionism was confirmed. 'Middle way' influences were riding high.[24]

Business and Heath-ism Mark 2: moving towards a débâcle

It soon became clear that the government's U-turn, once it accelerated from summer 1972 onwards, would have some awkward consequences. The highly interventionist (and non-consulted) Industry Bill, published in June 1972, led to predictable CBI and wider protests.[25] The economic expansionism, though congenial, would soon run into difficulties. Above all, the government's attempts at formal tripartism on pay and prices through the rest of 1972 were to draw the advanced revisionists into a tortuous, in some ways constraining web of often secret diplomacy. This would reflect both CBI modes of qualified co-operation with government and their own convictions. But it would also lead them towards a partial breach with voluntarism, and towards ever-increasing risks to their representative role as grass roots resentments mounted and the apparent business consensus began to fall apart.

In summer 1972 Edward Heath convened tripartite discussions about a voluntary incomes policy. The ensuing 'Downing Street talks', perhaps the most dramatic effort at voluntarist mutualism of the whole post-war period, strained the business side's capacities no less than the other parties'. The CBI team was cross-pressured and appears to have lacked both a single authoritative captaincy and the ability to cope with sheer surprise in a conjuncture which unprecedentedly tested both tripartite politics and interpersonal relationships.[26] After the talks failed in November 1972, the government crossed the Rubicon to a statutory policy which went through successive mutations as Stage (1), a pay-price-dividend freeze up to March 1972; Stage (2), low percentage maxima for pay and dividends, along with vetting of price increases by a new Price Commission, up to autumn 1973; and Stage (3), higher percentages for pay *plus* slightly more flexible price controls but covering more firms, from November 1973.

All these phases involved the CBI top group in complex discussions separately with government or TUC, or in tripartite form. These the group saw as unavoidable partly in deference to urgent government demands, partly to safeguard key business interests (particularly as the controls tightened and government began leaning towards the unions). But fears of the dreaded alternatives of runaway inflation or draconian deflation lent a new edge to the advanced revisionists' pursuit of a tripartite consensus for wealth creation and 'fairness'. Certain positions were regarded as non-negotiable, to be surrendered only under outright duress. These included a stricter control on prices than pay; a specious restraint on pay; permanent statutory control of either pay or prices. The underlying call to enhance, or at least defend, the profit and investment shares of national resources remained central, as did the avoidance of undue central *fiat*. To soften on these fronts would seem like surrender and, from the likely reactions of CBI members, 'unsaleable'. They would evoke more vigour as the prospect of a 'soft landing' to partial decontrol repeatedly receded and the government appeared to be moving to the left.[27] The following (typically capsulated) exchanges show the tough language being used privately to Edward Heath by late summer-autumn 1973.

PARTRIDGE: It is completely wrong to clobber industry as a whole for the minority.

ADAMSON: The utter disincentive to strive for greater efficiency; it is 100% confiscation.

HEATH: But how do you carry this psychologically with the wage earner?

ADAMSON: It is not an impossible PR problem for manufacturing industry. Problem area is capital gains.

JARRATT: Price Commission have interpreted rules too freely – or made them up as they go along . . . 15% of senior executives' time spent on [Price] Code.

MARSH: The Chancellor cannot sit back and see this shambles . . . deficits of hundreds of millions [in the nationalised industries].

O'BRIEN: Risks from further compression . . . greater flexibility needed . . . give more room for bargaining, though not free bargaining. (9 Aug. 1973)

CLAPHAM: See how to end policy – get off back of tiger.

ADAMSON: Distortion of demand . . . misuse of resources. (18 Sept. 1973)[28]

As before, there was dislike of a purely sectional stance (as might characterise 'a traditional employers' association'), and an eagerness to throw constructive proposals into the pool. A settled preference was for a form of permanent tripartite compact, to be largely operated by business and trade unions, at arms' length from government, and a new consensus-seeking organisation for distributional issues, whose range was envisaged, at various times, as including national bargaining guidelines, differentials, low pay, equal pay. In autumn 1972 Clapham suggested such a body to Heath, claiming that 'the combination of public opinion, consumer resistance and the supplier's sense of obligation' would act as 'the most effective sanction of a voluntary policy'. Through 1972 and 1973 further ideas were thrown up in higgledy-piggledy fashion: for longer pay settlements, synchronised pay bargaining, CBI monitoring of price changes, employer control groups to watch pay movements, TUC vetting of wage increases.[29]

More than anything else, it was the issues seen as fit for *quids* in return for others' *quos* that would measure the advanced revisionists' convergence towards Heath's 'one nation' phase. Some of the suggested reciprocities would point to moves mainly from government: substantial amendments to the Industrial Relations Act, concessions on VAT, council rents or pensions; action on property speculation and house prices; fiscal measures to protect the least well-off. Others invoked direct changes for business, unwelcome to many firms, unsuitable for 'bargaining' in a crude sense, but where the revisionists felt the general climate could be improved, the main example being employee participation (see below). Finally there were issues where a species of negotiation was envisaged (albeit with more or less scepticism as to the ability of the CBI to commit its own members, let alone that of the TUC or indeed the government to 'deliver' any *quos*). Here a leading item was control of dividends: generally viewed as economically obtuse but socially tradeable or 'the political price for a good deal'.[30]

As the top group pursued these moves, much business opinion seemed at first to follow them. Close CBI supporters included Watkinson, Robens, Caldecote, Marsh, Ezra. Another heavyweight, Brookes of GKN, soon became a vocal critic. Through 1973 a new senior economic committee under Alex Jarratt, with a higher-powered membership, showed strains over the workings of prices and incomes policy, while an offshoot Financial Policy Committee flirted with mildly monetarist ideas.[31] But anti-deflationism was still supreme. The advent as economic adviser of Donald MacDougall, the ex-Treasury mandarin and leading Keynesian – a determined opponent of 'beggar my neighbour' policies in the deteriorating international situation – helped to reinforce broad support for the government's expansionism, and the revisionists were still very much on top.[32]

Through the period many company chieftains expressed their views privately or semi-privately. Discussions about continued price restraint and a voluntary incomes policy in June–July 1972 provided a first litmus test, as the following extracts show.[33]

This philosophy is so important at the present time . . . We would hate to give the impression the cement industry couldn't join in a new Scheme [for price restraint] (*Sir John Reiss*, Rugby Portland Cement)

Why does the thought of a price and income policy raise such hysteria? The more especially when some form of price control exists even in the US, the bastion of capitalism, and in most countries in Europe, with the additional factor of Japan and Germany being disciplined nations . . . While a greater control of the money supply would certainly be effective, I do not believe it would be seen to be fair by the wage earner, who would respond accordingly. (*Sir Hector Laing*, United Biscuits)

[Supporting a temporary extension of voluntary price restraint] I do not agree with forcing Government to introduce its own price and wage restraint . . . likely for electoral reasons to be hard on prices, more lenient on wages. (*T. Pearce*, Esso)

[Explaining problems over costs and extreme trade union wage demands] I personally believe it is impossible to get worthwhile assurances of wage restraint from the TUC and that the Government has the clear duty to impose a freeze – however distasteful this would be to them, and for somewhat different reasons to us. I am convinced that the CBI's well meaning attitudes are being used by the Government to avoid taking a painful and necessary decision. (*Sir Maurice Laing*, John Laing)

Doubts about a policy so relying on voluntary co-operation . . . If there really is an emergency probable need to liquidate £ as reserve currency . . . And creation, perhaps temporarily, of a social economic council, with employers, unions,

Government officials, and perhaps City representatives . . . greater authority for
TUC which, in ultimate analysis, only beneficial. (*J. P. Engels*, Philips Industries)

[Demurring over continued price restraint] The fibres and textiles industries have
willy-nilly not only observed last year's CBI price initiative, but have had to put
up with, in many categories, very severe price erosion. (*Lord Kearton*, Courtaulds)

Further price restraint 'artificial' and would cause 'long-term damage' . . . Also
the secrecy of early discussion 'not in line with modern thinking about partici-
pative or consultative management and of the need in large companies to delegate
authority and responsibility'. (*Lord Pilkington*, Pilkingtons)

Past – and present misgivings . . . No help from TUC nor from Govt . . . Political
problem . . . Dangerous for CBI. (*Sir Archibald Forbes*, Midland Bank)

If this is last chance . . . we'll do so . . . Danger of social confrontation. (*J. O. Blair-
Cunynghame*, National and Commercial)

Through the first half of 1973, with an intricate Price Code and an
interventionist new Price Commission, the balance was shifting omi-
nously. While detailed concerns accumulated in both Council and private
meetings, some (probably under-recorded) fundamentalist opposition
was emerging at the grass roots: 'We who support capitalism cannot
support ending that system'; 'the whole policy is an attack on industry';
it was avoiding root causes 'which might lie in a policy of full employment
. . . and restriction of the normal operation of a market economy'.
Even someone like Charles Bell of Coats Patons, an admirer of Heath's
'one nation' mood, a critic of monetarism ('I remain an unrepentant
Keynesian'), who sought 'a fair system seen as such by all sections of the
community', would view the policy as 'contrary to the national interest
and inimical to GDP growth' in the long-term, 'especially in terms of
investment'. A few heavyweights began blaming the CBI itself or its leading group. The intellectual liberationist Ronald Edwards, execrating
'Government control of profitability', suggested that the CBI would fail
in its mandate to represent industry and indeed perform no service to
government by taking a 'middle road attitude'. John Davies wrote *via*
the Rank Organisation's Secretary that 'the policy of the CBI over the last
10 months as expressed by the Director General has appeared to be too
conciliatory to the pressures imposed on the Government by the Unions',
while according to Lord Kearton, the Courtaulds board felt that the CBI
had 'rather lost its way' and that 'some staff seemed more pre-occupied in
being a branch of Government than in representing members'.[34]

Then a conflict of principle came to a head in Tothill Street itself,
affecting the Taxation Committee chairman, Alan Davies, and the economic director, Barry Bracewell Milnes. Both men were dedicated free
marketeers as well as respected experts in their fields, who had long

maintained a liberationist redoubt within the organisation. In January 1973 the Taxation Committee's draft for budget proposals gave a central place to major reductions in capital taxation. Bracewell Milnes argued that this was 'more onerous than anywhere else in Europe,' with Estate Duty 'the biggest single tax problem for small firms', and Capital Gains Tax an 'absurdity', given the lack of real gains under inflation, and an 'injustice' to investors who 'among all sections of the community . . . are doing the most to keep it (inflation) under control'.[35] The conflict with the top group's 'middle way' approach was sharp. A more senior committee, including Partridge, quickly reduced the capital tax demands, cut out a plea for lower duties on tobacco (also 'wrong . . . in present circumstances'), and added proposals for VAT reductions on certain basic foods. Bracewell Milnes reacted furiously. Davies would fierily assert a link between wealth creation and tax reductions *tout court,* protesting that 'the CBI should avoid adopting the views of the Labour Party'. Campbell Adamson, equally angry, summoned Bracewell Milnes and insisted on his resignation. Behind this episode lay deep policy conflicts which had been building up for a long time. It left serious scars.[36]

More widely, there was irritability that steady growth and industrial peace both seemed as far off as ever. Productive investment was not taking off, whereas social resentments, diversionary speculation and a byzantine intrusion into private enterprise *via* the Price Code were growing. It could still be argued, of course, that the government had a fair chance of success given time; but it had little time left electorally or relative to the mounting international problems. For the advanced revisionists the situation was highly fraught. Tough talk in Whitehall or concessions won on the Price Code etc. were largely hidden from business constituents, many of whom unfairly blamed them for wider ills, while there was no onus on the critics to explain alternatives which, according to the revisionists, would threaten unacceptable economic and social costs.

Radical initiatives and final misadventures

Before reaching the final stages of the Heath government, it is necessary to mention briefly three major reforming initiatives which succeeded in exposing still more acutely the conflicts of ideas within advanced revisionism.

(1) In September 1972 a committee under Lord Devlin proposed changes in 'industrial and commercial representation': broadly, a tiered confederal structure with strengthened trade and employers' organisations which would belong to a merged CBI and Association of British Chambers of Commerce, with only the constituent units or

the largest firms as its direct members. This latest effort at rationalisation in a chaotic field soon evaporated into a vague rhetoric of 'discussion' or 'contact' and hopes of purely voluntary reform through a small advisory unit in the CBI.[37]

(2) In January 1973 a committee under Lord Watkinson produced a wide-ranging and imaginative report on the responsibilities of public companies. A 'code of corporate conduct' should guide directors on ethical or social issues 'beyond the immediate pursuit of profit and the requirements of the law', including greater attention to industrial relations and company-wide joint councils. Company boards should observe tenure limits for directors, separation of chairman and chief executive roles, and an increased role for non-executive directors. Shareholding, especially by the financial institutions, should become more active and probing. This project would not be without influence, but by autumn 1973 virtually everything in it had had to be watered down.

(3) In summer 1973 a report on employee participation reflected an urge to generalise the existing 'best practice' of many leading enterprises. It envisaged representative plant councils in all save the smallest firms, developing towards company-wide councils; increased information for employees; consultation on a wide range of specific issues; and all this to be gradually effected by persuasion and negotiation reinforced, however, by enabling legislation and an enacted, though flexible code of practice. This report, too, was largely squashed and the issue postponed.

(2) and (3) will be discussed in the next chapter, but meantime the politics require brief comment. Although government influence or thoughts of possible legislation played a part (and EEC factors in the case of employee participation), these were independent initiatives, reflecting deep prior convictions, particularly on the part of Adamson, Partridge, Clapham, Watkinson and O'Brien. Their defeat owed something to mistaken judgements: in particular, an over-ambitious coverage of company responsibilities within a single report, and the proposal for structured employee councils to apply to quite small firms, not just larger ones. More significant was the factor of deep-rooted resistances in major sections of the CBI. Yet this also appeared to owe much to a context of heightened suspicions of government and grassroots feelings in the CBI that further changes were being thrust upon them by the leading group.

These events, however, were soon overshadowed by the final turbulences of the Heath government: international crises, industrial relations disputes, the miners' strike, the 3-day week. The atmosphere in late 1973 and early 1974 often had a feel of Dunkirk or the *Blitz*. The backrooms at

Tothill Street were churning out rescue proposals relating to the next phase of prices and incomes policy, or the international economic crisis and monetary co-operation. The inner group was in constant touch with leading figures in government, Whitehall and the TUC as well as top industry. The emphasis had largely shifted to urgent, day-to-day fire fighting. By the turn of the year the CBI Council sometimes resembled a frenetic staff headquarters, with anxious intelligence of the latest events at the front hurtling back and forth. There were parallels to the bunker situation virtually a stone's throw away at Number 10 Downing Street.[38]

During this last phase the top group enunciated a form of radically-flavoured centrism. Close to Heath-ism Mark 2, in some ways this was sharper-edged on both 'firmness' and 'fairness'. It embraced (a now qualified) expansionism, appeals for social convergence and sternness towards exploitative minorities. From Clapham came a roundly didactic rhetoric, from Adamson a more clipped, puritan tone ('Some of the changes I am implying management will not like. Some the trade unions will not like, and some the government will not like. But this is a time for unity'). In private slightly more precision emerged. After Stage 3 there could be no return to complete free bargaining: pay determination would need recasting. More scope for business expectations, profits and investment would have to be carved out. The IRA should be extensively amended or (subject to a new tripartite compact) repealed, profits from property or financial manipulation curbed, a new consensus sought towards deciding differentials and a 'fairer' distribution of incomes and wealth.[39]

It was not unreasonable to envisage such a path being attempted by the Heath administration in its final stages or a new Conservative government under Heath, or even perhaps by a national coalition. The risk of a right-wing backlash in the Conservative Party was discounted; also, it appears, of a more left-wing Labour government. Although Labour enjoyed less esteem among revisionists than in 1963–64, superficial contacts with Opposition leaders may have helped the CBI leading group to overestimate the likely continuities to be expected from Wilson, Healey and Callaghan, and to under-estimate Labour's leftward and pro-union swings (see chapter 7). One way or another, then, a vigorous sort of political centrism still seemed feasible. By now, anyway, the advanced revisionists would find it difficult to adjust to anything else.[40]

The last weeks of the Heath government brought two dramatic misadventures along the interface between the CBI and national politics. Both were self-defeating, and profoundly influential in their different spheres. One misadventure was Edward Heath's, the other Campbell Adamson's. With regard to Heath, it is ironic that the issue which has been most identified with his government's final undoing, its failure to grasp the 'special case' lifeline offered to it to settle the coal industry dispute without loss of principle, should have been one where the CBI leaders advocated a settlement up to the eleventh hour.[41] This, in turn, made all the more ironic Campbell Adamson's mishap, in the midst of the subsequent general election campaign. Believing he was in a private meeting, he made some highly critical, albeit familiar remarks, off the record, about the Industrial Relations Act, only to find these headlined in the national press. Of various mitigations, not the least was a breach on the part of members of the press. But the result was a widespread, though highly unfair impression that he was taking sides in the election.[42]

Adamson at once offered to resign. Major support for him to stay came from senatorial figures like Partridge and Plowden, and from departmental heads and staff in Tothill Street. When the issue came to a Council meeting a sense of sympathy with Adamson was uppermost, only Brookes strongly protesting to the extent of walking out. Privately, criticisms ranged from the virulently extremist to the moderate.[43] Revisionists with strong Conservative ties, notably Watkinson, were resentful. The amount of clear and open CBI annoyance was not great. But Adamson's position was weakened and, though consoled by wide support and committed in a dutiful way to soldiering on, he knew as much.

Again, some part had been played by grassroots resentments at the involvements with the Heath government's reverses and at the leading group's high profile combination of central influence with reformist zeal. The incident itself was puny compared with the larger disappointments of 1973–74, over tripartite mutualism, socio-economic 'fairness' and business reconstruction. However, it made a curiously downbeat, incongruous end to a period which had tested advanced revisionism so dramatically in both intellectual and emotional terms.

6   Systemic change in capitalism?
The reconstructionists

> Business needs to be made responsible in its relations with the workers, the community and the consumers as well as to the shareholders – 'Company law . . . stands in need of drastic revision' with new forms of 'accountability' and public companies to become 'public trusts', with 'workers as full members' and 'shareholders turned into creditors'.
>
> *George Goyder*[1]

> The need is for a 'fairer, social and democratic society', 'one nation', 'competition in the market place but co-operation everywhere else' – 'a developmental, collaborative state'.   *Charles Villiers*[2]

As the UK's predicament seemed to worsen, so the hold on business opinion of moderate, gradualist, reformist ideas slowly weakened. The cause of gentle improvement, though still preferred by most, looked more and more battered. There was a mounting sense that a radical shake-up was needed, with remedies heroic or draconian. But liberationism was still not the principal shaper of this mood, nor yet fully ready to benefit from it. The triumphs of free market ideas in the '80s and '90s should not encourage one to overlook the many institutional and atmospheric obstacles these ideas still faced in the 1970s. Moreover, other types of radicalism were vying for attention. The time has come to consider a third long-established tendency of thinking, namely reconstructionism, as espoused by a few business leaders.

The reconstructionists were tiny in number: only four principal exponents emerge in this chapter *plus* six or seven others. They were most likely to have formed decided social views prior to entering business. Influences from Christian beliefs and social ideas were often cited; also inspirations from secular sources and social prophets such as Blake, Ruskin, William Morris, Tawney: though not so much from economists except, sometimes, Hobson or, rather more often, Keynes. A higher-than-usual proportion cited early exposure, in various ways, to class divisions, social conditions or forms of deprivation seen as unjust. Reconstructionists tended to gravitate early on to parts of business which they saw as consistent with their beliefs, run by like-minded leaders or amenable to their personal influence.[3] Most also started early in their careers in their activities of trying to persuade others. They tended to do so as relative 'loners', sometimes aided by small, congenial coteries but mostly in separation from peak organisations, strong interest groups or conventional party politics. Of eleven exponents referred to in this chapter, as many as eight produced books or major tracts; five produced several.

The reconstructionist viewpoint was not 'anti-business'. It accepted the 'basics' of devolved economic initiative, market institutions, private property, managerial co-ordination of firms. Even those who called themselves 'left-wing' or 'socialist' opposed superseding these processes by central planning, wholesale nationalisation or workers' control. But the reconstructionists' allegiance to the basics was severely conditional. What marked them out was a belief that the business-economic system needed both an internal overhaul and massive external safeguards and countervailing forces. They did not plan its elimination but were convinced that it should be suffused and encircled by superior social forces of higher quality than presently existed. Although sharing some ground with revisionism, in mood at least they were closer to liberationism, similarly challenging fundamentals and urging a radical shake-out of both cultures and structures but in a very different direction.

Much of the framework had been laid down by Samuel Courtauld in the midst of World War II.[4] Courtauld had called for less exploitative marketing; an end to the 'malignant disease' of 'gambling in industrial counters'; the worker's right to an increased share of rewards and 'to know all about the administration, policy and finance of the company', this being an end 'desirable for its own sake.' 'Businessmen should look upon themselves as do high officers in an army, as do leading statesmen in a government, as do the great men in the worlds of science and art; as men ... whose first motive is service to the truth of their metier and to the community'. Both 'worker directors' and 'government directors' should sit on large company boards.[5]

Courtauld favoured social security for the masses; public restraint of sectional interests ('no government can tolerate a free and irresponsible *imperium in imperio*'); and fair degrees of state ownership and control (though he stressed the dangers of bureaucracy). His ideas on education repudiated 'materialism.' 'Commercial education' was a bad thing: 'the trading and buccaneering instinct ... is quite highly enough developed in our civilization'. Its 'artificial fostering' would be both 'immoral' and 'economically unsound': 'better to teach the public to resist the blandishments of salesmen and advertisers'. Courtauld contemplated measures to restrict dividends at least in established large firms, with 'the total elimination of the speculator from the industrial field', and speculation in land foreclosed. Distribution and advertising costs should be reduced. 'The barriers of jealousy, suspicion and secrecy' should be broken down through much greater flows of information from companies to government, shareholders, managers, workers: 'In general, to throw light into every corner is the first step to true co-operation.' A proper representation of industry was equally a national concern, with regulated and 'responsible' trade unions and the FBI developed into the 'supreme' business organisation.[6]

Courtauld's vision featured major gaps. His lack of a bridging analysis between a Christian, Quaker ethical ideal and contemporary realities took much for granted: it offered little intermediate theory to evaluate either where the system was going or what trends might assist or obstruct his favoured causes. Reconstructionists within our period would mostly incline towards less directly religious language. They would also be more empirical or analytical, drawing on ideas of historical or contemporary dynamics, often adducing trends or cycles to support their case. None the less, many of Courtauld's themes would recur. And his vision of the primacy of values of community, democracy and justice would remain central for reconstructionists.

Social unity, democracy and justice as overarching goals

Reconstructionists shared with other groups an acute concern over Britain's economic performance, and some preferred remedies. They were insistent on the case for vigorous corporate enterprise and risk taking. They commended 'strong management' in business, with functional arguments favouring both high earnings differentials and powers of initiative for those at the top. Indeed, criticism of extreme egalitarianism brought supporters of the Labour Party among reconstructionists into direct collision with left-wing elements, as did their rejection of extreme nationalisation or central 'planning'. They tended to agree with revisionists on the case for cross-party consensus over many industrial issues: some reconstructionists would argue for radical institutional innovations to this end. Reconstructionists were no less concerned with issues of productivity, exports, training, rationalisation, innovation, research: many went out of their way to advocate scrapping managerial 'deadwood', promoting merit, or encouraging new small firms. However, a distinguishing mark was their strongly 'social' orientation even in these fields.

For the reconstructionists Britain's economic predicament was inextricably linked to their wider critiques over democracy, justice and civil society. Economic regeneration could not be tackled without radical improvements on those fronts. The 'class system' contributed to industrial strife, labour restrictive practices, conservative managements. Social divisions – inheritance, unequal opportunities, 'them and us', lack of employee participation – had pernicious economic effects. By the 1970s reconstructionists were not alone in believing that sectional interest conflict and excessive all-round expectations were major causes of inflation; and that crass defects and uncertainties over investment stemmed considerably from faults in the political system as well as cultural denigration of industry, over-mighty trade unions and outdated managements. The differentiation lay in the sharper links they drew and, still more, in their proposed remedies. To redress these problems the reconstructionists would return to their first base socio-political precepts. They would emphasise, yet again, worker and trade union incorporation, recast company structures, greater accountability, new cultures and institutions for economic and social co-operation.

However, greater democratic participation, 'fairness' and social unity, though critical for economic turnaround, were regarded as urgent for their own sake. Economic utility was important but not the primary test. In thus attributing primacy to certain social values the reconstructionists were at one with social idealists of similar hue outside business. They might find common cause with a 'Christian social' reconstructionist, a 'social' or 'left-wing Tory', a socially-orientated 'liberal' or 'radical', an 'ethical' or 'Christian socialist'. Often they would describe themselves partially or wholly in such ways, with an overall bias towards the 'centre–left' or 'left'. What was distinctive was the additional business component. This would include some insights from business experience. It would mean an insistence on a role for business in the sought-after new society. It would offer blueprints, seeking to extend or project the cherished social values in some detail to business-economic cultures and structures.

A typical starting point invoked values of 'one nation' or social integration. For some this went far enough to align with concerns for civil society or community in the traditions of Maurice, Scott Holland, T. H. Green, Durkheim or Tawney (though in so fragmented an area of theory such linkages were unlikely to be drawn directly). Here the statements were more purely normative: historical or social science-type arguments, if deployed, would relate to trends towards 'increasing interdependence', implying needs for greater contact or responsiveness between different interests. Reconstructionists were little inclined to cite a past 'golden age' of social solidarity, more disposed to draw on religious beliefs, gut ethical assumptions, or their own life or career experiences.

Such references included Ruskin's *Unto this Last* (George Goyder); 'common effort in war' or a college quad as 'the shape of fellowship'

(Peter Parker); the 'practical Christianity of Tubby Clayton . . . trying to reconcile man to man', 'a world without class distinctions' and 'war socialism' (Charles Villiers); 'a religious incentive to reconstruct a corrupt system', with 'guild principles and Christian principles one and the same' (Tom Heron); the civic mood of post-1945 reconstruction and 'service to the community' (Peter Thompson).[7]

In the area of 'justice' reconstructionists saw themselves as 'anti-privilege'. They tended to locate themselves within a long-familiar line of post-Industrial Revolution effort to overcome exploitation, class division or extreme inequality. Here again, formative influences were cited: of poverty in Lambeth in the late 1920s; of guilt at 'the part of luck in success', including one's own; of a 'shock contrast' with acute poverty in China; of 'a deep-rooted feeling that the workers, particularly in the coal mines near our home town, were not getting a fair deal', or dismay at 'guzzling', 'self-perpetuating oligarchies' and 'old boys' racket' in the City; of North Country boyhoods 'favouring a classless attitude'; of shame at conditions on West Indian sugar estates and exploitation of slavery by one's forebears.[8]

The reconstructionists would not add to the stock of macro-analyses or policy debates on anti-poverty or redistribution. They would, however, offer ideas on applications to the micro-levels they knew directly. One such was inequalities inside the enterprise. Here they favoured a reduction of divisions between 'staff' and 'labour' over social facilities or working conditions; fewer extravagant 'perks' for top managers; a sterner rationale for top rewards. Another stamping ground was 'exploitative finance'. While few went as far as Samuel Courtauld, there was sharp criticism of excessive returns to financial intermediaries or investors, and of the manipulation of take-over situations or share prices, divorced from economic progress or genuine risk-taking. Though such sentiments were not restricted to reconstructionists, it was they who sought to give them teeth, for example through stock market regulation, take-over curbs, increased disclosure, differential taxes or dividend limitation.

With regard to 'democracy', it was characteristic to argue outwards from long-established civic rights to suffrage and representation. For reconstructionists, the lack of complementary rights for employees at work was an anomaly; also an affront to contemporary expectations. Although business organisation was not identical with politics, here was a huge gap which should be narrowed, specifically through the introduction of constitutionally entrenched processes for representation and participation within the enterprise. This would also help to reduce social divisions inside the firm, to overcome 'them and us'. A subtler variant contemplated with dismay an unhealthy gap between 'power' and 'authority'. On the one hand, the power of workers and trade unions had greatly increased; but in the absence of legal regularisation such power could be, often was, exercised irresponsibly. For this reason, too, the enterprise needed to be reconstituted. Significantly, reconstructionists refrained from arguing for workers', let alone trade union control. This they saw as unworkable, adverse to clear decision making, even potentially selfish. After all, the enterprise also had responsibilities to consumers and 'the community', and these too required enactment, constitutional structures, supportive institutions.

Enthusiasms for democracy brought in their wake wider concerns about corporate power. According to one line of argument the power of the large public company was already much curtailed by consumer pressure, public opinion or government influence; according to another it ought to be so restricted. Despite some confusion between these two approaches, more or less resolved by distinguishing 'enlightened' or 'socially conscious' firms from the rest, the inferences broadly converged. Whether to reinforce an existing balance or to restrict excessive corporate power, changes would be needed in company law and management's formal responsibilities; also in the composition of company boards, in the information to be provided and in the public surveillance to be applied.

The political role of business was regarded as problematic. At the national level, policy effectiveness and democratic criteria both seemed to point to the necessity of business involvement in public affairs. Business's social enfolding or embedding, indeed, implied such participation. In an increasingly complex economy to rely on the 'invisible hand' was a recipe for chaos, injustice, division. Yet co-ordination by government would overload the state, over-centralise decisions and damage enterprise, while equally it was foolish to expect too much from legal regulation in view of the inadequacies of the law, its frequent rigidity or inapplicability, its inability to cope with new situations, unexpected crises or economic policy. Hence it followed that organised business, along with trade union and other interests, had a part to play in co-operating with government, contributing to public policy formation, helping to implement public policies or national interests.

Yet the existing system shortchanged this ideal as well as defying criteria of equity and democracy. The relations between business and government incorporated biases, even abuses. Business itself was anarchically organised and inadequately represented. Still more serious were secrecy, arbitrary influence or log-rolling, lack of parliamentary scrutiny and public openness, an absence of even minimal constitutional recognition. Therefore, if 'corporatism' meant the organised representation and participation of business and other sectional interests, then so be it, a large measure was unavoidable, indeed desirable. But 'corporatism' should be made more visible and open, more representative, accountable and 'responsible'.

Reconstituting the firm: multiple responsibilities, employee participation

The two principal developers of the reconstructionist theory of the firm, George Goyder and Wilfred Brown, did not come from business's top echelons. They were not economic diplomats, nor involved in the FBI, BEC or CBI, nor influenced by previous national policy involvements. Both had made their way as chief executives of smallish firms. Goyder, managing director of the British International Paper Company 1935–71, was both a debonair and an earnest figure, active in church debate, on the Protestant-ecumenical wing of Anglicanism, a social reformer. He had been influenced by observation of poverty at an early stage as well as culturally by Blake and Ruskin, economically by Hobson and Keynes, and in his business philosophy by Samuel Courtauld.[9] Brown, head of the Glacier Metal Company from the mid-'30s to 1964, was a leading management theorist as well as practitioner. A pithy, down-to-earth, free-thinking Scot, Brown was a Labour Party supporter who served in the 1964–70 Labour Government.[10] Both men were prolific expositors, publishing books and pamphlets, with the addition of sermons and church addresses in Goyder's case, political memoranda and correspondence in Brown's. They were fervent ethicists, with obstinate and imperious streaks, convinced of the rightness of their case.

Goyder's *The Future of Private Enterprise*, first published in 1951, had set a framework he would follow over ensuing decades. Authoritarian ideas in business and the concept of shareholder possession were 'as archaic as the 17th century doctrine of the Divine Right of Kings'.[11] The formal objectives of the public company ought to encompass wide social responsibilities. Criteria of justice, democracy and 'mutual aid' all required this; in secondary fashion so did contemporary realities. The company's duties should be to workers, consumers and community as well as shareholders: balancing or reconciling them was a major task for management, even 'its highest function'. Changes in the constitution of the public company would be needed: first, a General Objects Clause to enshrine multiple responsibilities in legal terms and, secondly, legislation to provide workers with equivalent rights to shareholders.

Goyder's proposed shift of power, resources and cultures went further. He sought to diminish or redirect the role of shareholders and dividends. For established large enterprises (as distinct from new small ones which needed a greater supply of equity capital) he proposed immediate statutory dividend limitation for those with extreme market power. Others would be encouraged to opt voluntarily for a system of reduced shareholder returns, effectively turning shareholders into creditors, with profit surpluses diverted to funds for employees in the form of shares or eventual retirement pensions. Companies that chose this path would earn a new, hopefully sought-after 'public trust' status. Those that failed to conform would be eventually compelled to do so, after a period of fifty years. Goyder added refinements: (a) worker directors on unitary boards; (b) supervisory boards where a strong desire for these existed, with 1/3 worker, 1/3 shareholder, 1/3 consumer, local or government representation; (c) greater salience for company AGMs as deliberative, reviewing bodies, again including a wider range of interests; and (d) a parallel legislative code for nationalised industries 'to ensure their accountability, efficiency and freedom from outside parliamentary or other pressure'. (e) Periodic social audits of large companies were a further feature, though outlined more vaguely.[12]

By this time Goyder's basic rubric of multiple responsibilities had become widely accepted as 'progressive' wisdom, sometimes reflected in chairmen's speeches, company codes or pressure group proposals. He had broadcast it consistently, without the moral hype of precursors like Courtauld, incorporating a wide sweep of both history and constitutional ideas, and he wrote well. However, his wider proposals were more difficult to understand, let alone accept, for mainstream business readers.

A different sort of 'redistribution to the workers' was advocated by the City radical Nicholas Davenport.[13] A leading stockbroker, investment expert and financial writer with Labour Party ties, Davenport opposed interfering with dividend variability, equity shareholding and capital markets. These should be retained as cardinal for a still-essential dynamic private sector, even 'the magic that makes it work'. *Pace* some socialist revisionists, profit incentives were, and would remain, central: high incomes for 'efficient profit makers . . . pillars of the trading State' should be welcomed by socialists. Davenport's other views on taxation were orthodoxly left-centre. It was his objections to employee profit sharing and his advocacy of a state unit trust that were distinctive. The former could benefit only a minority of earners: it would create 'a new privileged clique', 'bitterness', 'syndicalism in which management and labour gang up to exploit the consumer'. Correspondingly, even sharper objections applied to stock options for executives: 'bribes to the greediest', a device to 'get rich quick'. His central proposal would seek to combine robust stock market capitalism with collective values or 'securing a stake in the country'. It was a State Participation Unit Trust, independent of the

Treasury, investing in the best equities, with small units available over Post Office counters: it should fairly expeditiously accrue a large stake in investment for the ordinary public.[14]

Wilfred Brown, a better-known figure, advanced complementary ideas, though with some differences. His social scientism was greater than Goyder's, influenced by ideas of group dynamics and his long association with Eliot Jacques in the 'Glacier experiments' in his own firm. Brown's egalitarianism was deep-felt but not extreme. On income tax he started by opposing 'incentive'-based arguments for reductions, but by 1979 would criticise the 'excessively high direct taxation of private income'. On profits, too, he rejected left-wing crudities such as ideas of 'fair profits' tied to individual products. A progressivist with an optimistic streak, Brown believed in the improvability of human behaviour given changes in the 'social framework' and 'outmoded institutions'. The 'social priorities' of relationships, status, liberty, security, had to come first. 'It is the absence of national plans' on these issues 'that is harmful to our economic performance. We damage the latter by giving it too much priority . . . If we could agree to go hell-bent for human values at work we might well get the economic efficiency we need as a by-product.' 'Concentration on production, efficiency, budgets and the like, to the exclusion of human factors, in fact reduces efficiency.' It was necessary 'to institutionalise the methods by which due attention is paid to the human factors'.[15]

Brown's main contribution, over employee participation, owed much to his chief executive experience and tried innovations, albeit within a small-ish enterprise. He went so far as to claim that fuller participation, going well beyond conventional joint consultation, would enhance managerial (moral) authority as well as promoting justice and containing the power which had migrated to the shop floor. His stress on a constitutional system repudiated the older school of 'human relations', whose top-down concept of 'motivation' or 'education', with management posing as 'benefactors', he deplored as 'manipulation'. But believing in firm leadership and 'employment hierarchies' as well as responsibilities to consumers and the community, he rejected 'workers' control'. Brown emphasised the elective principle, grass roots participation and, again drawing on both theory and *praxis*, involvement in 'policy' rather than 'decisions'. Excepting very small firms, the core would be statutory works and company councils with wide functions of policy deliberation and implementation, distinct from the executive board. To this he added employee rights of appeal against unfair dismissal. While the details and timing of such company constitutions might vary, Brown saw both legislation and a special national commission as necessary to implement them. Voluntarism would be far from enough.[16]

Even while Brown was summarising his proposals in a book, *The Earnings Conflict*, events were conspiring against such ideas. The peak business bodies would stumble over them, the trade unions would be uninterested or cross-pressured, with prospects further stymied by 'industrial democracy' proposals first from the Labour Party, then the Bullock Commission, which Brown would deplore, viewing them as in some respects too extreme but in others not radical enough. It was Brown's misfortune to swim against the tide in other ways too. For example, he advocated schemes of job evaluation or group-determined differentials, as opposed to payments systems related to piecework, 'results' or 'productivity', whose absurdities and injustices he had good reason to dislike. But it was the latter which were on the increase. Ill at ease in politics, Brown had been uncomfortable at the Board of Trade. By 1975 his sense of a national moral crisis of 'greed' and 'a drooping sense of mission', including excessive trade union power, produced a private exhortation to Harold Wilson to 'lead the nation', 'transcend party politics' and pursue tougher policies towards sectional interests, finance as well as labour. Another idea, something of an *idée fixe* between 1973 and 1979, was a National Council for the Regulation of Differential Wages (NCRD). This scheme met with scepticism even among ideological allies, confirming an impression of idiosyncrasy: a pity, given the fertility of his other ideas.[17]

A new co-operative fabric: conciliar peak institutions and public stimuli

Some reconstructionists in our sample would engage in sweeping normative discourse about society or political economy. The management educator and retailer Grigor McClelland, for example, invoked 'egalitarian', 'democratic' and 'unity-seeking' values in general terms, writing mainly in his capacity as a Quaker reconstructionist in the Joseph Rowntree tradition.[18] It was more usual, though, to move to applications. Fred Catherwood, expressing broadly reconstructionist ideas between bouts of revisionist-flavoured activism in Whitehall, NEDO and the BIM, set out a Christian ideal of moral aspiration for society as well as managers (occasionally with prim overtones). He included universal social services 'financed by high and progressive taxation', 'a considerable redistribution of wealth and income' towards 'the under-privileged', 'some kind of national planning process', and a 'public code of conduct for industry'.[19] A concept for multinationals to behave in socially responsible fashion within developing countries, going well beyond prudent political calculus, would be affirmed by Jock Campbell of Booker McConnell, a vigorous articulator of business 'social responsibilities.'[20]

The women's clothes manufacturer and retailer, Thomas Heron, in a high church Anglican tradition of 'anti-capitalist' social thinking, would reaffirm a Christian social, guildist concept of economic reformation. Heron trenchantly criticised existing company governance as showing 'a strong resemblance to the activities of tribal councils and one-party totalitarian states'.[21] A Christian business group would pointedly see management not as 'the servant of the state' *nor* of 'the rich', but as a reconciler of 'all the interests which focus on the firm, for the advantage of the people as a whole'.[22]

It was not easy for reconstructionists to say distinctive things, however, complementing the familiar work of social theorists, about a new social context for business. This applied even in a field at the core of reconstructionism where business leaders could be expected to come up with useful ideas from experience and intuition as well as belief, that of co-operation between business, other sectional interests and the state. Here it would not be enough just to practise such co-operation, to understand its wider workings or to seek more of it, in a manner familiar with revisionists. Additional moral passion would be needed; also a critical, imaginative leap towards some concept of new cultural or institutional artifacts for co-operation. Two reconstructionists who took these further steps, with the ability and desire to develop a coherent model of their own, were Peter Parker and Charles Villiers.

Peter Parker would be the main exponent of a macro-conciliar approach to the civic inclusion and democratisation of business. His managerial career, featuring much precocity, included Booker McConnell for fourteen years, Rockware and Mitsubishi UK, with British Railway 1976–83 as the biggest test. From his secretaryship of the Duke of Edinburgh's Conference in 1954–56 onwards, Parker was an arch-networker. Ebullient, mercurial, affable, he exuded a mixture of communication as art form, communication as belief, and ideas for improving and widening it. A keynote was the 'economic, entrepreneurial and social' dimensions of management as ascending priorities, with 'social' at the peak. Themes of 'courtesy', 'connections', 'civility', 'putting, rather than knocking, our heads together' were celebrated. Parker's verbal artistry could run to a life of its own, with a polymath's range of authors cited and frequent ironies, aphorisms, plays on words: a whirlwind fluency could leave some hearers puzzled or rushed, if enlivened. A lesser interest in economics coupled with an elastic, markedly optimistic tilt in his thought made him the least astringent of reconstructionists, with some attendant dangers. It meant that description, prediction and prescription could blur or oscillate, with ethical preferences often emerging, in rather Whiggish, progressivist fashion, as benign unilinear trends: 'board agendas in the '90s'; 'a new push ... to be expected'; 'the age's priorities'; 'the rise of humanity in management thinking.'[23]

Parker was fascinated by the 'inescapable condition of interdependence', the 'public significance of all the major decisions of modern business'. Among his specifics were greater commercial freedom and a 'bi-partisan' settlement for transport as a 'national industry'; an amalgamation of trade bodies, with engineering as prime case of confusion to be redressed; and a huge, humanistically interpreted expansion of education. Parker vividly related economic to social malaise: 'economic weakness in our split society'; 'class-based and pickled in privilege as we are'; 'inflation as an expression of our social tensions'. For him the post-1960s crises were linked with party polarisation, policy U-turns and 'swirling' volatilities of interventionist bodies' combined with *stasis* over essentials, giving industry 'the worst of both worlds'. He sharply criticised a skewed tripartism, 'centralising ... power without guaranteeing adequate representation'; the decline of parliamentary control and its sheer remoteness from industry. His most distinctive proposal, however, was for a new conciliar, cross-sectional institution at the peak.[24]

Parker arrived at this proposal first through an analysis of 'paradoxes'. On the one hand, the inevitability and desirability of partially self-governing representative bodies in the interests of 'articulacy', 'an interdependent economy', 'government by consent'. On the other, 'the closed, remote, increasingly undemocratic influence of the big corporate trade union and industrial powers'. Not only were the TUC and the CBI inadequately representative in their own fields. Further, the system excluded other components of 'the national interest', consumers, the self-employed, pensioners etc. To cope with all this it was absurd to hanker after 'the golden age' of 'fully competitive markets or ... classical parliamentary democracy'. What was needed was clearer public accountability, 'better communication', measures for 'civilising and constitutionalising corporate power so that it is exercised responsibly'.[25]

Parker's model drew on previous UK advocacy and some West European precedents (for example, the French Economic and Social Council and the ECOSOC of the EEC), though without fully explaining how these could be improved on. He proposed a central forum of 200–250 members, 'spanning industry and commerce section by section, public and private, nominated by the various trade, professional and other associations and trade unions' but also including 'special, minority groups', not just the established bodies. This institution would be 'independent and advisory', 'a creation of Parliament but not part of it', with its own public platform and 'visibility'. It would deliberate such issues as industrial democracy, a wealth tax, differentials, the closed shop, nationalisation, the City of London, and would be consulted on guidelines for prices and incomes, budgetary and monetary policy.[26]

A part-complementary, part-different emphasis came from a sweeping critic of British individualism, Charles Villiers. Background influences on Villiers had included family traditions of public service, Oxford PPE, ideas of 'radical Toryism', and empathies with the ranks in his regiment during the war. After working in merchant banking Villiers became managing director of the IRC 1967–70, followed by related activities in Ulster, a further stint in the City, and chairmanship of the BSC 1977–82. A holistic sense of political economy was important for him; also overseas and particularly European models. A mutualist, relational ethos owed much to religious affiliations, from Toc H to convert Catholicism. Villiers' ideas mainly appeared in lectures in the 1970s and two books, in 1984 and 1992.[27] Eclectically wide ranging, not particularly good at projecting himself in wide terms, nor a specially agile thinker, though earnest and reflective, he would be easy to misjudge. A long phase of outward conventionality in the City was a factor here; so were public roles which constrained free expression, with his main policy contributions coming when less in the public eye. Villiers retained some slightly Edwardian, gentleman's club mannerisms, with an air of, say, Harold Macmillan. His radicalism did not quite attain a consistent, resonant style, but it was substantive and distinctive nonetheless.

Villiers insisted on a 'democratic', 'fair' and 'social' framework for 'wealth creation'. 'Social' meant reducing 'them and us', and 'a sense of national purpose', not 'selfish individualism'. 'Fairness' meant avoiding 'excessive personal wealth and poverty', and 'more for the poor and disadvantaged'. Villiers' belief in managerial initiative and 'a new spirit of enterprise' was matched only by his anger at the short-termism and sloppiness of large swathes of existing managements. Far from eliminating these weaknesses, market forces tended to be 'too slow in shedding duds at the top end, and too timid in encouraging the starlets further down the line'. This economic astringency persisted. Though not denying some merits to the Thatcherite regime, Villiers saw no fundamental improvement in the 1980s. To rely on 'fear and anxiety' to shift basic attitudes, as distinct from immediate reflexes, was inadequate.[28] The British economy still featured far too little risk-taking, investment and education and, above all, too little co-operation. Excessive 'individualism' remained his principal target. This he saw as a deep-rooted historical, cultural, almost 'religious' phenomenon in Britain. There was an element of inconsistency here. The implication was that major change would have to be medium- or long-term, with a sense of being a prophet, 'ahead of my time'. But Villiers was also eager for an immediate, 'get up and go', 'born again' national reconstruction: a conflict he never quite worked through.

Villiers exhorted 'co-operation' at virtually all levels except the competitive market, with qualifications even there. Inside the firm this implied avoidance of 'excessive privileges' for managers, greater accountability through 'tiered' board systems, statutory works councils and 'industrial democracy'. Next, whatever its past merits, grassroots entrepreneurial individualism now defied the needs of a 'more sophisticated', interdependent economy. This caused the small proprietor 'to flinch from the collaboration with others which growth, innovation and exports always imply', while keeping many firms from diversifying or moving up beyond one-person control. Even the agencies for small firms were too many and too separatist. At national level there should be 'continuous, trustful, well-researched collaboration between government and management', with a hope that (rationalised) trade unions would also join in these practices. Indeed, the co-operation he chiefly enjoined was to be economy-wide: 'a creative link between managers, employers, self-employed and government, workforce, shareholders, customers, schools, colleges', with government, civil service and management in the leading roles.[29]

To bring about such a complex fabric Villiers looked partly to a sort of cultural conversion, 'a new spirit', partly to a bevy of energisers from public institutions. He never deviated from a belief in the inescapability of government activism, its need to 'steer' and 'accelerate', to 'arouse and lead'. Some of the agencies he envisaged were pump priming (notably a large-scale, state-backed capital fund on West German lines, to lend at low interest rates to small business); others would be purgative (IRC-type action primarily 'to remove bad management before it is too late'). But they would also aim more directly at systemic co-operativism: an Industrial Co-operation Agency to promote 'employee participation' and to overcome the 'them and us' which he saw still existing in 'more than half British workplaces'; an ombudsman or tribunal to assess scandals, disasters and complaints about management performance; a SEC for the City; an intermediary board for nationalised industries; and an 'Economic Cabinet' at the peak, separate from the Treasury, staffed from business, academia, science, the unions. He saw major changes in political systems and culture as necessary for his 'developmental, collaborative state', with a lead from the top 'in the spirit of Roosevelt's New Deal, Adenauer's Germany, De Gaulle's France and modern Japan'.[30]

Constraints on reconstituting the firm

The reconstructionists, then, had plenty of ideas both for recasting the firm and for changing the socio-economic context. But how far were their chosen audiences, as distinct from small coteries of initiates, ready to hear? The answer is, very little, at least for the stronger measures they anticipated or the larger models they portrayed. Neither the business nor the wider cultures seemed capable of digesting their wider message. Sometimes they appeared to realise as much, at other times they preferred to forget it or, more likely, decided to compromise and work with others in the interests of partial changes. In the rest of this chapter we consider the sort of obstacles they faced, starting with their more accessible ideas for reconstituting the firm.

In this area some parallel influences were at work. Radical, if often vaguely rhetorical aspirations had been expressed by John Marsh at the Industrial Welfare Society, a considerable influence on 'progressive' human relations circles in the 1950s.[31] His successor, John Garnett, director of the Industrial Society through most of our period, a more down-to-earth figure, was a believer in staff-labour equalisation and would be a fervent missionary for human and industrial relations priorities, though some of his more far-reaching proposals would fall on stony ground.[32]

A major test soon appeared for corporate reformism. It came through the medium of an inquiry in 1972–73, chaired by Lord Watkinson, into 'The Responsibilities of the Public Company'. This exercise was sponsored by the CBI under its advanced revisionist leadership of the time (see chapter 5), another stimulus being possible EEC implications for UK company law. A further key influence was a series of consultations on 'business ethics' at St George's House, Windsor, which had started in 1967.[33] Significantly for reconstructionist ideas on the firm, the Watkinson inquiry laid bare fundamental contrasts with other philosophies of the public company. It sidestepped some reconstructionist preferences. Of the five main issues it tackled the fate of three would be instructive. On two others which went to the heart of reconstructionist beliefs, huge roadblocks would be thrown up by business commentators or on the Committee itself.

On the fundamental objectives of the company a chasm soon opened up. A reconstructionist minded element on the committee showed its colours from the start. According to one member, 'The basic structures and method of the private sector', 'a malaise affecting the joint stock company . . . and with it the greater part of our economic life', needed 'continuous reform', so that 'the company has to be given a conscience', or as another member put it, a breaking down of 'inequality . . . unnecessary secrecy . . . and *apartheid*' between 'all the interests involved in running a company'.[34] But at the other extreme a pure doctrine of shareholder hegemony was expressed mainly by the Stock Exchange: 'If we want a free enterprise society . . . the primary objective should be to maintain the concept of proprietorship', whose dilution 'would endanger provision of share capital by diminishing rewards and damage confidence and expectations'.[35] A subtler conservatism accepted the idea of additional, lesser duties to employees or other interests, but it saw these as reconciled in practice with shareholder primacy and profit-maximising: the workings of 'enlightened self-interest', legal safeguards already in place or existing pressures from public opinion, should render major changes unnecessary.[36] As for the leading group on the committee, this was revisionist and keen on moderate 'self-reform'.[37]

At first the committee flirted with the idea of an ethical 'code of conduct', already bandied about at St George's, Windsor. This could 'clarify external responsibilities', 'avoid government regulation', promote 'self-restraint in the public interest' or recognise 'duties beyond both immediate profit and the requirements of law'.[38] However, the 'code' proposal ran into much criticism. If it looked to the politically anxious like a Trojan horse for state intervention, for radicals it was too vague, while to others again it seemed merely irrelevant: unnecessary for the well behaved and unlikely to influence the buccaneers. If extra obligations were required of companies, surely to enact these legally would be more straightforward, even more correct constitutionally? Even advocates of the 'code' agreed it would need 'backing up'. Predictably, it was dropped, with only abstract principles retained.[39]

The second idea, largely tangential to reconstructionist aims, was to involve the investing institutions in more active surveillance. These would stop being sleeping shareholders and assume monitorial roles in the companies they invested in. More ambitiously, some mixture of the CBI, the major financial institutions, the Stock Exchange, the governor of the Bank of England or a new disciplinary panel would act as 'watchdogs' to 'police' the new code or punish 'breaches' of it. This proposal, however, excited industry suspicions of City interference. Its main proponent, Watkinson, an enthusiast for the revisionist notion of a (collectively conceived) 'private enterprise capable of its own self-reform', did not appear to understand the City's workings. Fears as to 'sanctions' came from the CBI grassroots, along with wide scepticism as to whether institutional shareholders were 'equipped to become the consciences of the nation'. Neither the Governor nor the Institutional Shareholders' Committee nor the Stock Exchange was favourable, showing a reluctance to judge ethical standards, a feeling that this was not appropriate for investors, that it would be inconsistent with monitoring efficiency.[40] As the theme of City policing faded, increased reliance was placed on the third idea, of non-executive directors (NEDS) exercising a greater role on company boards. This prescription would persist long after the Watkinson inquiry, though from the start key insiders had strong doubts as to its potential feasibility and scope.[41]

A fourth theme, employee participation, revealed strong reconstructionist leanings among some members of the committee. 'Far too many directors . . . think their workers are 'hopeless', forgetting 'there are only bad generals, not bad soldiers.' 'Employees invest . . . their skills and themselves to their company – in fact, are contributors of capital . . . Shareholders can buy one share on a Monday, attend its AGM and ask questions and vote on Tuesday, and sell shares on Monday, while employees have no right to question Directors at all.' 'If people lose their jobs they may be losing not just their jobs but part of themselves.' There was a need for 'position and status' and 'some sort of membership of the firm'. Here, too, some revisionists were quite sympathetic, for example Geddes. Watkinson himself argued that a 'firm responsibility' should be put on the board, particularly the chief executive, for industrial relations, 'joint consultation and disclosure' to employees.[42]

The idea of 'worker directors' on existing company boards was not favoured. It was disliked not only by conservatives but also by pragmatists who perceived little trade union support for it, and by reformers on the grounds that 'worker directors' would form an artificial top dressing, peripheral to the real business of participation 'from the ground up'. Even Goyder and Wilfred Brown had not put them uppermost. Instead, the committee 'strongly favoured Company-wide joint councils, with full disclosure of information' and plant councils, both on ICI lines.[43] Here, then, common cause could be found with revisionists. But in wider business circles there was opposition to the 'employee participation' proposals, particularly from small firm elements, and once they reached the CBI Council, they had to be watered down.[44] The official CBI policy that emerged was tepid even by revisionist, let alone reconstructionist standards. George Goyder, for one, would dismiss it as still shareholder-dominated, antipathetic to 'social accountability' of management, and out of line with European trends.[45]

A final idea got closer to a full reconstructionism of the firm. It offered a constitutional route for the public company's plural responsibilities, not only to employees. A consultative body would exist for each major company, each main interest group being represented alongside top management. This would not solve the inevitable conflicts in decision making, though it could assist consensus-seeking, gulf-bridging, deliberation, holding the executive to account. Some near-reconstructionist sentiments were voiced in its favour. It fitted with a 'team', 'non-separate', 'equal' approach to 'all the interests in society involved'. Again, 'whether or not it contributes much to the running ... of companies', 'it brings together in a large number of small groups, each of which has a collective responsibility (however nebulous) ... the way in which human understanding is built up and divisions come to be healed' and 'national confrontations' reduced.[46] Others on the committee, Benson, Orr of Unilever and Shawcross, at least wanted it studied. Clapham was favourable; so were senior people from several leading firms including Imperial Group, BICC, Lucas, Reckitt and Colman, and ICI, in the last case in the form of a 'trusteeship council' to include 'community' as well as employee, shareholder and management representation.[47] Initial CBI soundings did not suggest overwhelming grass roots opposition, though majority support would have been another matter if the idea had got further.[48] None the less, the idea got short shrift, notably from Watkinson. The Interim Report dismissed 'the supervisory board' as weakening 'the link between executives and shareholders' and diluting 'the feeling of management of total responsibility'.[49]

That much business opinion would find the idea indigestible, let alone unfit for legal enactment in 1972–73, is hardly surprising. A suitable UK terminology was lacking. The 'two-tier' or 'supervisory board' suffered the misfortune of being foreign and cumbrous-sounding, associated with widely feared EEC proposals, smacking of a threat to strong decision making by a unitary company board. It would arguably do less to advance employee participation than effective machinery inside the firm. Over the next twenty years or more the supervisory board was destined to become something of a punch-bag for (often inconsistent) disparagement. The make-up of such a body was bound to be problematic, although the German *Mitbestimmung* (management, shareholders and workers each having one-third representation) could have offered a viable compromise. The failure of the idea within the business community in 1972–73 left a gap soon to be filled, all too contentiously, by the largely tangential 'red rag' majority proposals of the Bullock Committee (see next chapter). It also starkly revealed the constraints suffered even by micro-reconstructionism in this period.

Prophets in the wilderness?

Reconstructionist ideas on the wider political economy fell on even stonier ground. Intellectual coherence often accompanied their specially wide conceptualisation of the social and political context. Part of the heavy price for this, however, was a lesser attunement to detailed economic processes and policies. Above all, the reconstructionists stood at awkward angles to existing conventions and institutions. They tended to be stymied by cultural, organisational and political isolation as a small minority cult, with consequent difficulties over a strategy of persuasion.

It was hard to find wider intellectual currents to sustain their position. No equivalent developed to the degree of rapport, in certain areas, between revisionists and some Keynesian economists. Reconstructionists whose antecedents included early twentieth century social liberalism, national guildism or Christian socialism would find no leading contemporary movements to link up with. A helpful factor would have been a strong tradition of thinking about 'democratic corporatism', as in parts of Western Europe and Scandinavia, but this was lacking in the UK. So was a parallel brand of trade union radicalism. Neither left-wing nor right-wing trade unionism would appeal to the reconstructionists, while moderate reformers among summit trade unionists, for example Woodcock, Feather, Murray, might find closer affinities, at least operationally, with the CBI revisionists. Only a few academic thinkers offered significant overlaps. Phelps Brown was a sympathetic figure on industrial relations. Andrew Shonfield provided a wide perspective on economic policy, trends and institutions with considerable affinities; but he was intellectually aloof as well as lacking in the social vision and ethical thrust which reconstructionists prized so highly. Perhaps significantly, two outstanding observers of the British system with more complementary or congenial prognoses, albeit at some distance from business, were foreigners; Samuel Beer and Ralf Dahrendorf.[50]

The lack of an attractive overall label was unhelpful. Even revisionists, despite much definitional vagueness, could usefully huddle under the loose ideas of 'middle way', 'moderation' or 'centrism'. But reconstructionists would find it hard to encapsulate their triple allegiance to the inter-related values of democracy, 'fairness' and social unity: a single short term could easily over-emphasise just one. An umbrella description could be too reductive, as with Villiers' 'co-operative, developmental state', while the mediocrity of 'mixed economy' was a caricature. As for 'capitalism,' with all its attendant ambiguities or traumas, the reconstructionists were hardly alone in showing some disarray. On a broad, mutable definition of 'capitalism', confined to the business basics, a few resorted to qualified or secondary uses of the term: on an adversely loaded interpretation, others saw themselves as clearly 'anti-' or 'post-'. But others again, perhaps wisely, avoided the term.

The difficulties reconstructionists faced in getting their ideas accepted in the peak organisations of business have emerged several times in this chapter. Such difficulties applied to Peter Parker in the BIM in the mid-1980s, and to Hunter Johnston, Richard O'Brien and Peter Thompson, for example, at various stages in the CBI.[51] They applied even where popularity and effectiveness were achieved in other ways within these bodies. Most reconstructionists preferred to steer clear of them. Some were obstinate 'individualists', so that organisations of any kind would be difficult, though ongoing personal contacts were characteristic among themselves. Differences with business colleagues would also be experienced within smaller coteries. They could be found in the smaller Christian forums, for example, particularly St George's, Windsor, and the Christian Association of Business Executives, where radical reformers were in a minority and a restricted 'business ethics' more prevalent.

Within the party system reconstructionists prospered least of all the ideological tendencies. Some abjured party connections altogether. Even strong commitments did not prevent major disappointments, with no 'wing' of any party seeming capable of welcoming reconstructionist ideas. Goyder found Liberal Party circles in the 1960s too syndicalist, and remote from the realities of large-scale business; Catherwood migrated from Conservative to near-Labour, and, by 1979, back to Conservative, though remaining a strong critic of free market extremism; Villiers, styling himself a 'left-wing Tory', akin to Ian Gilmour, had some social democratic sympathies.[52] Most of the rest were Labour supporters, sometimes with SDP phases in the 1980s. Often, however, their Labourism was uncomfortable. Traditional 'Clause Four' socialism was out of bounds for them, making for distances from, say, Gollancz or Lipton. They did not usually find natural allies among prominent Labour sympathisers in business, who tended to be conventional in both business and party terms. Nor, perhaps most disappointingly, did the currents of revisionist socialism provide much support. The Labour revisionists appeared culturally distant, politically constrained, their energies drained by party controversies, sometimes almost too eager to embrace markets in simplistic fashion, more often unable warmly to embrace private enterprise as a condition of greater radicalism over its reconstruction.[53]

Behind all these problems lay difficulties over strategy and time scales. The reconstructionists were the least well endowed in numbers and resources of all the tendencies yet the most far reaching in their ambitions for change. Most of them were deeply engaged in business operations while proclaiming their nostrums. On the one hand, it seemed natural to concentrate on trying to persuade business constituencies, typically in Fabian, piecemeal fashion; on the other, there was a strong case for cutting free and reaching out to wider audiences with a longer-term, prophetic, even 'counter-cultural' message that demanded outside allies and focussed on the interdependence between business and socio-political categories of transformation. This dilemma would be difficult to face and even more difficult to resolve.

7 Turmoil, realignment and recovery: British business 1974–1979

In this chapter we move back to historical chronology for a critical period which deployed all three tendencies of opinion analysed so far and which catalysed major attitudinal shifts across the board. Labour's fragile victory in the general elections of 1974 abruptly ended the period of high tripartism described in chapter 5. With Labour in power with a bare majority of seats, a period of political instability seemed likely to last for several years. The context was one of accelerating inflation and unemployment, a tight squeeze on corporate profitability, and widespread industrial conflict. Many business leaders believed that the time had come for a radical overhaul in their relationships with government and the public. Optimistic hopes of a leading role in tripartist arrangements, dating from the early 1960s, largely broke down when faced with manoeuvres between the minority Labour government and the TUC to engineer the 'Social Contract' by the summer of 1974. The demotion of business interests seemed confirmed by the government's first budgets, which appeared in the guise of vote-seeking exercises at the expense of a corporate sector facing bankruptcies, higher taxation and salary squeezes for high earners.

During the years 1974–79 the scope for a socialist-business entente appeared to diminish further. At no stage did such a concept loom large for either side as it had done at least initially during the 1964–70 period. Though eventually extracting concessions, sometimes more so than was admitted, organised industry saw the government successively distracted by large spending ventures, by the crises of 1975–76, by the further cliff edges of cuts and 'freezes', narrow majorities and industrial unrest, while all the time looking nervously over its shoulders at the unions. Militant-sounding schemes for planning agreements, financial intervention and industrial democracy were initiated, only to reveal divisions inside the government, ensuing in much watering down or backing off as business angrily protested. The CBI leadership would lock with the government in relations of anger, sullen acquiescence or recoil, or at best joint crisis management. The initial shock of dealing with two robustly left-wing ministers, Tony Benn and Michael Foot, soon gave way to reasonable working relationships with ministers such as Eric Varley, Shirley Williams or Edmund Dell, while behind the scenes Wilson and Callaghan could be reassuring, with Denis Healey in particular, despite his astringencies, often confidingly forthcoming in private about the government's difficulties with the unions and the left.[1] But the circumstances were such that no real convergence could develop.

Realignments of business opinion were soon evident. A large number of businessmen began to speak out for liberationist-type policies, in contrast to their muted interventions under the previous government. The traditionally inarticulate small business sector would acquire a collective voice in the IOD and within the CBI. By 1979 the momentum developed by liberationism appeared such as to alter the balance of opinion within the business community and sufficient to influence the incoming Conservative government. Yet despite much confusion, the period also witnessed a recovery of the revisionist position, which achieved a more realistic appraisal of what could be done to reform the economic system through its favoured methods of education, persuasion and gradual change. Both the CBI and a more active British Institute of Management (BIM) developed public profiles which suggested they could influence the policies of an incoming government.

The manner in which business presented itself would become at once more coherent and more variegated. The peak organisations would be prepared to collaborate on such issues as the Bullock Report on industrial democracy and budget representations, against what was seen, at least initially, as a wilfully unsympathetic government. At the same time their rivalries and disagreements persisted. By 1979 it could be argued that the CBI, BIM, and IOD all offered distinctive formulations about the policies required for domestic recovery. This process can best be described as one of 'co-operative competition', with business leaders competing to influence politicians and public opinion, but within an implicitly agreed framework that the crisis of 1974–76 required a more robust assertion of what 'business' provided for society and what it should expect in return. There was, typically, much talk of educating public opinion about the 'economic facts of life' and demanding that the creation of wealth should have precedence over schemes for its distribution. It was a time for reasserting business basics. But the underlying, long-term differences between revisionists, liberationists and reconstructionists did not recede.

Sharpening perspectives

Shock at the economic situation was intense, particularly in 1975–76, later recalled by the intellectually independent banker Jeremy Morse as the nadir of UK post-war performance. Disillusionment with government intervention, already strong in 1972–74, became further reinforced. Indignation over high taxation was to reach a peak. Not least came a major shift in perceptions of trade union power. To describe this whole mixture words like 'terrible', 'disaster', 'near despair' were not infrequent in the interviews conducted for this study. Some now moving into top positions in their companies, for example Michael Edwardes, Terry Beckett, Peter Walters, would have their attitudes strongly shaped in varying ways, as would emerge by the 1980s.[2]

Social defensiveness was giving way to a more assertive stance. In January 1975, under the aegis of St George's House, Windsor, some leading reformers, including both John Partridge and Wilfred Brown, agreed that 'in view of increasing pressures on companies from government, there should be a change in emphasis to a more traditional role . . . to enable our society to rediscover the virtue of the industrial process itself'. For established revisionists in particular the period incorporated much pain. They found their views hardening on industrial relations, often in spite of themselves, as one by one they faced sharper labour militancy in their industries: Maurice Laing in construction, Lord Caldecote in Delta Metal, Michael Clapham in printing. The seasoned tripartist Alex Jarratt later described how a sense that 'the unions were running the country' would reinforce his shift of beliefs towards both competitive forces and managerial authority.[3] The mixed economy enthusiast and business ethicist Fred Catherwood would move to an astringent attitude on the 'imbalance of power'. In the traditional bastion of Quaker social conscience, Cadbury's, now Cadbury Schweppes, there was 'a growing disillusionment throughout corporate management' at an older 'Cadburyism', a 'hardening of managerial attitudes and tactics'. Others talked in the interviews of feeling 'embattled', 'appalled' at pay demands or 'stupid strikes'. Although the remedies suggested for excess trade union power varied widely, right across the spectrum there was agreement that 'things could not go on as they were'.[4]

After the 1974 elections there was a feeling that overt 'neutrality' and under-publicised lobbying had undermined rather than bolstered business representation. As a result, a greater effort was made by business interests, representational, corporate and individual, to publicise their case. The peak bodies would publish more policy documents, and those in the form of manifestoes or as polemics. The CBI and IOD would make greater efforts to exploit connections with the media, and both the CBI and BIM used national conferences to launch their new platforms. Businessmen used their annual company statements to criticise government policy and decry the denigration of business in British society.[5]

Advantage was taken of any opportunity to promote diagnoses of the 'British disease' and possible solutions through newspaper columns, publications of the new right-wing think tanks such as the Centre for Policy Studies (CPS), and through public platforms like the Ashridge and Stockton lectures. Awards such as the Hambros' Businessman of the Year and AOI's Free Enterprise Award offered new platforms to promote the excellences of business in an unsympathetic environment.[6] The House of Lords also saw an upsurge in interventions of this kind by business peers.

To an unusual degree, business leaders resorted to political concepts or overtly ideological language, often in the name of 'anti-[economic or political] ideology'. Some of their rhetoric grew rotund, moralistic, even apocalyptic. Among reconstructionists, sweeping prescriptive books were written by George Goyder and Wilfred Brown, while Peter Parker and Charles Villiers delivered seminal lectures. Leading independents with national profiles spoke out. Exponents of the main tendencies searched for new and higher ground, often expressing familiar ideas in more radical terms. Liberationists became bolder, less conservative, more populist. Some leading revisionists retreated from ideas of reflex mediation and moved towards advocating major changes in the political system. If consensus and continuity were to be achieved, it seemed to them, radical structural reforms would first be required.

Among independents, Arnold Weinstock emerged from his usual silence to lambast the two main parties and advocate coalition government, based on a long list of agreed priorities, as 'more flexible, pragmatic and directed to the public good'. Lord Robens' brand of independent centrism went much further. He urged a scheme, evoking Churchill and World War II, for a five-year Council of State comprising all parties and none, trade unions and business, which would forego 'politics' and 'doctrinal economic ideologies' to concentrate on a single aim, 'the economic battle'; then, given 'an united effort ... turnaround could be dramatically quick'. James Goldsmith entered the fray with a cocktail mixture of proposals for a reformed House of Lords, laced with populist ideas for national referenda and US-style primaries.[7]

Amongst liberationists, a few advanced spirits were talking of a new 'people's capitalism'. Nicholas Goodison, chairman of the Stock Exchange Council from 1976, was one, while Nigel Vinson pursued more radical themes of wealth redistribution, wholesale transfers of public assets, and a new economy of liberated small entrepreneurs and 'participant' groups. The successful entrepreneur John Hoskyns, who had previously shown mildly 'social democratic' sympathies, developed a vigorous argument for radically reducing trade union power and changing the whole landscape on individualist and free market lines.[8] At the same time, some illustrious revisionists were becoming politically bolder. The cause of electoral reform or PR was favoured by Plowden, Partridge, Cadbury, Maurice Laing, Arthur Knight. For a time, too, a wider spectrum drawn to this banner included Weinstock, Joseph Lockwood, John Sainsbury, Nigel Broackes. Within the CBI itself, a working party under Lord Caldecote was privately advised by well-known political scientists with 'centrist' preferences. Its report, drawing on West European models, advocated both electoral reform and limited public funding of political parties in the interests of 'moderation and stable policies'.[9]

The cultivation of public opinion would operate in harness with a growing sensitivity to opinion at the business grass roots. The three main organisations, the CBI, IOD and BIM, would all undergo major internal reorganisations, directing their energies to policy proposals and to winning a wider degree of public support for business. Such actions would be taken not merely to check the perceived excesses of a Labour government. After 1976 the political threat posed to business by government policies grew negligible, whilst the concessions gained were substantial. Hence the enthusiasm devoted to new policy documents and manifestos ceased to be largely defensive, and became part of largely unacknowledged debate to influence the Conservative leadership. Previous experience suggested that that influence needed to be asserted at an early stage in the policy making process to be successful with a future government.[10]

Labour in power 1974–1976: confronting 'Bennery'

In 1974 the prospect of actively influencing government policy seemed illusory. The CBI in particular was surprised by the extent of the Labour leadership's deference to trade union and left-wing elements. Cabinet ministers still received CBI delegations but showed little evidence of acting on their representations. The agreement of the Social Contract in the aftermath of the first election appeared to confirm pre-election declarations that bilateral negotiation with the TUC would largely supplant tripartist consultation. The apparent dominance of the left threatened withdrawal from the EEC and the implementation of protectionist measures to overcome the economic downturn.

With evidence of corporate profitability in crisis, Denis Healey's budgets in March and July 1974 offered scant comfort. Corporation tax and higher rate income tax were both raised and exchange controls tightened (despite the fact that neither budget was deflationary). Fiscal strategy appeared to be geared exclusively towards the Social Contract.[11] With declining opportunities for new investment, it appeared that the expansionist policies desired by the government to ride out the post-1973 downturn could only be achieved by allowing a major expansion of the public sector and of private consumption. By the autumn of 1974, as the corporate liquidity position reached its nadir, intense efforts were made by the CBI to win concessions on stock appreciation relief, and a cut in corporation tax.[12]

This difficult situation was exacerbated by a lack of focus within the CBI. Campbell Adamson's public comments on the Industrial Relations Act compromised the attack on the new trade union privileges promised by Foot, and relationships with the Department of Employment and Productivity deteriorated. There were growing calls for internal reform within the CBI to improve its campaigning stance and to consult more with the militant grass roots. Important divisions of opinion remained over the extent to which the CBI should publicly commit itself to a more rigorous incomes policy or campaign for relaxations in price control. Tensions also surfaced over macro-economic strategy, with the CBI leadership, backed by their new adviser, the magisterial senior economist Donald MacDougall, supporting non-deflationary measures to sustain output through the world recession but, in contrast to Healey's strategy, to ensure a fiscal bias towards business investment rather than general living standards. However, liberationist voices both within and outside the CBI urged bolder cuts in public expenditure and a stricter control of the money supply.

The CBI leadership was therefore forced to look for an issue which could boost business morale, whilst building connections with potentially sympathetic Cabinet ministers.[13] The activities of Tony Benn at the Department of Industry offered an obvious target for ideological counter-attack. Benn's proposed Industry Bill was the most debated issue in 1974, becoming the point of departure for a business *ralliement*. In retrospect, evidence of Benn's isolation in Cabinet, and the ease with which he was manipulated by Wilson and Healey, puts the CBI's claim to have been the main influence on the 1975 Industry Act's emasculation into perspective. However, it is important to understand how shocked revisionist-inclined businessmen had been by Benn's plans for a National Enterprise Board (NEB) and for planning agreements with leading companies. For revisionists, successful supply-side measures required voluntary action by firms and trade associations. Benn challenged these beliefs with his view that UK business was sufficiently inefficient to require a degree of central direction, though less through nationalisation than equity stakeholdings in 'strategic' firms via the NEB and the policing activities of planning agreements.

'Bennery' thus constituted the greatest challenge and opportunity to business until the Bullock report in January 1977, though unlike Bullock, Benn's policies appeared to stand a real chance of legislative enactment. Initial attempts by the CBI to establish a negotiating position with him got nowhere.[14] But the CBI conducted a largely successful campaign against Benn by involving a wide swathe of big companies: its consultations with members also revealed a desire for a more aggressive free enterprise campaign which the CBI felt unwilling to engage in with a general election pending.[15] When Benn's white paper, *The Regeneration of British Industry*, was published in August 1974, it had been already toned down by Cabinet committees, with compulsory planning agreements disappearing.[16] The campaign against 'Bennery' in 1974–75 marked a tactical rather than an ideological watershed for most business leaders. Meantime, militant voices would have to rest content with largely illusory threats of withdrawing compliance from government policies.[17] On the other hand, the experience of Benn had undermined some of the more complacent revisionist beliefs about industrial policy. Thus the Industrial Strategy between 1976–79 enjoyed none of the high hopes invested in similar projects in the 1960s.

Increasingly, there was a business consensus that the dominant theme in the near future would be the 'balance of power' between state, unions and business. Practically all business leaders believed that a fundamental disequilibrium had opened up. For reconstructionists this reinforced long-standing ideas for a new social settlement, including greater integration of both unions and business. For liberationists it demanded major legislative curbs on the trade unions; an overhaul of the taxation system; a new macro-economic framework geared much more to price stability; recognition of the claims of the entrepreneurial/proprietorial business leader who, for them, led the way in wealth creation. Revisionists would share this concern to shift resources and attention to wealth-creation as part of a restored balance of power. They, too, would require a dominant role for business in economic strategy and, in contrast to the revisionism of the 1960s they would be less accommodating to the trade unions. Yet they believed that tripartite collaboration and rational persuasion would be sufficient to reform the pay determination system, and that forums such as the NEDC could be effective in difficult economic conditions. Revisionism was chastened but its conviction that the 'balance of power' ultimately demanded mutual accommodation remained.

Although differences of opinion were developing in the CBI which would harden into something like factionalism for the rest of the period, the leadership was probably correct in judging that most members wanted them to work for tax concessions, and for a more formal means of wage restraint. The CBI made its first breakthrough in the November

1974 Budget with the provision of tax relief for the value of company stocks and relaxations on price control. Although the Employment Protection Bill went ahead in 1975, together with the nationalisation of the airframe and shipbuilding industries, there were successes with the EEC referendum and the removal of Benn. The most promising development in 1975 was, however, the agreement with the TUC for wage restraint, based on a £6 flat rate increase, to combat inflation rates running at over 25 per cent. A modest rapprochement with government was confirmed by the Chequers meeting in November which set up the Industrial Strategy on more consensual and conventional lines, with private management playing the key role. In early 1976 the CBI president, Ralph Bateman, could present to Council a long list of concessions obtained, to silence the grumblings of the minority who believed an opportunity for stand-off had been wasted. Bateman contended that the CBI 'had brought about a complete U-turn in the Government's economic strategy', at a time when the Conservatives were 'demoralised'.[18] The traumas of 'Bennery' appeared to be over.

A new regime at the CBI: Watkinson's recovery act

The events of 1974 had not precipitated a major change in the CBI leadership which still had distinctly revisionist sympathies: Clapham, Adamson, O'Brien, Cadbury, Partridge, MacDougall, Swinden. They were temperamentally unwilling to launch the 'free enterprise' campaign demanded by liberationist voices in 1974. Grassroots discontent was not calmed, and criticisms of the manner in which the leadership represented the member firms grew. The Smaller Firms Council (SFC) was particularly outspoken over what it saw as inadequate CBI responses to the new government.[19] At the heart of their criticisms, shared by many regional councils, was a rejection of what was seen as complacent elitism at Tothill Street. The failure to take a more political stance during the election campaigns was deprecated, and traced to an ideological unwillingness by the leadership to assert 'free enterprise' values. There were demands for a president's committee to be established to ensure that such a voice was heard publicly.[20]

Richard O'Brien, chairman of the Employment Policy Committee, also experienced 1974 as a year of frustration. He saw evidence of a reaction against formalised incomes policies within Council and the economic committees. The EPC, underpinned by the Social Affairs Director, Alan Swinden, felt its views were being by-passed to accommodate free market critics. It remained a persuasive advocate of the 'national' responsibilities of the organisation, insisting 'the impulse had to come from the centre, from the CBI and the major companies who were in a position to resist inflationary wage claims and were prepared to do so'.[21] Powerful voices could still be mobilised in Council to back a new incomes agreement. Other leading figures, such as Adrian Cadbury, remained committed to wage-push explanations of the current inflation, partly because an insistence on monetary measures alone in 1974–75 might have had dire consequences for the beleaguered corporate sector.[22]

By the summer of 1975 opinion in the CBI appeared to be moving towards a more formal incomes policy (including the retention of price controls). In May 1975 Partridge's proposal of an inflation target and pay limit over a twelve month period was endorsed by Council. With inflation reaching 25 per cent in May, the CBI moderates believed a turning point was in sight, with a restored tripartism as a likely consequence. Talks between the CBI and the TUC took place on a possible framework for a counter-inflation policy. Although the CBI decided to accept the unwelcome pay sanctions, the leadership believed that its opinions on this issue were now being treated more sympathetically by the government.[23]

In 1976 the CBI reached a turning-point. Adamson retired as director general, and O'Brien left the EPC for the Manpower Services Commission. The departure of Adamson was symbolic: despite his huge contribution and high public reputation, the struggles of 1971–74 had weakened his position internally. After enjoying considerable discretionary powers under sympathetic or hands-off presidents, he did not welcome the arrival of an interventionist president, Lord Watkinson, with whom his relations were cool. Watkinson's succession in summer 1976 was to have critical importance for the CBI in this period, together with the recruitment of John Methven as director general.

These appointments came against the backdrop of the 1976 IMF crisis which forced the government towards much more deflationary policies, distancing itself from the TUC in the process. Favourable policy changes for business were accompanied by an increasingly introspective and reactive cabinet. Thus the business counter-attack against the Bullock Report in 1977 was to meet with surprisingly little resistance from Government. This defensiveness boosted business morale, and it was after 1976 that 'cooperative competition' between the CBI, BIM and IOD acquired momentum as the two latter groups emerged onto the public arena. Events thus conspired to give business leaders a real sense of optimism about changing the balance of power.

It was a challenge that Watkinson and Methven took up with enthusiasm. Although neither had clear liberationist sympathies, both understood the sense of grievance from many businessmen that the CBI had failed to convey its strategy of the balance of power to a wider audience.

Methven, recruited from the Office of Fair Trading, had had a back-ground in the legal department of ICI.[24] An able networker, he had a sharper style than Adamson. He, too, was a committed centrist, carefully non-party political. But an ethically earnest 'social' flavour and design were less evident. Some would detect in him a greater degree of flexibility towards free market ideas, though ideologically Methven was hard to pin down, seeming to sympathise with people of rather differing views. In his no-nonsense style and pursuit of internal organisational changes, such as the CBI's move to Centre Point, he resembled John Davies. His methods were not always welcome to the CBI staff, but won considerable plaudits from the grass-roots.[25]

Lord Watkinson believed that more open politicisation would help to influence the thinking of the Conservatives. Watkinson was a Conservative meritocrat who had risen to cabinet rank in the 1950s. Since leaving the cabinet in 1962, he had become a top, publicly articulate industrialist at Cadbury-Schweppes. A spare, forceful, magisterial figure with unrivalled experience and an imperious streak, he inspired not so much affection as wide respect. Watkinson was firmly committed to concepts of socially responsible private enterprise, industrial policy, a tripartism weighted more towards business. More than any other revisionist so far, he allied this vision with a clear political standpoint. Loyal to memories of Churchill and Monckton, he believed that 'one nation' Toryism was as likely to have a constructive impact through business politics as through party politics.[26] His contribution at the CBI would be to harmonise a relatively militant rhetoric with a continued representational role and a blend of policies appealing to liberationist business opinion but without conducting a U-turn in policy.[27]

Although loyal to the traditions of CBI revisionism, Watkinson was to give the organisation a new style through his operations both at the heart of government and with the grass roots, often attended by the maximum of publicity. He wanted a CBI which was 'militant and activist', 'more initiatory and less reactive'. The CBI would 'go public' on all major policy issues, with the President 'a powerful instrument of policy'.[28] A number of reforms were initiated: membership was further extended into the financial and retailing sectors. A President's Advisory Committee, set up in 1976, marked an important step away from the dominant role of the director general practised by Adamson, even though the PAC was dominated by long-established revisionists. To convey these policies to a wider audience, Watkinson established the national conference in 1977 (which launched the first *Britain means Business* document), while Methven greatly improved relations with the media.[29]

These reforms demonstrated Watkinson's belief that revisionism had to be presented in a more forceful way without truckling to the grassroots. He believed that business should develop its own constructive agenda on industrial and employment policy so that the CBI could help to determine future government policies. His 'one nation' ethos was apparent in his view of the Industrial Strategy, which he believed a future Conservative government would have to work with. At a period when talk of coalitionism was common, he exploited the rhetoric of national unity to bring the CBI back into the public eye, and to engage relatively smoothly with the government. Although considered by some to be authoritarian or over-impulsive, his political ability and deeply held beliefs would leave a strong mark, though he was to overestimate the potential for his ideas and even for his own staying power: he had to retire early from the presidency in December 1977.

The Labour government had promised that industrial democracy legislation would form part of the original Social Contract, but had done little on the issue until discontent in the Parliamentary Labour Party led it to establish the Commission on Industrial Democracy in the summer of 1975. It appears that the government hoped to relegate the issue to the distant future. The Commission was given unusually slanted terms of reference: to find the most effective means of introducing employee directors onto the boards of large companies. Chaired by Lord Bullock, it began taking evidence in early 1976, and reported in January 1977. The CBI responded with vigour to this overt challenge. It was an issue where Watkinson could rightly claim expertise, and he took a leading role in reconvening the Company Affairs Committee and Employment Participation working party to draw up an alternative policy. He welcomed the Commission to the extent that it 'frightened the CBI membership into a realistic consideration of the problem' of participation.[30] Throughout 1976, when it became increasingly clear that the Bullock majority would advocate the imposition of worker directors on a unitary board, the CBI leadership promoted 'participation agreements', reflecting the genuine enthusiasm of some, the tactical necessity of others.[31] Unlike the previous debacle in 1972–73 (see chapter 6), the small firms were protected from these provisions and barely participated in the debate.

Once the Bullock majority report was out, the CBI launched a highly public counter-attack.[32] Watkinson involved non-CBI members in his campaign, and used the proposals to damage the credibility of the government both in public and private.[33] With the government's embarrassment evident, the stylised intransigence of Watkinson and Methven probably had a significant effect in burying many long-held doubts about the CBI's ability to defeat head-on, rather than merely qualify, unwelcome proposals. The white paper on Industrial Democracy published in summer

1978 as the government's belated response, saw little weakening in business resistance.[34] However, even this stance proved inadequate for CBI members, with the 1978 Conference rejecting the idea of legislative fallback for participation agreements, and the issue was shelved as the election approached. A considerable propaganda victory had been won, but one which demonstrated wide, previously latent hostility to the genuine desire of the architects of the participation policy to increase employee involvement, by legislation if necessary.[35]

An adapted centre ground and its critics; the CBI policy programme

The CBI's continuing revisionist sympathies were demonstrated by the energy expended on the issue of the reform of pay determination (RPD) between 1977 and the 1979 election. The prevailing scepticism about returning to free collective bargaining has already been mentioned, and the CBI believed that some form of incomes control would still be vital for counter-inflation policy. Most revisionists were, however, keen by this stage to get away from price and dividend controls, as no longer appropriate to the worsening position of corporate profitability. They believed that the inflationary shocks of 1974–75 had led to both employers and employees understanding the need for a flexible but coordinated institutional framework for wage bargaining, but lacking the long-term instruments with which to achieve this.[36]

The CBI had introduced its ideas in *The Road to Recovery*, and substantiated them in *The Future of Pay Determination* in 1977. They involved parliamentary and tripartist surveillance of wage bargaining, based on 'objective' economic appraisals of annual wage settlements. Although the instructions then given to bargainers would be voluntary, a greater degree of informal pressure would operate, accompanied by larger bargaining units and pay settlements synchronised in a shorter pay round. The process would be strengthened by stricter parliamentary control of public expenditure. However, the success of the RPD proposals would correspondingly downgrade any calls for trade union reform, and advocates urged the CBI away from the latter approach.[37]

Although initially well received by most of the CBI committees, the proposals ran into opposition both from members who wanted short-term relief for pay flexibility and from those who opposed such 'corporatist' ideas in principle.[38] The SFC in particular offered trenchant opposition, clashing with the EPC. Some SFC members criticised the RPD proposals as a throwback to an earlier 'corporatism': 'the CBI was promoting the virtues of the market economy and it was therefore essential it did not adopt a line on pay that was at odds with it'. Such was the SFC's hostility that it published its own paper on pay in 1978, explicitly reject- ing the official line on pay reform, maintaining that 'pay bargaining in Britain has gone wrong primarily because . . . the effectiveness of market reforms has been undermined or deliberately stymied'. For SFC liber- ationists such initiatives made them feel their views were at last being taken seriously.[39]

This criticism was increasingly shared by other CBI members. At the 1978 national conference the majority for the RPD proposals was small, reflecting short-term frustrations at incomes policy.[40] During 1979 the leadership reduced its aspirations to the much more modest ones of pay conferences on wage inflation and the EPC was forced to admit that the proposals had expected too much of 'educative potential and human goodwill'.[41] With the pay bargaining ideas running into trouble and employee participation downgraded by 1978–79, the debate on the balance of power increasingly focussed on trade union reform, which the EPC had previously ruled out as inimical to RPD. The issue had not been prominent in the Road to Recovery, and the EPC took no initiatives until the manifest public hostility to the unions after the collapse of Phase 4. Eventually, a Balance of Power Steering Group was established in January 1979, chaired by Alex Jarratt, to consider the CBI's attitude to picketing, secondary action, secret ballots and the closed shop. Its recom- mendations, though moderate compared with forthcoming develop- ments in the 1980s, were felt to be closer to Conservative Party opinion.[42]

On macro-economic policy the CBI leadership promoted eclectic policies to maximise unity. The basic Keynesian policies advocated in 1972–74 gave way relatively painlessly to a more modest strategy for cut- ting public deficits and inflation to assist an export-led recovery. The debate on 'monetarism' was heard especially in the Financial Policy Committee, and radical tax-cutting solutions were presented by the Tax Panel.[43] Inevitably, though, demands for long-term financial stringency were counterweighed by those closest to the industrial front line, in the Economic Situation Committee, as well as by the CBI's economic advisers (MacDougall, Dermot Glynn, Brian Reddaway). As chairman of the umbrella Economic Policy Committee 1974–79, the eirenic Adrian Cadbury, sought to balance these conflicting ideas.[44] Meantime, argu- ments like the Bacon and Eltis thesis, first published in 1976, were help- ing to shift the economic blame from business's shortcomings. By tracing post-war economic decline to the squeeze on profits of the 'marketed' sector due to the expansion of the public, 'non-marketed' sector, their arguments accorded with the gut feelings of most businessmen. The solu- tions advocated, including major cuts in public expenditure and employment, and a shift to industrial investment from public and possibly private consumption – were also in line with mainstream business understandings of the 1974–75 crisis.[45]

The *Road to Recovery*, published in autumn 1976, was an attempt to appeal to all sides on economic policy. It assumed that higher rates of growth were feasible, with more resources shifted into industrial investment. Public spending, reined in by a greater use of the cash limits system, would be held to current levels, hence falling quite dramatically as a share of national income by the early 1980s. Taxation levels would correspondingly fall: public borrowing would be cut and stabilised. Investment incentives and a continued Industrial Strategy would assist sufficient gains in industrial performance to cope with exchange rate appreciation once North Sea oil gradually influenced the economy. 'Monetarism' as such received little mention, beyond the now familiar support for more reliance on monetary policy in economic management. The document was clearly intended to influence Opposition thinking, and it enjoyed public backing from the BIM and the IOD.[46]

Between 1976 and 1979 the CBI was able to achieve a high degree of public purpose. The boost to organisational morale by a skilled leadership did not, however, develop an ideological consensus. Pay bargaining reform had been seriously compromised by liberationist critics; work on trade union reform had been delayed; employment participation had been embraced, then demoted. The CBI had re-established its credentials as a 'national' organisation, though at the expense of coming to terms with the possibility of a more confrontational approach from its external or internal critics. Liberationist critics, always vocal in Council, the economic committees and SFC, were able to have their views taken more seriously. On the other hand, most of the leading figures were still revisionists, still maintaining a gut belief in growth and economic pluralism, constructive engagement with government, whether Conservative or Labour, and a redrawn national consensus, not a decisive break with the past.

Towards a liberationist alternative: the IOD 1974–1979

Under the Spears-Powell regime the IOD had long retained its traditionalist character, with shortfalls in both research and propaganda (see chapter 4). Moreover, as the rule of Powell drew to a close in 1974, the depth of the Institute's financial problems became clear: declining membership rolls were not reversed until 1977.[47] The time for a major overhaul had come.

Rejuvenation was largely the work of three men, Lord Erroll of Hale, chairman of Council until 1976, his successor Denys Randolph of Wilkinson Sword, and a new director general, Jan Hildreth, appointed in 1974. The key initiator was Erroll, like Watkinson a former Conservative cabinet minister turned industrialist but with more free market and right-wing views.[48] A tall, dapper, bonhomous figure, a shrewd talent spotter with considerable political *nous*, Erroll was efficient in the chair, though not so much a public articulator of ideas. His long association with the IOD reflected abiding allegiances to private enterprise and Conservatism: it also gave scope to a zest for quiet influence. He had long been impatient with the old guard of 'septos and octos' under Powell and Spears,[49] and the palace *coup* he helped to engineer in 1974 resulted in a major change in direction for the IOD.

The new director general, Jan Hildreth, enthusiastically set about rebuilding the Institute. Hildreth was engaging and mercurial in style, with a genuine interest in ideas. He represented very much a new broom who aimed to change the rather stuffy image of the IOD, with sometimes abrasive effects. By background (EDCs, London Transport, John Laing), Hildreth might have been expected to have revisionist sympathies, and it appears that he originally wanted to work closely with the CBI and BIM as part of a coordinated strategy.[50] However, he was to sound increasingly liberationist in his monthly column in *The Director*. Though controversial as an administrator, he was to be successful in shifting energies into more public channels.

Between 1974 and 1979 the leadership revived the IOD, restoring its financial position, setting up new branches (especially in the south-east), taking a public stand on issues like Bullock, and adopting a more ideological line in its publications. This contrasted to the situation in 1974 where both money and ability appeared to be lacking to intervene in the November general election.[51] Although still under-resourced on research, Hildreth promoted a distinctive voice through his columns and a greater use of the media.[52] A move from Belgrave Square to Pall Mall produced a more businesslike image. Denys Randolph, chairman from 1976, devoted himself to building up grass roots morale. Strong links were maintained with the Conservative backbenches, a leading role being played by Cecil Parkinson MP, the leader of the IOD's parliamentary panel since 1972. *The Director* continued to attract a diverse readership under the polymath George Bull, and greater use was made of intellectual talents such as those of Alan Davies, the leading tax expert, and Barry Bracewell Milnes, the ardent free marketeer. Although the IOD was seldom able to engage in the type of policy sophistication of the CBI, it could claim to set out distinctive positions on such issues as taxation, 'customer democracy', trade union reform and deregulation.[53]

Hildreth paid particular attention to the views of the 'entrepreneur-proprietor' strand of business opinion, and the wider vision of 'popular capitalism', as also expounded by Nigel Vinson at the CPS.[54] Incomes policy and industrial strategies were denigrated, a radical rethink of the nationalised industries and state provision was promised. Deregulation and deep cuts in taxation (especially for investment income) were strongly pressed in a spirit of entrepreneurial revivalism. Erroll had recently complained, following a familiar rubric, that the director was 'the victim of a social trend to despise the very concept of leadership'.[55] Hildreth suggested the basis of the ideological counter-attack. Long-term economic success would only return when the micro-environment for growth took priority over collective would-be manipulation:

Only when individual entrepreneurs find it in them to respond to the challenges of creating new markets to serve with new products will the economy demonstrate vigour and growth again. For too long we have been seduced by siren voices singing salvation from the efficiency of mature and over-mature elements in our economy. We have forgotten that the innovation and risk of the new remain the other leg upon which the prosperity of the new must be built.

With the creation and development of small firms, the new economic environment would not require any central guidance on promoting growth: 'governments have little power over growth, over our success in finding ways of supplying each other with more goods and services. In this, we depend on the enterprise and energy and energy of individual citizens minding their own business day-by-day. We have to be self-standing.'[56]

This 'heroic' view of the business leader emphasised that a decisive break, as much cultural as legislative, would have to be made to restore the 'balance of power'. Whilst the IOD's proposed measures in the 1970s were milder than those of the early 1980s, especially on taxation, their self-confident tone was significant, particularly when related to underlying economic prospects: the IOD Council did not discuss macroeconomic policy in great detail before 1979. As the IOD's evidence to Bullock contended in its defence of a micro-view of 'customer democracy', what mattered was that the firm should not be deflected from its essential economic purpose.[57]

The culmination of this approach came after Hildreth's resignation, when the IOD published its *Business Leaders' Manifesto* for the general election. This was still cautious on some fronts. No specific proposals were made for denationalisation or privatisation, though this was set as a goal, and nothing said about marketisation of the public services or welfare. More radical changes, however, were proposed than in the corresponding manifestos of the BIM and CBI. The IOD proposed an immediate abolition of all price control, deep cuts in taxation, with income tax assessed on a 50:25 per cent ratio of top to basic rate, a reduction of the role of the NEB to a 'casualty station', cuts in capital taxes, market disciplines into the public sector, especially the local authorities, a balanced budget, and an end to most subsidies. The spirit of the entrepreneur in the small business permeated the whole document.[58] Whilst such ideas could never have been fulfilled between 1974 and 1979, they did leave the Institute well placed if a new Conservative government were to adopt a more radical posture than that assumed by the CBI.

The BIM: managers' union or new revisionism?

In this period the British Institute of Management followed much the same path in developing a campaigning identity as did the IOD, though with different ideological aims. Organisational reforms in 1974–76 carried out under the BIM chairman Fred Catherwood, and its new director general, Roy Close, allowed it to undertake a direct representational role on behalf of managers.[59] This would involve a sometimes uneasy balance between revisionist-type proposals on incomes policy, employment participation and a national economic forum, and a forthright demand for boosting the incentives for all levels of management. Catherwood embarked on a new incarnation at the BIM as an industrial-managerial leader, urging both a reformist, centrist position and an end to the socio-economic plight of middle management. In this task he was aided by the diplomatic and energetic Close, and by Derek Ezra, the chairman from 1976–78, a dedicated tripartist with wide Whitehall contacts.[60] The BIM could also call on talents as diverse as Peter Parker, Michael Edwardes, the small firm financier Larry Tindale, and Lord Croham.

The aspirations of the BIM leadership until 1979 were to become a source of new policy making, to act as a complement to the CBI on major issues, and to boost managerial morale by demonstrating an aggressive line on managerial incentives, which could not always be a priority of the CBI.[61] Although the BIM leadership were concerned that inaction would lead to their representational role being usurped by white-collar unions,[62] they were keen to avoid the appearance of a 'managers' trade union'.[63] They hoped to act as a 'third force', which for many in the leadership meant occupying the middle ground. As Close put it, 'the whole BIM approach is one that the true interest of both sides cannot be in conflict and the BIM has constantly been attempting to get rid of a 'both sides' concept". The wisdom of this approach appeared to be confirmed by surveys carried out of managerial opinion on key political and economic issues during the period.[64]

The BIM leadership, which was not exposed to the sort of grass-roots pressures of the CBI, saw the necessity of publicising business opinions, which offered an alternative to the liberationism of the IOD. This was a product not merely of functional representation or that nationalised industry bosses were important in the BIM, but reflected the established revisionist (occasionally reconstructionist) pedigrees of the leaders. This could be seen in the generally moderate tone of the *Managers' Manifesto* in 1978 (penned by Ezra), in the proposals for employment participation, and in the strong support given to incomes policy. Inevitably, however, divisions opened up between 1976–79 over such issues as tax cuts, macro-economic policy and reform of pay determination.[65]

Initially the BIM had responded to the crisis of 1974–75 with a sectional defence of the interests of the professional classes, hit by inflation and tax rises. In the succeeding years there were predictable disputes over the degree to which the income tax system should be reformed and whether budget submissions should ask for tax cuts as a means of income restraint.[66] Some, like Catherwood, Austin Bide and Leslie Tolley, believed that the issue of managerial tax rates was sufficiently vital, to allow the BIM to take a more decisive line than the CBI. Others, however, were as keen as CBI revisionists to maintain self-restraint on pay as part of a wider strategy to rebuild tripartist bridges, though with a greater managerial involvement.

The BIM's search for influence endorsed continuing efforts at tripartist reform.[67] Although attempts to be represented on the NEDC failed, the BIM's commendation of the Industrial Strategy saw it engage in consultations with NEDO.[68] It developed policies of reform of pay determination which were close to the CBI's.[69] The BIM was able to formulate a distinctive and potentially influential line with its proposal for a national economic and social forum, which would discuss wider issues than the RPD forum wanted by the CBI (though falling short of reconstructionist ideas such as those of Parker: see chapter 6). With a membership of up to 200 people, who would be consulted by government on the propriety of relevant economic and industrial legislation, the forum promised to end consultation 'behind closed doors, and limited to the CBI and TUC, and about which very little was known'.[70]

Although the forum idea was to be something of a BIM mainstay in the early 1980s, there was a sense in which it missed the mood of the moment. Leslie Tolley caught this when he attacked the pursuit of 'over-consultation': 'any new Government will want to show it was there to govern, not to set up new avenues of consultation'.[71] As the BIM still lacked access to the main tripartite forums, to continue to advocate such a policy was risky when opinion within UK management was shifting to a more confrontational stance by the winter of 1979.[72]

By the time of the 1979 election the BIM had been reasonably successful in achieving a representational voice. Meetings with the chancellor over budget proposals had become standard, an independent voice had been conveyed during the Bullock debate, connections with the media improved and the quality of its research enhanced (especially through the ESAC, formed in 1976 by Catherwood). The BIM could have influenced future policy thinking, partly as an ally of the CBI, partly through developing some of its own ideas. On the other hand, the revisionist emphasis was never as forthright as the liberationist one in the IOD, due in part to greater exposure to different opinions but also, importantly, because it would be difficult to construct an ideological defence of the highly ramified managerial class as compelling as that devised by the IOD for the company director. Internal divisions between public and private sector managers, combined with ideological differences on such issues as taxation and incomes policy, also tended to mute its campaigning role.

Conclusion

By late 1978–79 'cooperative competition' was becoming more competitive than co-operative. Policy differences over trade union reform and incomes policy sharpened as the election approached and the urge to influence the Conservative Party increased. In the CBI this sense of urgency led to serious internal conflicts, and to the dropping of more contentious policy platforms on pay determination and employment participation. There was some sense of a dormant and under-articulated liberationism about to awaken, demonstrated by the increasing ideological significance of the small firms. Even more important than changes in attitudes among the previously active was an expansion in overall articulacy, both public and organisational, from previously less vocal quarters, most of them broadly liberationist in sympathy.

But although the ground had shifted, the major divergences remained. The basic enthusiasms of reconstructionists persisted, while the traditional sources of revisionism remained strong. Even in late 1978 and early 1979 it was not unreasonable for revisionists to believe that a new Conservative government would be susceptible to their influence. In the end, however, it was the failure of revisionists to understand the sheer depth of disillusion of liberationist opinion, and that of its party political allies, which placed them in a weak position in 1979. Despite the tactical or rhetorical efforts to adapt to free market critics, they could never really take seriously the liberationist desires for 'disengagement' and free market breakthrough. Moreover, the possibility that tripartism would wither into insignificance, and industrial and incomes policies be officially dismissed, would have constituted a rejection of most of what they had worked for since 1960.

8   Business and early Thatcherism

The Conservative victory in the 1979 election had come at a moment of apparent widespread consensus within the business community. There was a common feeling of exhaustion and disillusion with previous governments, with better treatment expected from the new one. The 'balance of power' was expected to shift at last in favour of business. Immediate and welcome changes were forthcoming on personal taxation and price control, and the government was soon showing a resolute determination to reduce trade union power. There was, therefore, something of a honeymoon period in late 1979, warmer and more hopeful than in 1970. Business leaders had been almostly universally supportive of the Conservatives in the election, and many expected the beginning of a new era of co-operation to replace the failures of the past decade.

Yet the fund of goodwill was not indefinite. Doubts existed from the start about the government's economic policy, and many business leaders felt a vague unease about its overtly 'ideological' stance on a range of issues. Many appreciated this determination but felt it was ignorant of industrial realities, where the situation seemed more than ever volatile. Within twelve months these doubts would lead to open criticism as the economy entered the deepest of post-war recessions. Business seemed to suffer most initially but found the government apparently unyielding in its policies. Business critics of the government would find themselves criticised by newly assertive liberationists, convinced of the rightness of the government's policies for business and the economy. The parting of the ways when it came was to be dramatic, seeing some of the most controversial and heated debates within business since the early 1960s' revisionist rethink.

Revisionism at bay

Revisionism still appeared to be a powerful force within business. The rethink of the late 1970s had left it apparently revitalised and more in tune with other business points of view. Although revisionists were now

142

more aware of sharing political space with liberationists, they were still convinced that they predominated in that space. The CBI and BIM remained under the control of 'moderates', despite an official hardening of positions on several issues in an effort to make revisionism appear more realistic and less temporising. Even though the Conservative leadership seemed determined to occupy a position further to the right, the experience of repeated political cycles since the 1950s reinforced a hope that U-turns would follow.

Revisionists were now warier of the mutualist rhetoric of the 1960s and early 1970s; they were concerned not to appear to appease the trade unions for the sake of tripartite consensus; and they were much more sceptical about 'virtuous circle' concepts of economic expansion. Evidence about corporate profitability, investment, and managerial reward suggested that business had sacrificed too much in the previous two decades. Hence the corrective measures that the Thatcher government offered were warmly welcomed. On the other hand, revisionists were equally convinced that reversing economic decline would be painful for industry in any circumstances: hence the need for a government sympathetic to continuous formal consultation and dialogue with business to see through the difficult changes. With all interests needing to be flexible and cooperative, a tripartism inspired by revisionism would still surely be essential?

Revisionists expected the more militant free market rhetoric of Margaret Thatcher and Keith Joseph to diminish once the realities of office were faced. Yet they had no desire to experience another complete U-turn, sending economic policy into confusion. So although there was keen desire to criticise the government's more dogmatic positions, they hoped to do this carefully through usually private channels. Alternative proposals should seem reasonable and tailored to the government's own ideological predilections; escape routes should be offered rather than ultimata laid down. But the grim facts of recession, already apparent by the summer of 1980, followed by a mixture of economic shell shock and political confusion over the ensuing two years, would elicit a deeply ambivalent response, part plain dismayed, part eager to snatch at any sign of recovery. Soon, too, the revisionists would be faced by the sombre reality of 'disengagement'.

In such circumstances the 'loyalty' of business, expressed through the traditional channels of the CBI, could no longer be guaranteed. Some in the CBI and BIM believed that there should not be a special relationship with the Government because the short-term costs were likely to be so high. Campbell Fraser had told the 1979 CBI conference that the new government was 'not our government' and to see it so 'would be to add further to the polarisation that had torn the country apart'.[1] Criticism of Conservative governments was always more difficult because of the presumption of common interests; and the Thatcher government, by trying to do much for business, yet in large part, it seemed, misdirectedly, caused private turmoil about the degree of criticism to offer. Considerable attention was given to discerning the relative degrees of doubt of each government minister and how this could be exploited. In private, anguished affirmations of support to the government co-existed with grievance at the latter's failure to respond. Polarisation undermined revisionism because it forced an unwelcome choice on ultimate loyalties to be made: either support the government in public, criticising it privately, or declare opposition publicly and lose the chance of immediate concessions.

The government's design of 'disengagement' of the state from industry (and vice versa) wounded revisionism at a sensitive point. It discounted the constant exchange of information and opinion between business and state as a key to economic success. A return to separate spheres of competence, with government setting a rigorous (highly non-discretionary) macro-economic framework to which business was supposed to adapt, freed from 'interventionist' constraints and relying on its animal spirits, was not compatible with the revisionist view of the complexity and interdependence of economic knowledge. Whilst they felt sympathy for the critics of state failure, revisionists still urged intervention, albeit of a more limited and expert sort. Governments could redesign industrial strategy, paying more attention to 'sunrise' industries and offering 'near-market' assistance for industry as a whole. Unlike most liberationists, they believed that the current brand of counter-inflationary policy would impose excessive costs, and that an oil-inflated exchange rate would be more an indiscriminate destroyer of manufacturing than a salutary disciplinarian for the under-performing. Further, the still powerful position of the unions in 1979 suggested no rushed counter-offensive, but rather measured laws and extended persuasion. Government should accept that wider education for economic change would require dialogue and some joint action with the trade unions to avoid an eventual political backlash.

For revisionists, to transfer resources to industry was not to offer privileges to the business elite but to lay down national seedcorn for the future. They felt unembarrassed in asking for 'business budgets' and infrastructure spending which would lower unit costs. Revisionist macroeconomic thinking retained its eclecticism. In particular, the unexpected depth of the recession brought many business leaders back to first-order Keynesianism as the safest way out of the morass. Criticisms had been made of the likely effects of high interest rates even during the 'honeymoon period', but as recession bit hard in the first part of 1980 these became more prevalent. Indeed, the CBI revisionists found some surprising allies in many of the regional councils, together with sections of the SFC and the EEF.

The effect of monetarism as actually practised gave rise to a number of different responses. Some business leaders accepted the government's assertion that tough monetary policy was needed but felt that the disinflation should be gradual, as originally intended, and supplemented by countervailing fiscal advantages to business. There was a strong feeling right across the board that the time-scales necessary for adjustment had been understated, and current 'rational expectations' theories, influencing the government's conception of disinflation, caused particular unease by their seeming naïveté, for example in relation to UK pay psychology. Worries about the mechanistic conception of monetarism, on the grounds it was 'academic' and ignored the practical experience of business, extended to strong government sympathisers like Brookes, Hector Laing and Nigel Vinson.[2]

Within the revisionist camp there were still many mainstream Keynesians, believing that expansion out of recession was still feasible. With much support amongst professional economists and opposition parties, this group enjoyed more influence than might have been expected from the late 1970s. Such veterans as Lords Robens and Plowden strongly urged the case for old-style demand management in the PAC, with powerful intellectual support from Donald MacDougall. But many more business leaders with basically revisionist sympathies were simply perplexed. They felt bereft of moorings, veering in the space of a few months between support for big boosts to public investment and demands for minor changes to interest rates, so uncertain were they about the economic situation (*a fortiori* once the recession had become international). 'Reconstructed Keynesians' like Terry Beckett, Adrian Cadbury, Ronald Utiger, and many in the Economic Policy and Situation Committees, felt that old-fashioned Keynesianism could not be restored, also viewing its props of incomes policy and planned expansion as too hazardous. They tended to prefer a more overt commitment to low inflation, an effort to change government policy at the margins, and a stress on managerially-led micro-transformations.

A reformist agenda did still exist. Both the CBI and BIM believed that reform of pay determination institutions was essential, and they still saw value in a tripartist-inspired industrial policy. The CBI saw itself as part-begetter of such a package: the government was still expected to consult it, rather than other business bodies, over major economic decisions. It retained its NEDC monopoly throughout this period; its budget submissions and industrial surveys were taken seriously by the Treasury and the press; and it still assumed priority in access to civil servants and ministers. Yet Thatcherite ministers would not expand 'consultation' beyond these limits and in so doing undermined key revisionist tenets. The desultory treatment of NEDC, and what appears to have been limited discussion of CBI economic proposals, reinforced this prospect. The government's assumption of tough conflict in the process of economic change would challenge and eventually overcome two decades of revisionist encampment in Whitehall.

Revisionist perplexity was accentuated by growing internal differences. Liberationist sympathisers in both the CBI and BIM had acquired influence in the 1970s. Following the rhetoric of these organisations' leaderships before and immediately after the 1979 election, they might have expected loyalty to the government. Annoyed when this proved not to be the case during the recession, they were critical of 'backsliding'. Opinion in the CBI Council was now more factional, more willing to publicise differences: there were resignations whenever anti-government gestures appeared to be made. The reactions to Terry Beckett's 1980 Conference speech typify the political tightrope the leadership was forced to walk. The number of critical and sympathetic letters received by Beckett was approximately equal. Supporters spoke of a sense of relief that the government had at last been challenged; the 'bare knuckles' speech was 'splendid and courageous', and praised its 'sound and thunder'. But the speech cost the CBI several leading members. Critics were 'extremely surprised and upset', condemning a pugnacious and disloyal tone.[3] Further ructions ensued over the leadership's reactions to the 1981 Budget and its routine but awkwardly publicised meeting with Labour shadow ministers in 1982.

These considerations inhibited revisionists from taking a bolder path. Their apparent temporising, however, also reflected genuine intellectual or political uncertainty in the face of both an ideologically assertive government and persistent recession. Although dismayed by the costs of recession, many still wanted to see the government succeed in its basic aims. Public criticism was a painful necessity, best undertaken with 'commonsense' alternatives, tailored to seem 'responsible' and offering no hostages to other political parties or the unions. There would be a much less tolerant attitude to economic risk-taking, which some had seen in the CBI's reactions to the Heath government's earlier reflation. These attitudes were exemplified by the major CBI policy document of 1981, *The Will to Win*. The product of considerable research effort, this was drawn in careful technocratic language, presented in the format of a 'business plan' for the UK. Its arguments about the role of manufacturing in the economy and its support for education and training and industrial policies anticipated many of the arguments of the later 1980s. Yet every effort was made to avoid an ideological breach with the government. It was assumed the proposals could be tacked on to existing policies without a U-turn. The government, though, proved unresponsive and the document had less impact than had been hoped.

The regime in control up to the mid-1980s ultimately saw its role as diplomatic bridge-building with the government, softening the hard edges of government policy, while tempering the more ignorant reactions of members towards the government, whether naively enthusiastic or over-critical. None of the presidents had the political flair of a Watkinson or the ideological overview of an Adamson or Clapham. John Greenborough (1978–80) was most attuned to the government: a bluff, good-natured former oil company chairman, he functioned best during the honeymoon period and relied heavily on John Methven. His successor, Ray Pennock, (1980–1982), a former deputy chairman of ICI, faced more difficult times with private frustration and public diplomacy.[4] Pennock, though critical of monetarism, was able to win the ear of the Cabinet 'drys'. He was seen as 'a liberal at heart', voicing ICI traditions of 'progressive' management and with a keen enthusiasm for employee participation and continuing dialogue with the TUC.[5] Campbell Fraser of Dunlop (1982–1984) had more wholly revisionist sympathies.[6] A self-proclaimed 'one nation Tory', an applied economist in the Keynesian mould, as CBI president Fraser supported reflationary public spending and industrial policy: he faced a less than congenial situation, preferring the grass roots to contacts with government. His successor in turn, James Cleminson of Reckitt and Colman (1984–1986), a safe pair of hands and able bridge-builder, would be economically 'dryer'.

The director generals were more obviously exposed to the political convulsions of this period. John Methven, who continued in office until his untimely death in April 1980, strove for unity as the onset of recession loomed. His well-known 'last-chance saloon' speech to the 1979 conference, insisting that economic revival was essentially the responsibility of management, had marked in many ways the apogee of CBI loyalism to the Thatcher government. Trusted by the prime minister, understanding if not necessarily sympathising with the government's more radical enthusiasms, he appeared to have the making of an arch-reconciler of the divisions which were soon to break out within the CBI, though whether this quality could have survived the recession is less clear.

His replacement, Terry Beckett (director general 1980–87) was the most formidable and widely experienced senior industrialist to occupy this role so far.[7] Beckett's early training had been in engineering and economics. Within the multinational culture of Fords he had moved from on-the-ground production at Dagenham, through US-style marketing, to the 'hot seat' of headship of Ford UK in the 1970s, gathering a reputation for 'firm but fair' industrial as well as public relations. A commanding, rugged figure, Beckett exuded the image of a bluff, disciplined but intellectually acute fieldmarshal of industry. His regime at the CBI would increasingly enlist blue-chip company chairmen while drawing skilfully on backroom expertise, notably from MacDougall. He would emphasise tough-minded analysis and problem solving, and what he regarded as the CBI's 'crown jewels' of economic information, forecasting and education of both public opinion and firms. Beckett was down-to-earth, programmatic, pithy, incisive.

This man, perhaps more than anyone else, was to epitomise the hard choices faced by organised industry in the early Thatcher period. He confessed later: 'We were faced by real dilemmas ... trying to persuade the government to adopt policies we thought were beneficial, but to avoid being excessively critical because we believed their overall aims, though not their tactics, were right.'[8] Philosophically, Beckett was pluralist liberal: an early intellectual influence had been Popper. His experience in the motor industry in the 1970s had convinced him of the need for major changes to restore individual enterprise, attack inflation and curb the unions. A committed centrist, though more from empiricist 'anti-dogmatism' than any reforming 'big idea', Beckett's perspective was 'industry and the economy' rather than 'values and society'. For him the keynote was the centrality of dynamic, intelligent industrial management for Britain's economic regeneration. His approach to the worlds outside business and the economy could seem less coherent and sure-footed than his predecessors'. His limitations included occasional verbal gaffes, a seeming ill-at-easeness in Whitehall, a lack of ability to resonate some deeper chords. But these were in large part the reverse side of his strengths. He was to win widespread respect for tenacious advocacy of the cause of industry, often seeming a lone strong voice for moderation in the surrounding conflict.

Revisionist strands were still strong. Donald MacDougall remained highly influential as economic adviser, firmly propounding much of the more typical Keynesian medicine during the recession. The Economic Committee chairmen, Ronald Utiger of Tube Investments and Kenneth Durham of Unilever, showed mainstream revisionist scepticism of 'monetarism'. Adrian Cadbury, and the elder statesmen Plowden, Caldecote and Robens, remained on hand to urge more eclectic economic policies in the PAC. The battle-hardened Alex Jarratt maintained a tightrope consensus on industrial relations reform as chairman of the EPC.

Revisionist activism in these years typically went on behind the scenes, pleading with the government to lower interest rates, stressing short-term economic stimuli, so that much of the public thinking of both the CBI and BIM emerged through budget submissions. The etiquette of courteous CBI meetings with Labour frontbench economic spokesmen continued, and these showed a shared commitment to some form of reflation, though with considerable differences as to its amounts and forms.[9] There was a feeling that Labour had moved away from their post-1976 'responsible' attitude to public finances, while similar suspicions were voiced of the TUC's 'highly inflationary' proposals.[10] There is little evidence of interest in the SDP, which some business leaders did join, and the degree of interaction with Conservative 'wets', despite the sympathies of some of the CBI leaders and staff, remains unclear. Only Prior was in direct contact with the CBI as a minister, and other leading Cabinet dissidents, by their personal distance from business or economic experience, might have been considered dubious allies. Much of the CBI's behind-the-scenes advocacy would be directed towards undogmatic 'centrists' in cabinet.

Revisionism also remained entrenched in the BIM. Its leadership had considerable opportunity to promote its own agenda in view of the size and heterogeneity of the managerial membership and their widely varying experiences during the recession. Its energetic and persuasive director general, Roy Close, was a convinced centrist: some of its better-known figures, Derek Ezra, John Harvey Jones, and the reconstructionist Peter Parker (see chapter 6), were openly critical of Thatcherism. However, the BIM also had less revisionist voices, including James Ball, the influential economist, chairman of the Economic and Social Affairs Committee (ESAC) 1979–82, who was highly sceptical of the reflationary packages proposed by some members. His ESAC successor, though, the ex-mandarin Lord Croham, was a mainstream Keynesian and tripartist, who emphasised the role of infrastructure investment for economic recovery. In addition, a momentum for ideas like the national economic forum and employee participation was maintained in the BIM through this period. More than any other factor, however, limited resources would prove a stumbling block. Financial problems would weaken and eventually put paid to the BIM's public role, and its chances of being an alternative focus for revisionism.

The policy response of the revisionists

Conservative intentions for a more formalised monetarist experiment had been known before 1979 but seldom explored as likely policy experiences. Neither the dominance of the economic ministries by 'monetarists' nor the Medium Term Financial Strategy (MTFS) seems to have been predicted. CBI economists remained highly sceptical of the sterling M3 targets, and there was perplexity at the government's shift to a less discretionary macro-economic framework at a time of unexpected external pressures on sterling through North Sea oil and international recession. Initially, both CBI and the BIM had argued for a 'flexible but tight' monetary policy.[11] This reflected a belief that public sector inflation could be brought under control more rapidly than proved to be the case, and that the government would offer countervailing fiscal concessions to business in the interim.[12] Radical critics of the government strategy would be upbraided and the CBI evidence to the Treasury Select Committee in 1980 was relatively supportive. Having said this, there was little intellectual commitment to explicitly monetarist ideas at any time.

The Economic Directorate had sounded a critical note from the start, insisting that the policies would only work 'painfully and slowly at the expense of intolerably high unemployment, stagnation, business losses and bankruptcies'.[13] Sceptical industrialists asserted that the PSBR 'should not be a theological belief', and CBI revisionists felt encouraged by the support they received from independent figures like Jeremy Morse in the NEDC.[14] By summer 1980 concern about Minimum Lending Rate (MLR) and the exchange rate was intense and had leaked into the media, although privately the CBI's language was still tempered.[15] Initially, Geoffrey Howe had seemed sympathetic to industry's plight but the failure to get interest rate cuts in autumn 1980 led to the fateful 'bare knuckles' speech at the 1980 Conference.[16] Both Pennock and Beckett were more vocal in demanding immediate concessions through a 'business budget' and a major cut in MLR. The 1981 Budget confirmed, however, that this more critical stance had failed, thereafter leaving revisionists with the awkward choice between sullen acquiescence or arguing publicly for a major reflationary boost.

Rhetorical rigidity about the MTFS targets coupled with their flexible interpretation in practice frustrated reflationists: they felt it was 'oversimplified to say that a lower PSBR necessarily means lower interest rates'.[17] Yet even when opposition to government was at its height, the CBI leadership faced influential government loyalists in Council. Indeed, after the 1981 Budget the Council was so divided on its response that there was an effective agreement to disagree. The minutes noted: 'Members of the Council wanted Government to succeed in its objectives; there was disagreement about the steps needed for this'.[18] The economic committees tended to be particularly divided on this question, but in the more revisionist-inclined PAC, as well as the economic staff, the desire for fairly large reflationary boosts through infrastructure expenditure was insistent.

The failure of the CBI to influence the 1981 Budget and the defeat of the 'wets' in the cabinet reshuffle in autumn 1981 appeared effectively to rule out any major reversal in economic policy. Even so urgent pleas for changes mounted. By late 1981 Pennock was privately warning the government that the 'general impression was that we are not getting any- where'.[19] By the time of the 1982 Budget the leadership was able to call on support from the regional councils and some SFC members. Howe was warned there would be 'a parting of the ways' if the budget was not pro-business. Minor increases in interest rates provoked sharp responses ('a disaster for manufacturing industry'), and if PSBR was not increased 'social strains would become intolerable'; 'ample room' for a stimulus was believed to exist every year. Doubts about the strength and character of the recovery remained into 1984, and all budget submissions from both BIM and CBI were expansionary in intention up to 1985.[20]

Revisionists did make an impact with their proposals for increased capital expenditure by government as a demand stimulus and means of reducing unemployment. Urging infrastructure projects ahead of per- sonal tax reductions appeared suitably 'long-termist', even unselfish. The BIM asserted that 'our managers who are at the sharp end of recovering prosperity said "put infrastructure first", even ahead of increasing their own pay'.[21] The CBI's proposals reflected a deep pessimism about the prospects for domestic manufacturing, and infrastructure public works were expected to have only modest effects on growth and employment. Doubtless this caution reflected the belief that a fragile coalition of busi- ness opinion had to be held together by pragmatic proposals, though it left outside observers uncertain where the CBI stood.

The trimming of proposals to diminished expectations and a fragile organisational unity was also evident in relation to incomes policy. The reform of pay determination had been a major plank of the CBI's new thinking (see chapter 7). Concern with inflationary pay settlements was a major feature of CBI debate in 1979–80. The government was roundly excoriated for allowing excessive public sector wage settlements while punishing a more 'responsible' private sector with a high MLR. Much effort was made to educate companies about pay inflation through a series of pay conferences. Yet institutional reforms, such as those proposed at the time by James Meade and his colleagues, aroused little interest. 'Incomes policy', indeed, now seemed rather *passé*: the CBI had not dissented when the government ruled out a formal pay policy soon after taking office. The EPC no longer devoted much attention to the issue, and it was regularly criticised in both Council and the annual conferences:

the key policy document *The Will To Win* noted there was 'hardly any' support for institutional reform.[22] Although some of the old guard continued to believe in its necessity (e.g. MacDougall, Hugh Weeks), more influential figures like Beckett and Jarratt accepted that the time for formal incomes policy was over.

The national economic forum, previously seen as the pinnacle of the pay determination strategy, wilted to a shadowy existence in CBI thinking. Originally charged with characteristically revisionist tasks of economic education and reconciliation, its identity grew ever more tenuous after 1979. At the same time CBI interests in industrial policy survived, leading to dismay at the attitudes of some ministers, but the mechanisms for such proposals were conceived in traditional terms, the CBI leadership preferring its established role in the NEDC. Attempts to persuade the government to extend the scope of tripartism had got nowhere from the very beginning, despite the belief that some such action was feasible and urgent in relation to wage costs.[23] More innovatively, the BIM advocated a 'Standing Industrial Conference', supplementing the NEDC (on which it was not represented), to encourage a wider discussion of 'an explicit, coherent industrial policy'. Such views were stated more robustly by independent revisionists like Arthur Knight, David Orr and the ex-head of NEDO, Geoffrey Chandler. But as the BIM discovered, and as did Arthur Knight with his proposal for an industrial policy think-tank, these views were unwelcome to the CBI leadership.[24]

Yet again it was the issue of trade union reform which threw up some of the toughest divisions. Although the pristine certainties of the IOD (see below) were avoided, the belief that the unions had a wider political and economic role to play was uttered *sotto voce*, if at all. Such hesitancy was heightened by major economic policy disagreements with the TUC. As a result, revisionists were willing to back the government's gradualist approach to trade union legislation, especially under the trusted Prior. There was still some desire to strengthen union leaderships by making immunities more conditional on following observed procedure, hence promoting industrial peace through responsible officials. Grassroots pressure had led to the creation of the Balance of Power Steering Group, chaired by Alex Jarratt. But this committee backed off more contentious areas like trade union democracy and abolition of the closed shop, the perennial favourites of Council dissidents.[25] A desire to stall on this issue was suggested by the fact that the committee did not report until summer 1981. The final report's emphasis on employers' insurance funds and linking immunities to exhaustive procedures, while opposition to the closed shop would only be 'principled' and with secret ballots barely discussed, confirmed many liberationist suspicions.

The Employment Policy Committee had generally taken a moderate line throughout, preferring codes of practice to legislation on closed shop and picketing, and a minority was even sceptical of the value of legislation on secondary action.[26] Reluctant acquiescence to the 1982 and 1984 Employment Acts reflected a desire by the leadership to avoid 'too much emotion' or a sharp, open breach with the TUC, and anticipation of later repeal by a Labour Government. The CBI leadership was prepared to wait on events in pressing for legal changes but, as always, a considerable minority demanded more enthusiastic backing for immediate measures. The BIM found itself under similar pressures.[27]

The shifts on industrial relations were mirrored by attitudes to employee participation. Both the CBI and BIM were now more divided than before on the idea of a positive, semi-statutory policy in this field. Some revisionists, including Pennock, remained strong advocates at least of an activist voluntary policy, mainly as a means of educating for industrial change. The legislative back-up of the Watkinson era was, however, dropped. Opposition to EEC proposals such as Vredeling became fiercer than in the 1970s. The BIM retained legislative backup for longer, but even it moved away from its 1970s positions. Behind these moves, however, lay new competitive pressures and more abrasive labour market conditions. Top-down notions of 'briefing groups' and a managerially mobilised 'involvement' of employees were increasingly typical; ideas of structured, conciliar, semi-constitutional participation were on the wane. The more radical policy had never commanded a convinced majority, and by this time the tides of a new 'toughness' in industrial relations, along with the recession, were running strongly against it.[28]

Liberationism tested: pro-Thatcher business leaders

A profoundly different ideological and emotional atmosphere prevailed in the liberationist camp. The introspection, perplexity and heartsearching of revisionists was hardly in evidence; there was a widespread feeling among liberationist business leaders that, quite simply, their moment had come. They exploited this feeling to the full; they were more outspoken in the press than before, they challenged revisionists directly within the organisations; they began to enter the corridors of power in Whitehall. Most importantly, non-business opinion seemed interested in what they were saying, and at last the highest powers in government visibly shared their values.

Within a few years the liberationists had changed perceptions of the place of business in political debate. Civil servants seemed interested in hearing the proposals of the IOD, as did foreign business leaders. Radical proposals on taxation, privatisation and union reform would be heard sympathetically at the heart of government. In the process much enjoyment was to be had in debunking the old idols of the 'corporate state', while the discomfiture of revisionists, after years of political condescension to 'free enterprise' businessmen, was hardly a source of regret. The painstaking, unrewarding concentration on short-term analysis of many revisionists was to be countered by sweeping, manifesto-like, if vague proposals for the long-term economic revival of the UK.

The election of Margaret Thatcher presented what seemed like an unrivalled opportunity to entrench liberationist values among far wider sections of society. The necessary changes would have to be 'cultural' as well as economic. The language of 'popular capitalism' was present amongst liberationists from the very start; suggesting a strategy of creating financial stakes in the capitalist system through self-employment, privatisation and share ownership. This was a 'hearts and minds' approach, arguing for boldness in changing the balance of power in society. As Lord Erroll contended, 'Britain was a capitalist country, in which it was to be hoped that the majority of people would come to think of themselves as capitalists'.[29] Business itself had to take a wider role, refraining from demanding small, specially tailored advantages from government, and, unconstrained by considerations of social unity or political balance, be prepared to criticise vigorously other interests like the unions.

The liberationist conception of 'loyalism' to the government was to back it in adversity as fair-weather business allies faded away, whilst insisting that its radical agenda be pursued with greater zeal. The IOD claimed later to be the government's 'radical conscience', never afraid to remind the Conservatives of their ideological obligations. Walter Goldsmith (see below) fretted about the government's amateurish presentation of its policies and its failure to create 'a vision for the people' during the recession. There would be much frustration about the pace of change and the potential for back-sliding while fears of an eventual anti-business backlash were discounted in the belief that the Thatcher experiment would be a last chance for liberationist ideas to take hold.

The political importance of business support could seem critical, especially with the CBI leadership pressing hard for some form of policy rethink. It might have been expected, given the mutedness of liberationism under previous Conservative governments, that, faced with deep recession, business leaders would argue the case for a major modification of policy. But although some were later to express doubts, at the time the facade of unity was impressive. The strategic interventions of Walter Goldsmith, and of newly publicly involved figures such as John King and James Hanson, were of considerable importance for morale. They urged an uncomplicated commitment to seeing through tough economic policies, and insisted that business was prepared to make sacrifices for long-term gains. Thus King spoke characteristically when he urged, after resigning from the CBI: 'in our hearts we all know there must be pain and suffering as we strive to return the country to the position where we are once again creating wealth by our own efforts'. The moralising tone prevalent in earlier liberationism was accentuated by evidence of the difficulty of the task facing the Thatcher government: Ian MacGregor welcomed a return to the 'original verities' of free market capitalism, while Geoffrey Howe was warned never to fall for the 'soft-option' of reflation.[30]

Much of the interaction between liberationist businessmen and Thatcherites was informal: this partly reflected a preference of Margaret Thatcher for taking personal advice from trusted supporters. Some of these were in politically strategic roles in the nationalised industries, such as Ian MacGregor, Lord King and Graham Day, others personified the risk-taking entrepreneurial executives admired by No.10, such as Lord Hanson. Some were to operate in complicated interstices between government, think-tanks and business, where there were unprecedented opportunities for making reputations. An example was the Argonauts, a CPS-run think-tank where business leaders could discuss long-term plans with free market ideologues. Others, such as Nigel Vinson, and Nicholas Goodison of the Stock Exchange, reached this type of audience directly with their own policy proposals on share-ownership and private pensions.[31]

Nevertheless, the main thrust of liberationism was conducted through organisations. Although sympathisers in the CBI exercised considerable negative influence over the policies of that organisation, here it was the IOD which played the leading positive role. The IOD established itself very quickly in the early 1980s as the government's most reliable supporter and as a source of new ideas. A major part of its success derived from the efforts of Walter Goldsmith, its director general from 1979–1984, the most outspoken liberationist of early Thatcherism.

Goldsmith was a bold, perhaps almost revolutionary choice.[32] He came without the usual credentials either of blue-chip business, Whitehall or political know-how, or economic expertise. He had been chief executive of Black and Decker, influenced by a tough stance on trade unions and by some US management ideas. His background and style could hardly have been more different from the elitist 'English gentlemanliness' previously regnant in Belgrave Square or at 116 Pall Mall. Goldsmith could seem brash and flamboyant. His family roots were Jewish; also north London, self-made. He was self-consciously 'anti-establishment' while also keen for acceptance. Goldsmith identified with values of tolerance, self-help and small firm individualism, with ideas of both history and economics correspondingly circumscribed. He had been much influenced by US ideas of entrepreneurial capitalism, the 'New Right' and tax revolts while working in California, as by the general anti-statist reaction of the 1970s.[33]

Goldsmith could set up strong resistances both internally and publicly, sometimes even among supporters, often being regarded as pushy or aggressive, with a tendency to 'shoot from the hip'. He had, however, a keen appreciation of how best to exploit the IOD's limited resources. Its concentrated power structure, along with much support from Denys Randolph and, more particularly, the influential elder statesman Lord Erroll, gave him the freedom to roam wide politically. Drawing on the work of fervent researchers, his very uncomplicatedness of perspective helping to exude a sense of mission and excitement. He would be a potent symbol of the small entrepreneur streak in liberationism, a leading proponent of 'popular capitalism', and a radical supporter and goad for the government.

Goldsmith aimed to emphasise proposals for a small core of policies by repeated forays in the press, short policy statements, and meetings with ministers. It is unlikely his zeal was always welcome to them. Lacking the capacity or even the desire to undertake full-scale macro-economic research in competition with the CBI, he preferred to concentrate on trade union reform, privatisation, tax reduction, and 'popular capitalism'. The structure of the IOD, with its less developed consultative procedures, gave wide scope for such initiatives. A small, committed research team, including Andrew Hutchinson and the tax theorist and free market intellectual, Barry Bracewell Milnes, gave devoted support. Goldsmith intervened constantly in the press, often wrong-footing the CBI and reminding them that their 'monopoly' in this area was gone. A real rivalry developed between the two organisations, with Goldsmith relishing the role of unwelcome upstart.[34]

The executive committee and the Council both acted as testing grounds for Goldsmith's ideas but there was rarely need to dilute his proposals because major open divisions on these bodies were rare. The IOD continued to hold convivial Annual Conventions rather than the party-political style conference of the CBI, which was vulnerable to the exposure of divisions. However, grassroots misgivings about some of Goldsmith's moves were probably greater than appeared. Activity was directed towards showing consistency of purpose and commitment to specific goals. In the face of criticisms for ignoring grass roots industrial difficulties during the recession, probably more extensive than was officially admitted, Goldsmith could always point to an increasing membership for vindication, despite some resignations; and since membership was personal it suggested that joining reflected a certain ideological sympathy. CBI staff may have criticised the IOD for lacking the weight to have a national voice, but by 1983 they were being forced to move towards positions already adopted by the Institute. For his part Goldsmith attacked the CBI variously as a remnant of the 'corporate state' and a spokesman for 'older declining industries', especially nationalised ones.[35]

The IOD's policies veered closer to 'New Right', US-style 'supply-side' economics than did those of any other business group. Their emphasis on the huge creative economic and business powers to be released by radical tax reform reiterated familiar liberationist beliefs. Goldsmith, however, stood out by arguing for drastic reforms even in the depth of a recession. This reflected the belief that the Thatcher government offered a one-off chance to shift power permanently towards the free market. There was to be popular incorporation into the 'capitalist' system, a set of values and relationships which ran much deeper than the immediate needs of business. This could only be realistically done through creating financial stakes. The economic changes brought by the recession saw a shift to new high-tech and service industries: they made existing firms more productivity-conscious, unemployment would be cut only if small firms and self-employment were expanded. The public sector would have to be emphatically prevented from taking up the slack.

IOD tax proposals were deliberately drawn up to be dramatic and overt, in marked contrast to the alleged 'tinkering' of the CBI's submissions.[36] IOD budget representations insisted on cuts or reforms in personal and capital taxation in every budget submission between 1979 and 1983. The explicitly pro-business packages of the CBI, for cuts to NIS and corporation tax, were deprecated with a rationale from Goldsmith which serves to illuminate sharply how liberationists viewed the relationship of business to other interests. The CBI's view was wrong, he claimed, 'because it is based on the fallacious concepts of corporatism. There is not a separate business interest that needs to be restored to ... prosperity at the expense of employees and customers. The interests of business are not competitive ... but complementary and even identical with them'.[37] Goldsmith persuaded a group of leading executives to write an open letter urging income tax cuts as better for boosting demand than a reduction in the NIS. Thus, although welcoming the cut in NIS in the 1983 Budget, the IOD would have preferred the money to be used on basic rate reductions.[38] There was deep unhappiness about the government's failure to cut public expenditure ('recession has been all the more severe ... because the Government has not contributed its share'); hence more radical approaches would be necessary, including 'the withdrawal of government from complete sectors of activities and even the closing of whole Departments of State'.[39]

From an early stage liberationists argued that tax cuts could be afforded via speedier privatisation, and claimed cutting taxes would take pressure off wage claims.[40] Reduced taxation would also stimulate employment and, even if higher demand increased import penetration, eventually this would encourage foreign firms to invest directly in the UK.[41] Ultimately, some in the IOD took this permissive view of tax reduction to a striking extreme by claiming that the PSBR could be increased if only the additional public debt were used to fund tax cuts.[42] Despite these radical proposals, bound by overarching loyalty and in contrast to other bodies, at a critical moment the IOD publicly defended the 1981 austerity budget.[43] The blunt insistence on annual tax cuts did not meet universal approval within the IOD: some felt it compromised counter-inflationary credentials.[44] But calls for radical tax changes always made a public impact. Practically all liberationists disparaged the cause of public capital expenditure: they were suspicious of the uses to which new funds would be put, suspecting that it would fall into the hands of the nationalised industries or be captured by public sector unions in the form of pay.[45]

Liberationists, in line with earlier views, did not take much interest in macro-economic debates about the exact instruments of monetary and fiscal policy. This reflected not only lesser economic expertise than, say, the CBI economists', but the belief that salvation would come through more fundamental changes than merely, say, a few interest rate cuts or a declining exchange rate. 'Monetarism' as a theory did not occupy much time. Unlike some free market economists, liberationists were not drawn to discussing new proposals like monetary base control, still less once the initial monetarist experiment had disappointed. Concentration on such issues could also be self-defeating if it exposed the leadership as indifferent to the problems of interest rate-hit small firms. Eliminating inflation was to be in a context, first and foremost, where business was freed from the burdens of taxation and regulation.[46] Even so, the fundamentals of government policy were diligently defended, and alternatives denigrated. The CBI's call for a 4 per cent cut in MLR in autumn 1980 was condemned as 'crassly irresponsible' by Goldsmith, and liberationists tended to content themselves by blaming the depth of the recession on excessive public expenditure.

Liberationists shared Keith Joseph's views about disengagement from industry. No long-term future for tripartism was envisaged, industrial subsidies via regional policy were condemned and bodies like the NEB considered ripe for abolition. The NEB issue focussed a highly symbolic conflict between its chairman, the revisionist Arthur Knight, who wished the Board to act as a public entrepreneur for 'sunrise' industries, and John King, its deputy chairman, who wanted it reduced to a 'casualty station' for a few failing firms prior to its abolition.[47] A tense battle in late 1980 brought victory to the latter.

Arguments for a national economic forum were obviously unacceptable, promising 'even more state intervention in the economy than at present' and giving a platform for unsound TUC policies: a point of view fully in tune with that of Thatcherite ministers. Both deregulation and abolition of wage councils were advocated.[48] As for trade union reform, liberationists backed a 'thorough' policy which emphasised 'good laws' rather than voluntarist 'good practices'. Not only would the unions lose immunities for all but narrowly defined trade disputes, internal union organisation should also be legislated on. They accepted a step-by-step legislative approach but went further than revisionists by insisting on wider measures and clearer timetables. Both the IOD and the SFC were highly critical of Prior for failing to provide this, and the Institute constantly assailed him for lack of boldness.[49] The proposals for trade union democracy and closed shop abolition were seen as essential supports for this policy. The IOD claimed to be 'openly and fearlessly critical' of union leaders, not afraid to attack particular individuals, and it took an aggressive line during the steel strike and the TUC Day of Action in 1980,[50] while also supporting employers who used the new legislation during disputes.[51] Although Norman Tebbit was to provide most of what the liberationists wanted, two IOD proposals went further than government policy, for legal enforcement of procedure agreements and no strike agreements in the public sector.[52] The IOD's enthusiasm for hard-line reform remained undiminished for the rest of the decade, and it saw the CBI moving belatedly towards its position.

Privatisation was advocated enthusiastically for its revenue creating potential for tax cuts while there was a strong conviction that even failing nationalised industries would benefit from a quick transfer to the private sector.[53] However, privatisation does not seem to have featured much as an imaginative way of creating a new class of share-owners even though the 'capital-owning democracy' was a keystone of liberationist thinking.[54] By extending ownership of shares, boosting private pensions and encouraging self-employment in various forms, the 'values of capitalism' would be inculcated for the longer-term. It would also make the more traditional advantages offered to business more politically acceptable. A populist streak was displayed in other ways. Small investors would come to challenge the hegemony of the institutional shareholder; a new class of entrants to business could be created, perhaps using redundancy money to restart their careers; communities could be drawn to local firms by local investment trusts; employee shareholding might contribute to better industrial relations. It would bring individuals face to face with 'the dynamics of risk and return' for the first time, and it would change the views of economic success of both public and business.[55]

9 New orthodoxy? Muffled dissent?

By the late 1980s and early 1990s there was a growing sense that a major change was taking place in Britain, something of a watershed. Conservative governments were not only laying low the trade unions, reducing taxes on the wealthy, and privatising; they were displaying an ethos with marked 'business' associations of a particular kind. It was significant that Margaret Thatcher and 'Thatcherism' should both symbolise and proselytise a certain form of business culture. In this could be detected something of a Finchley suburb or a grocer's shop in Grantham, the 'self-help' spirit of Samuel Smiles, admiration for US Reagan-style capitalism, the sense of being self-made and populist and still 'anti-establishment' even after storming the heights of power. Although Britain had had prime ministers from similar backgrounds to Thatcher's, none so closely retained or consistently exalted this constellation of values. In 1990 she departed, but her project lived on. Both in the government and the Conservative Party the ideas of individualism and the free market now seemed firmly entrenched.[1]

Alongside the economic cross-currents referred to in the last chapter, significant institutional shifts were taking place. A greater degree of business–government bilateralism was shown by the downgrading of the NEDC and political marginalisation of the TUC. The fiscal system had shifted in favour of corporations, and, more markedly, high earners. Income differentials were widening sharply, and top managerial rewards shooting upwards. Privatisation was enhancing the sway of commercial or competitive values, particularly in the utilities. Trade union legislation, deregulation, stand-up industrial fights in the early 1980s, and, above all, high unemployment, had brought about a dramatic shift in the balance of power in the workplace. Finally, under the patronage of the state, certain categories of business influence seemed to be advancing in other parts of society.[2]

In this chapter we examine the pros and cons of the hypothesis that a new orthodoxy was now dominant in the business community, a primacy for liberationism. This hypothesis does not impute a seamless homogeneity, still less an unqualified victory, to the idea of a free market business primacy. Its claim is that liberationism, as a broad constellation of ideas, was 'winning the argument' within business, both positively and by default. Positively, by evoking enthusiasm or widespread passive acquiescence, bolstered from outside by favourable government and public policies, and by general international trends; by default, in the absence of coherent alternatives from the other tendencies and with the latter showing signs of being defensive, timorous or cowed. Comparisons are tempting with the revisionist orthodoxy of the 1960s and early 1970s. Then revisionism had exercised a public voice within and on behalf of business. It had been able to rely on ascendancy in the peak bodies and privileged access to government, together with sympathetic currents or exemplars overseas, and a principal adversary relatively in the wilderness.

Our understanding of these years remains sketchy. Archival sources central to our study run out by 1985/86; hence evidence is removed of internal cross-currents and debates in the peak bodies and there has to be greater reliance on published sources (press reports, publications, memoirs etc). In any case, a fair evaluation is difficult for such a recent period. On the other hand, this study has built up a considerable evaluation of relationships between published and 'internal' opinion, for example in the CBI, which are unlikely to change that much. The interviews with individual business leaders provide clues to privately held views compared with public statements. Much can be inferred, if only indirectly, from forms of secrecy or what is *not* said; from language or rhetoric as well as content; also from the ways in which basic conceptions of the firm are formulated. Hence, it is reasonable to attempt a provisional assessment of the new orthodoxy thesis, although readers will find greater caution in this chapter's tone.

The *prima facie* arguments for the new orthodoxy thesis appear quite forceful. Government patronage at the highest levels, a close accord with the ideology of a party enjoying repeated spells in office and a wider sense that 'socialism' was in retreat internationally can all be adduced in its favour. To some extent the 'market globalisation thesis' appears supportive, though this could be two-edged, arguing against business ascendancy in a particular country. It may be thought that business circles would be strongly attracted by the apparently sweeping gains to business from free market policies. A new consensus would surely be gathering round the favourable changes in taxation, top rewards, privatisation, deregulation, and workplace power.

Arguments can be enlisted relating to both pendulum-swinging and ideological 'long-cycles'. The previous orthodoxy, with its pursuits of a 'mixed economy', full employment and a mildly egalitarian welfare state, had lasted from the 1940s to the 1970s. Would not a reaction last for a comparable time? In addition, were not business self-interests more powerfully tied to the new order? When business saw itself as weak and under attack in the 1970s increasing militancy had resulted. But a reverse situation of greater power, status and resources would surely engender mainly quiescent or protective attitudes. Even business people who suspected the pendulum had swung too far the other way would find it hard to urge relinquishing the gains: those fearful of counter-reactions would find it difficult to express their views or to obtain a hearing.

Yet there are also strong arguments against the new orthodoxy thesis. These focus most obviously either on the scope for divergence between two types of free market ideology, the government's and business's, or on evidence of policy failures. Business critics, on these interpretations, might see government as too wrapped up in irrelevant ideological designs or less committed than hoped to specifically business understandings of the free market project. A liberationist hegemony in business would be less likely on account of the failings or cross-currents in economic performance, the damage to less favoured business sectors, the discontents of manufacturing interests. On top of all this, a still larger reason for discontent existed. Still far distant, it seemed, was the crucial liberationist goal of large reductions in overall taxation and public spending. Surely, then, a 'realistic' basis for a sense of 'winning' would be lacking?

A less obvious critique would see 'victory' as pyrrhic, subjectively unsatisfying or illusory or transient for large numbers of the business elite. Success could be psychologically confusing, victory would lead to complacency, business might be unable or unwilling to 'take the crown'. The advantages of political salience, high rewards or workplace power might not outweigh a day-to-day business atmosphere which was still highly insecure and driven by competitive pressures, perhaps more so than before in consequence of global trends. Behind much of all this lies the alternative of a more 'opportunistic' interpretation of business attitudes, and a suspicion that ideological interests in business might eventually prove ephemeral. Perhaps, after all, the controversies of the 1960s and the turmoils of the 1970s were exceptional? Perhaps there would now be a return to more normal detachment in the business community, a sense of ideological exhaustion, even an 'end of ideology'? There might also be feelings of fragility about the victories gained or their likely future costs. Business leaders could be influenced by Schumpeterian-type arguments to the effect that capitalism's new, harder mutation would tend to be self-stultifying on account of its excesses, its hurts to other interests, its undermining of supportive social institutions, the adverse reactions it could set in train.

Continued organisational distance on more liberationist ground

In this period both the CBI and the IOD exhibit some changes of style, emphasis and tactic under successive leading groups which have little to do with ideology. Differentiation between the two organisations is partly imposed by sheer pressure of competition for influence and memberships. Moreover, their rivalry shows signs of extending to an issue whose ideological implications are unexplored or unclear, that of closer European union. Previously, business opinion has tended to follow the CBI's official commitment to economic-technocratic support for the EEC. By the early 1990s the IOD turns 'Euro-sceptic' on monetary union, along with some leading independents, while the CBI remains broadly committed, but still no ideological battle is joined.[3] Despite all this, however, a central ideological trend amongst the peak bodies is clear. There is a preservation of distance on familiar lines but on ground that has significantly moved towards liberationist ideas.

Institutionally, the strongest voice for business liberationism in the late 1980s and early 1990s is still the IOD. Here the desire for minimalist government, stripped down to 'law and order, low taxes, sound money', remains undimmed.[4] A retreat from fiscal progressivity culminates in the call for both steeply reduced and flat rate taxes. Privatisation and deregulation remain as central passions. Thus in 1986 there are demands for large-scale privatisation of health, education and welfare, in 1990 for corporation tax to be ended and for the public spending percentage of GDP to be halved in fifteen to twenty-five years. Featuring at various times are calls for 'zero inflation', 'wholehearted support' for the Community Charge, market solutions for environmental protection, and 'a department of state to promote market at home and overseas'. Further massive privatisations, including coal, railways, post services and the motorways, are still being urged in 1992.[5]

From most of all this the CBI still maintained a discreet distance, its tradition of anti-extremism still evident. Yet the terrain for the contrast had changed. The CBI's traditionally pluralist macro-economic mix showed a shift of emphasis from growth and employment towards anti-inflation. Whereas in the early 1980s its statements had still assigned a broad equality to high employment alongside other macro-goals, later this was no longer quite the case. By 1986 a narrower range of anti-unemployment measures was envisaged compared with far-ranging proposals in 1983.[6] Expansionism was more subdued. If the CBI continued to ask for slightly more emphasis on growth towards budget time when it saw government policies as too tight, fears of inflation generally loomed larger, not only during the 1988–89 phase when they were more colourable. The continuing hope for a higher, steadier, non-inflationary growth rate (and hence, to a large degree, for lower unemployment) moved to the old, staple and longer-term aspiration for higher investment. Here the CBI still gave central place to the 'investment gap', particularly in R&D and new products, and, significantly, it pushed educational priorities and a 'skills revolution' upwards to a full equality with other national aims, though there were familiar 'voluntarist' limitations in its approach to training, leaving to more independent voices the case for a levy to ensure that the training free riders or 'poachers' played their part.[7]

It is over social affairs and privatisation that the shift of ground appears more clearly. A lesser role for the trade unions: an explicit disowning of tripartist consensus-seeking: official acceptance first of NEDO's reduction, then its demise: increased vagueness over employee participation, although the CBI's own studies reveal limited progress on 'upward communication and consultation', let alone formal representation: a greater emphasis by contrast on employee shareholding: adoption of ideas of labour market deregulation and 'flexibility': a hard line on EEC social regulation on such things as parental or family leave – all these are evidence of the trend.[8] There is a parallel over privatisation. While the sweeping evangelism of the IOD is avoided, here too the emphasis shifts. Whereas in 1985/86 a continued role for the public sector is forecast in a 'mixed economy', with no pleas for further changes, by 1991 privatisation 'has been a success which should continue with coal and rail'.[9]

It may be objected that official statements by both bodies provide insufficient evidence: the continued existence of sizeable minorities of dissenters in the IOD, perhaps more particularly in the CBI, would be understated. But our earlier evidence suggests that published positions could not grow too far divorced from an internal balance of opinion, or at least not for long. They would typically represent a leading group consensus as to what the majority of the membership would want. Thus it is not unreasonable to interpret the CBI's public platforms over a fair period of time as broadly representative of a genuine shift of grass roots opinion.

Revisionist ideas were dealt yet a further organisational blow during this period. There was a virtual disappearance from the public policy stage of the BIM. After the mid-1980s that body withdrew from taking major stands on issues of macro-economics, infrastructure, industrial policy and social dialogue. The BIM returned to an earlier, almost exclusive focus on professional issues of management status, training and education. For this a mixture of interrelated factors appears responsible: intensified resource constraints following a financial crisis and an internal rationalisation; leading figures who are less interested or prominent in public affairs; but again, in all likelihood, a liberationist-leaning drift, or at least a sense that previous stands at odds with the new regime had had disappointing results and were less likely to succeed in the future.[10]

The industry revolt: rearguard action or new ideological divide?

The early 1980s had seen widespread anger and dismay at the heavy blows dealt to manufacturing by government policies on top of international trends (see last chapter). By the mid-1980s a considerable movement for protest and redress was developing. The question arises as to whether this 'industry movement' had the effect of seriously undermining business support for the Conservative government. In a wider sense, did it appear to threaten the liberationist influence or perhaps even create a new focus for ideological conflict?

A cultural divide between industry and finance was an old story in Britain, almost a *hiatus* of sentiment and values. On the one hand, 'the City' was seemingly aloof and publicly reticent, its public policy influence largely exercised by proxy through the Treasury's preoccupations with money aggregates, anti-inflation and international markets. It characteristically saw itself as cosmopolitan, an advance guard for British economic power, and its sharper elements were critical of the less dynamic parts of industry. Industry, on its side, tended to view 'the City' as a cockpit for short-term asset shuffling, footloose international money, predatory takeovers, and easy or exploitative wealth. Since 1960 such attitudes had often emerged from business leaders.[11] Now, in the 1980s, came the harsh blows to much of manufacturing, the large, ostentatious gains for finance and services, and an official policy seen as deliberately biassed towards the latter.

The results were stormy. Business leaders would speak out for industry through House of Lords evidence and debates starting from a milestone report in 1985 by the Select Committee on Overseas Trade, chaired by Lord Aldington, through the 1986 Industry Year organised by Geoffrey Chandler, and the press. Front runners in the Lords were the senior revisionists Benson, Caldecote and Ezra, and, elsewhere, Monty Finniston. Interventions came from the leading independents Kearton and Weinstock, the latter emerging from his lair to lambast the policy of sacrificing industry and employment to excessive anti-inflationism. But some veteran liberationists also rallied to the banner, notably Lord (Ray) Brookes, a robust defender of heavy industry from the old right-wing, and Lord (Hector) Laing, a stern critic of City opportunism: both deplored the stripping-out of industrial capacity and the human effects. The doctrine that services would compensate was ridiculed: 'a satellite economy'; 'one cannot run a great nation on takeaways or the people who clear up the mess afterwards'. The harshest rhetoric was directed at financial interests: 'short-term-itis' (Aldington); 'predator disease' and 'shares now regarded as counters to be traded in a bazaar' (Benson); 'short-term manipulation of share prices' (Pennock); 'millions made in the City through mere transfer, privatisation and mergers' (Kearton); 'institutional shareholders have too much power' (Laing).[12]

The counter-response was less striking. In the Lords, government supporters and free marketeers did little more than accuse the Select Committee of ignoring a 'secular shift' to services and hankering after a return to 'talking shops' or the 'artificial stimulants' of dependency-creating government subsidies. Elsewhere there were some robust defences of the City, ranging from gung-ho praise for 'the young man in the Porsche, trading paper' as a source of 'greater value' (Castleman), through familiar rationales for take-overs (Leigh Pemberton), to blanket claims that the City was 'doing well by manufacturing interests' (Cuckney).[13] A CBI joint task force, with a large contingent from top financial institutions, sought to pour oil on the waters, criticising what it called a 'pervasive mythology' of City defects and proposing, anodynely, improved City-industry communications.[14] With a very few exceptions, neither self-criticism nor significant reformism emerged publicly from leading figures in banking or investment institutions, let alone the financial markets. Again a lack of clear, collective public representation of financial interests was evident.

The industry champions called for 'greater continuity' at the DTI (a notorious short-stay centre for ministers), and a 'stronger industry voice' inside government. They urged tax breaks for R&D, a bias towards long-termism in Capital Gains Tax, and tighter restraints on take-overs. Inclinations for new public bodies or sources of finance were understandably muted, reflecting memories of the 'lame duck' experiences and lavish subsidies of the 1970s. There was, however, little follow-through of the astringent criticisms in relation to dividend levels, share prices or investment policy. Few concrete proposals emerged to redress the forces singled out, on the stock exchange or among institutional investors, as favouring myopia, casino-type gambling or indifference to industry's need for long-term competitive strategy.

By the early 1990s the industry advocates could claim some public policy gains and a new emphasis at the DTI (and an impact on the opposition parties). Extreme indifference to manufacturing had retreated, along with obliviousness to competitor countries' more active industrial policies.[15] Also, the movement had given a platform for some wider discontents, particularly providing frustrated revisionists with an opportunity to regroup and regain a measure of high ground. However, it did not add significantly to the familiar store of prognoses of the UK economy. It can be seen as largely defensive or restorative, and it offered little ideological depth. The cardinal question of overall positioning was left open; of whether business, its balance redressed back towards industry, would or should be parallel, pivotal or tributary in economy and society. Hence the pro-industry stance could be embraced promiscuously, from all ideological quarters. The government were able to absorb much of the argument. It is hard to see how the essentials of liberationist aspiration and belief were undermined.

Lesser articulations, differing significances

An apparently puzzling tendency requires cautious interpretation. There is a drop-off in the overall supply of open, sweeping policy declarations, in books, pamphlets or set-piece lectures, as compared with the 1960s and 1970s. Indeed, judging by these forms of direct evidence, ideological excitements of all kinds appear to be receding. After Charles Villiers' *Start again Britain* (1984), there is no major 'state of the nation' tract or book from any business leader. The occasional, ideologically flavoured personal memoir is no substitute for the political economy credos offered in previous phases by, for example, Kipping, Maurice Laing, Watkinson, Robens, Bolton, Chambers, McFadzean, Parker. This phenomenon, of course, has to be carefully interpreted. In particular, examination is needed of currents below the surface and forms of indirect evidence (see below). However, even the more limited direct sources tell a story of a kind. Lesser articulacies, though characteristic of all the main tendencies of thinking, seem to convey differing significances.

It is hardly surprising that no frontal challenge to liberationism would come from 'independents'. As before, a small number of individuals made (usually fitful and fragmented) policy statements cutting across, or even at odds with, the usual categories or mainstream bodies. Whether such interventions were flamboyant or idiosyncratic, crudely self-serving or intellectually free thinking and eclectic, almost by definition they would be unlikely to cut coherently or sharply to the bone. One leading independent was James Goldsmith, diversifying from a conventional right-wing capitalism towards social tradition, national self-sufficiency and ecology, and thence to passionate Euro-scepticism.[16] A broader based independent was Michael Edwardes, with a strong managerial reputation, eclectically wide-ranging in his views on politics and the economy, who had already offered penetrating observations of the British malaise in his book, *Back from the Brink* (1983). Like Goldsmith, Edwardes had become a vigorous Euro-sceptic.[17]

In a different category again was the intellectual banker Jeremy Morse. A quietly effective board-room operator, studiously thoughtful, Morse enjoyed small circle dialogue but felt an aversion for larger public stages or missionising. Economically cautious, he had tended towards restrictionist, moderately deflationist views in the 1960s and 1970, while being forwardly cosmopolitan on international monetary co-operation. By the 1980s and 1990s Morse had come to adopt a broad, cyclical prognosis of finance capitalism, seeing both macro-economic 'rough' and greater competition as unavoidable to redress previous failures but also predicting much re-regulation of financial markets in the interests of 'order' and 'long-termism', and reaffirming high trust, bankerly 'business ethics', influenced by religious beliefs. Morse's dislike of tendencies to 'feed the powerful', which had favoured earlier rapport with the interests of finance, shareholders and free market ideas, now brought fastidious suspicions of excess. A moderate conservatism, solicitous of 'balance', would induce unease over social divisions or counter-reactions; a sense that free market Conservatism had 'pushed too far'; a degree of 'one nation' recoil.[18]

A more open challenge could still have come from individuals in the ranks of revisionism. Yet the revisionist leaders of the 1960s and 1970s were now ageing or retired. The memories of depression, World War II and national rebuilding which had helped to form their beliefs were fading. The parallel institutions which they had relied on, in the last resort, for pursuits of mutual accommodation were receding or absent. Their tripartite commitments and beliefs in both incomes and industrial policy had been downgraded. Unsure of their position, many revisionists had lost their political bearings, variously discouraged by the failings of the Conservative 'wets', a leftward-marching opposition and the uncertainties of the Alliance.

A vintage note came from Lord Benson: 'management must show greater willingness to work with, instead of independently of, government and unions'. The ex-mandarin and banker Lord Roll warned against monetarism and market dogmatism, reasserting classical Keynesian views. The staunch revisionist Lord Caldecote, while praising parts of the new regime, sounded the old notes of horror at severe deflation and unemployment as both 'waste of effort' and 'seeds of anarchy and strife'. But overall counter-proclamation was lacking. When a large group of business leaders openly supported the Conservatives in the 1992 general election, but within a context of free market individualist ideas, the names of more centrist-inclined Conservative supporters like Lords Aldington,

Prior, Nelson and Sieff were notably absent, while many other old-guard revisionists had their heads below the parapet.[19]

A leading re-interpreter from 1981 onwards was Arthur Knight, author of a substantial book on industry and government, and long active in CBI counsels. His chairmanship of Courtaulds had been followed by the bruising NEB debacle of 1980–81 (see last chapter). Knight's concepts of improved 'capitalism', rational enquiry and collective business action were in a classic revisionist mould, to which he added a utilitarian tone which 'avoided moralism' and stressed 'enlightened self-interest'. Exemplifying a chastened, slimmed-down emphasis among revisionists, Knight downplayed both macro-economics and national mutualism. His centrepiece was the improvement of corporate economic performance via 'the controlled use of departures from market forces' (whose inadequacies he stressed, notably capital market ignorance and myopia). The main agents were to be groups of platonic-minded industrialists, influencing public policy, *plus* collective leverage on firms by the investing institutions (by now he felt the CBI was 'too heterogeneous' to provide a cutting edge). To this Knight added a stress on worker participation, a cautious interventionism which had slightly advanced by the early 1990s, and an increasingly European framework for thinking about both industrial policy and 'social cohesion'.[20]

Intellectually, it might be thought, such ideas could well contribute to a new form of revisionism, socially slimmed-down but geo-politically extended, should conditions turn back in its favour. The distance from liberationism was clear. However, time would be needed to develop the implications. The tone was cautious, still imbued with 'non-ideology'. Nor was this untypical. In a wider sense, no battle cry was being articulated against liberationism, as distinct from sharp sallies against current trends from leading individuals.[21]

A more subtle possibility was raised earlier, that liberationism in business circles might lose coherence or even fall apart, whether from complacency, confusion or disappointment at slow progress. Indeed, liberationism in the 1980s and 1990s was showing a tendency to divide into 'wings'. A three-way division was emerging between, in broad terms, moderates, triumphalists and ultras. Among the moderates, Lord (Hector) Laing would criticise excesses of short-termism, boardroom greed and neglect of employee welfare[22], while Lord (Nigel) Vinson, a persistent decentraliser, would worry about a tendency for competition and deregulation to re-concentrate power.[23] Triumphalists, by contrast, would assert a seamless robe of ideological-political consistency between liberationism and the government. Thus, Eric Pountain's defence in 1994 of Tarmac's renewed large gifts to the Conservative Party on the basis that the government's nature as 'free market, capitalist' left no alternative. Thus, too, Lord Hanson's mixture of rapport at No 10 with open funding and defence of the government as both free market and successful, and Lord (David) Young, equating a socially pervasive 'enterprise culture' with Thatcherism in action.[24] A third sub-tendency, ultra-liberationism, was to be found not only in the IOD but also in parts of the CBI and in 'new right' pressure groups, for example the Adam Smith Institute (ASI). Here greater free market militancy would be urged on both government and business itself. An example was Dick Giordano of BOC, who had invoked free enterprise as much more than 'just another economic system', urging 'greater aggressiveness' over both privatisation and trade union reform, and implying high confidence in the power of legislation to bring about 'social change'.[25]

A sophisticated exemplar of this stance was Sir Peter Walters. A brilliant meritocrat who had risen fast within the byzantine milieu of BP to become its chairman at fifty-one, Walters was able to draw on a respected record of commercially orientated rationalisation of his company as well as an incisive intellectualism. As with many others, his free market militancy had really taken off through infuriation at both trade union power and government intervention in the 1970s. By spring 1979, attuned to the oil industry's internationalism but also politically near explosion point, he had been ready to emigrate. By the early 1980s, debating national policy in the CBI's top echelons, Walters found himself 'a hawk' on trade union legislation, worried that 'trench warfare' with government was 'getting nowhere', 'heart-searching' over Keynesian theory (though half accepting it intellectually, 'I just felt in my heart that government could not spend money acceptably'), and eventually discovering the IOD as 'a freer spirit' closer to his beliefs, 'a Sherpa organisation' with more central access and influence. By 1995 Walters had developed a coherent position on the intellectual wing of the radical right, passionate in the cause of drastically reduced government, regarding the civil service as the next lion in the path after the trade unions, crediting income inequality with great potential for voluntarist 'compassion', and persuaded that because of 'inbuilt tendencies in every democracy in the opposite direction', it was economic and political freedom that needed constant, radical reinforcement.[26]

There was, however, little in any of this to make people change basic allegiances built up over long periods. Liberationism (and in another sense the Conservative Party) had always been capacious enough to accommodate considerable differences of emphasis. Even a lower level of liberationist proclamation from public platforms would not necessarily damage the project. Though lamented by some ultra-liberationists, this could be consistent with a maintenance or even an increase in less obtrusive forms of moral or intellectual (not to mention financial) support.

Some senior liberationists were helping the now highly influential and diversifying right-wing pressure groups or think tanks, whether as Council members, sponsors or subscribers of funds. Those associated with the CPS, which admitted 'drawing most of its financial support from businessmen', would include James Goldsmith, Stanley Kalms, Cyril Taylor. For the AOI they would include some new entrepreneurs like James Gulliver alongside old-guard patrons from City, construction or brewing dynasties. For the more militant ASI they would include Austin Bide, James Goldsmith, John Greenborough, Ian McGregor, Clive Sinclair, Robert Taylor. The more long-established and ecumenical IEA had among its pillars Ronald Halstead, Gerry Norman, Peter Walters. Such channels could have the advantage of providing a less exposed vehicle for ideological profession, in-group 'correctness' or, in some cases, debate on public issues.[27]

Larger numbers appeared to be abstaining from public involvement. Non-participation continued to be a widespread assumption among liberationist-minded business leaders or, as with a job-obsessed leading entrepreneur such as Alan Sugar, a declared preference.[28] It did not prevent Sugar, and many other significant figures who normally lay low, from declaring themselves publicly for the Conservatives on liberationist ideological lines in the 1992 general election.[29] More activist colleagues might regret a lack of involvement from such quarters at other times. Ironically, though, this came closer to the central ethos of free market theory itself.

Currents below the surface

As to privately expressed viewpoints the evidence from the interviews which formed an adjunct to this study are of some relevance. Among the subjects discussed in the interviews were the benefits or failures, as the business leaders saw them, of public policies in the 1980s. An open-ended question on these lines, seeking to pick out broad views on 'plusses' and 'minusses', was put to thirty-six business leaders. Only rough-cut answers were sought and given, and the sample was not necessarily representative, but some interesting indications emerged on the spectrum of attitudes, cross-currents and, not least, contrasts between public and private profession.[30]

Among the benefits of the period an overwhelming majority of interviewees put first the reduction of excessive trade union power: 'a drag', 'a menace', 'a scar', 'a wound', which had been 'removed', 'broadly solved' or 'brought into proportion'. The explanation most cited was 'firm government action', particularly Margaret Thatcher's 'courage' or 'single-mindedness' on industrial disputes; not so much new industrial relations legislation or mass unemployment. Next in order, a perceived increase of confidence, enterprise and energy in much of British business: 'something of a revolution', 'get up and go', 'self-employment', 'management with its balls back', 'a larger number of internationally top-performing companies'. Some went wider, seeing 'a new sort of realism' in the economy, indeed 'an increase in national pride'. Third in order of praise came privatisation. Even previously sceptical non-liberationists admitted varying degrees of conversion to privatisation, though doubts were quite frequent on all sides as to both methods and possible excesses.

It was not feasible to discuss economic policy and performance adequately within the short format. Though the relevant answers on 'enterprise' were positive, comments elsewhere were critical, notably on recessions, monetarism, industry damage, the 'Lawson boom'. Only a few mentioned the Conservatives' tax changes for companies and individuals, though a fuller survey would probably have shown wider praise on this front. No one mentioned as major achievements either market/competitive approaches in the public and social sectors, or changes in political power relating to local and central government. Overall, what stands out on the side of perceived 'plusses' is a high degree of favourable consensus on privatisation, 'enterprise', and more particularly the taming of trade unionism, all cutting across the ideological spectrum, though with very different inferences drawn on future policy.

On the side of the volunteered 'failures' or 'disappointments' there was frequent mention of education and training ('serious', 'horrible', 'desperate shortage', 'largely a government failure'). A large minority picked out excessive management rewards in some quarters ('overdone', 'absolutely mad', 'greed', 'dreadful', 'an appalling example', 'a source of envy and divisiveness', '5% for you, 50% for me stinks, the negation of leadership', 'scandals in the City', 'brings capitalism into disrepute'). On issues of political economy balance a deep cleavage was apparent. Some said there was still too much government, too high general taxation. Others put more emphasis on poverty ('people lying in streets', 'cardboard city', 'shocking') and social division ('too much for the rich', 'declining sense of community', 'north/south contrast', 'the nation too divided', 'social systems neglected'). Many saw doctrinal excesses ('too much disengagement', 'driving too far the other way', 'risks of a bad reaction', 'reverse side of the coin of their good ideas', 'market oversell', 'want middle way back', 'bayonetting the wounded, going too far against the unions'). Sometimes ambivalences about Margaret Thatcher and her leadership

were added in the context of comments about either divisiveness or ideological excess.

Perhaps greater significance arises from contrasts with public statements and the light shed on muffled viewpoints, particularly of 'social'
or 'centrist' categories of dissent. On the one hand, among the ultra-
liberationist critics, those who privately thought government policy
hadn't gone far enough on taxation and public spending, most had voiced
such views in public or had close links with bodies collectively proclaiming their views. But neither of these factors applied in the same way to the
'social critics'. Those concerned about social division or ideological
excess had shown greater reticence and lacked such outlets. Whilst a few
could have pleaded long retirements from both business and public life,
most had not declared their views forcefully in public for reasons which
require further comment.

In some cases formal Conservative Party allegiances and desires 'not
to rock the boat' may have contributed. In quite a few other cases, current high profile chief executive positions could have counselled restraint.
Yet these explanations do not seem adequate if only because they do not
seem to have deterred ultra-liberationist critics. Fear of opprobrium
in the business community seems more likely, (small 'p') political caution,
discomfort at unfashionability. The organisational shortfalls were also
relevant. To 'come out' could identify one with anti-government political
parties, something to be avoided for its own sake, downplayed or, where
it existed, kept covert. In contrast to the liberationist camp, no organisation or leading group was available as support, symbol or 'cover' for
expressing such viewpoints *qua* business leader. Isolation would be more
palpable, risks of mass media misrepresentation greater. To repeat, the
evidence from interview sources alone is far from conclusive. Overall, however, support emerges for a thesis of asymmetry in the public expression
of dissent, with non- or anti-liberationist forms of critique understated.

Diverted dissent, reframed rhetorics

Two final questions relating to the new orthodoxy thesis raise more indirect possibilities. With both we return to the domain of public expression
but in search of subtler meanings. Was anti-liberationism becoming more
fragmented, localised or diverted to sub-issues? Was the language of individuals or organisations, even on micro-concerns, shifting towards liberationist ideas, whether from infiltration, conversion or tactical efforts to
persuade?

It was not without significance that by this time veteran reconstructionists were tending to divert their energies.[31] Nor that potential successors

to them were lacking. Three relative newcomers to the national scene with reconstructionist inclinations wrote books on business and society, but with a relatively limited focus. The ICI chairman and high profile communicator John Harvey Jones went widest over a primacy of the social, couched in communitarian terms: 'I share, therefore I am'. But though he made no secret of his opposition to 'Thatcherism', his books were not on political economy but mainly primers for cultural or institutional changes within business as well as human interest narratives of his own career.[32] Anita Roddick's assertion of business social responsibilities in her *Body and Soul* added the ingredients of feminism and environmentalism, alongside a colourful success story, but again the stress was on a 'can do' business self-improvement alongside or ahead of changing social values, not a restructured framework.[33] Peter Thompson's lively paean to employee participation, action-centred round the National Freight Corporation, followed much the same path.[34] The food manufacturer Christopher Haskins, an outspoken reconstructionist, would prove exceptional in pungent advocacy of active government, the EEC Social Charter and a minimum wage, attacking 'social exclusion' and describing much current business orthodoxy as 'hogwash', 'evasive' or 'crazy.'[35]

Meantime micro-conceptions of the firm, previously distant from macro-policy issues, were being voiced with wider reverberations. In the 1960s economic-technical conceptions of the firm (see chapter 1) had tended to be expressed in quasi-non-ideological terms, coolly, even clinically. Now, it seemed, they were being voiced both more often and more robustly. *Management Today* saw a 'new breed', combining 'the work ethic, entrepreneurial spirit and sheer opportunism': but in some quarters the last attribute was not far from being extolled. Two themes were being declared more explicitly and unapologetically: the doctrines of shareholder supremacy and a 'tough' personnel policy. The former was exemplified by Stanley Metcalfe of Rank Hovis MacDougall (pronouncing 'making money for the shareholders' as central) and John Cuckney (on 'the paramount importance of the owners of the business – the shareholders'). The latter occurred against the backcloth of a symbolic shift in management language from 'human relations' to 'human resource management'. It emerged in a sharply defined 'economic man' view of the workforce voiced by Ian MacGregor, and in Alan Sugar's open pride in 'doing without the paraphernalia of staff relations, personnel management and trade unions'.[36] It would be hard to find comparable swingeing proclamations from such senior levels in the earlier period, either for the doctrine of shareholder possession or the cult of autocratic governance.

A subtler counterpart was emerging elsewhere. This was an apparent tendency for challenges to the hard-edged new-style economism to become subdued or diffident. If technical-economic conceptions of the firm were taking on liberationist overtones, there is some evidence that social conceptions were shrinking in both content and style. Long-standing counter-proposals for social responsibility, employee advancement or boardroom restructuring were being recycled in attenuated forms. They were also being re-packaged within different terminologies, as if partly to disguise their parentage or to imply a fashionable novelty. Such processes, of course, were hardly unique to business anti-liberationists. To some extent they mirrored changes in political debate as significant ground was ceded to an apparently ascendant market individualism by its opponents. Within business both a slimmed-down reformism and a semi-muffled critique of liberationism were notable features.

In the field of 'corporate governance' ideas for change had retreated a long way from earlier revisionist schemes. Thus, Adrian Cadbury's reflective outline of corporate 'social responsibilities' in *The Company Chairman* in 1990 covered a narrower front than that contemplated privately by his revisionist colleagues within the Watkinson Committee in 1971–72 (chapter 6). 'Cadbury-ism' represented a watering-down even of that enquiry's final, official consensus: it focussed on issues of boardroom-shareholder relationships and NEDs.[37] Much social idealism was being concentrated on local rather than national issues, through the efforts of Business-in-the-Community. The socially conscious RSA initiative, *Tomorrow's Company,* attractively restated ideas of multiple stakeholding and reciprocity in general terms. Its invocation of mutualist themes was, however, confined to a micro-corporate framework (the *firm* as 'inclusive'), without sustenance from shared macro-understandings. 'Inclusiveness' was promoted to companies with a primary emphasis on profitability, competition and, above all, long-run maximisation of the market value of the equity, or 'shareholder value'. The latter phrase was applied across the board, including to employee, educational, environmental and community activities, being elevated to *mantra* status.[38] Such instrumentalism was frequent in reformist quarters.[39] The IPA was more forthright in its pleas, backed by revisionist-leaning business as well as trade union leaders, for 'social partnership', 'two-way communication and information' and 'some representative structure' for the workforce. Even here the content was thinner than in the 1960s or early 1970s proposals put about by the Industrial Society, the BIM or the CBI.[40]

The BIM's earlier 'humanistic' stands were not being repeated by its successor organisation, the Institute of Management. The Industrial Society, still a bipartite body and for long an outpost of 'human relations' enthusiasms, continued to defend a role for the trade unions, but the brave new worlds of its leaders in the earlier period, featuring staff-labour equalisation, a non-fluctuating wage and national-level mutualism, with calls for 'duty', 'service' or 'anti-materialism,' were now barely evident.[41] Such terms had been quite frequent in business circles previously, along with 'society', 'stewardship', 'fellowship', 'caring', 'consent' or 'human fulfilment' and liberal uses of 'social' (bracketed with 'conscience', 'service', 'responsibility', 'justification', 'involvement'). Now they had faded with few, if any, obvious substitutes. Social notes were being sounded *sotto voce*. Thus, John Quinton, 'Nice does not equal wet', and the chief executive of the Co-op Bank, Terry Thomas, dismissing 'social investment' as 'for the birds, the public sector or charity', denying he was 'a fervent disciple of the co-operative movement', and characterising himself as 'a popular capitalist'.[42]

More than symbolic, perhaps, were mutations within discussions of 'business ethics'. At St George's House, Windsor, active in this field since 1967, private conscience-searching continued over business's socio-ethical shortcomings; but a series of conferences on 'Attitudes to Industry', extending over many years, would lay more stress on criticisms of Whitehall, education, the professions, the intelligentsia, the churches, for their under-valuations of business: an emphasis which long survived the defensive collective *ralliement* of the 1970s, showing no signs of let-up even by the late 1980s. Conference briefs at St George's stipulated, for example, extension of an 'enterprise' climate 'to the whole community', 'a moral underpinning for an enterprise society and market economy'.[43]

A *Code of Business Ethics*, published in 1973 by the Christian Association of Business Executives (CABE), had observed 'a growing number of businessmen of all creeds and none . . . searching for higher motives', with profit as 'a legitimate stimulus, a measure of efficiency and a pre-requisite for growth' but 'not the primary end', and 'business as a service, a vehicle for social change, a means for the fulfilment of human personality and community'. CABE had long incorporated differences, mainly between voluntarist 'change of heart' attitudes, and more radical reconstructionists. Its partial offspring, the wider based Institute of Business Ethics (IBE), kept more to a limited 'business ethics', avoiding the issues of overall business influence and aiming 'to emphasise the essentially ethical nature of wealth creation' as well as promoting 'the highest standards of behaviour . . . the best ethical practices', reinforced by appeals for business support on grounds of corporate image, strategic prudence or fears of public criticism.[44]

It is doubtful whether, on any of these fronts, the relevant elites were moving far out of step with less senior colleagues. In 1987 a CBI portrayal of the views of 'below age 35 business leaders' spoke of 'a merito-cratic society where innovative work and competitive enterprises provide

work for those who seek it; a society ... committed to wealth creation
...which recognises that people are the prime asset in attaining that goal,
not a cost', with company commitments at the core. Such stripped-down
language was now typical. In the same year the BIM's profile of the views
of 3,000 managers described urges to smaller firms and enterprise culture, personal autonomy, independence: it pictured 'an increasing
remoteness of national service, Wartime values and experience of real
poverty', though expressing caution as to how far this was political fashion or some more fundamental trend.[45]

Much of this could be seen as a predictable reaction away from attitudes now regarded as too defensive, deferential or derivative. Earlier
business formulations had often drawn imagery from non-business
sources. Descriptively or ideally, business would be likened to army,
empire, commonwealth, orchestra, school, social or public service. Such
imagery would now feature much less, if at all, given an apparently more
favoured ethos of business as distinctive, unapologetic, self-contained or
at least much more self-standing.

Liberationism had tapped into this seam and seized an historic opportunity with zeal. In the process it had left its opponents relatively winded,
drawing them onto its own ground, even infiltrating their redoubts,
despite its own travails or internal divisions. The costs or benefits of its
success were still open to questioning in the business community, let
alone how far that success would be historically sustainable or defensible.
Crude triumphalism was less frequent than might have been expected.
Some individual voices were chipping away at what they saw as the social
narrowness of the new order. Many difficult issues remain unanswered,
and much more evidence is needed. Meantime, however, a provisional
assessment would surely find more going for the hypothesis of a new
orthodoxy than its rivals.

10   The significance of business ideology

The time has come for a final evaluation. How effective was the communication of ideas by business leaders and their organisations? How far did they contribute to public policy and to wider thinking about 'capitalism' through the period? What wider lessons emerge from the business social ideas in general, and the tendencies of revisionism, liberationism and reconstructionism?

These are not simply questions of historical fact, they also contain a normative charge and value implications. It can be argued that in public policy areas relating to business well developed contributions were needed from business itself; all the more so in view of the gravity of the UK's economic problems. Wider considerations can be adduced as well, relating to civic debate, democratic pluralism and informed social choices about 'the system'. Such criteria tend to suggest that, whatever the prevailing regime, unorthodox, 'anti-establishment' voices needed to be, and still need to be, available and articulate. Not the least significant are issues relating to business power, utility or legitimacy as raised by the ideologies themselves.

Not everything has been included in this study even in relation to business leaders and public affairs. The whole business elite could not be covered. Although a study of ideas cannot ignore issues relating to the 'influence' of ideas, our treatment of this aspect has had to be limited even allowing for the difficulties of reliable investigation of 'influence', particularly for such a recent period. We have not covered the politics of trade associations, industries, local or regional business. Nor has our study extended to the twilight world of business and politics: funding of political parties, company or trade lobbying of parliament or government, informal contacts, log rolling or 'sleaze'. Such issues remain to be uncovered and interpreted: they would probably show business leaders in a greyer light (though not only them). Therefore, our claims cannot be pressed too far. However, we have shown that social ideas and ideological differences were a significant influence on a prominent section of the business elite and on their national organisations. Indeed, we would argue that without the ideological factor neither the leaders nor the organisations can be properly understood.

As to the influences on ideology, this study has not supported 'economistic' or 'reductionist' theories of business or interest groups: those which assume that even here business agents are creatures of 'profit-maximising', power-seeking or pure corporate interest. It has emerged repeatedly that ideological beliefs, along with 'public interest' orientations, tended to travel beyond purely corporate or economic factors. Much of the evidence for this rests on the extent to which both public concerns and deep value preferences were voiced 'behind the scenes' or within the private or semi-private exchanges among individuals and within collective bodies. We have not found the 'industry' influences on macro-ideology (as distinct from trade politics) to be very significant. In this context a chicken-and-egg problem often exists: an individual's initial choice of sector to work in may already be highly value-laden. Industry factors appeared less important than company cultural influences in some cases, typically varying *within* industries. They were considerably less important in overall terms, we would argue, than influences on beliefs earlier in people's lives, political or religious allegiances, personal mentors or role models, the 'encompassing' or enlarging processes often evident in the peak organisations, the sheer play of intellect and emotion as public policy issues, with their own logics, were grappled with, often under pressure.

As to the patterns of ideology, our findings differ from some familiar assumptions. Business social ideas assumed forms unpredicted or even denied by mainstream theories of business and political economy. Their sharpest contradiction was of what is perhaps the biggest 'ideology about business ideology', the thesis of homogeneity or consensus. But they did not dissolve into polyglot amorphousness either. Rather, the ideas expressed by business leaders demonstrated at their core a riven and divided quality yet also a firmly patterned shape. They turned out to be contoured around three main tendencies. These tendencies – revisionism, liberationism and reconstructionism – formed contesting ideological claims. Indeed, they were sufficiently at odds to justify a picture of British business as internally divided on basic principles or truly 'in contention' about 'the system'.

The rhetoric of business: practicality before principle?

The overall impediments to ideological articulation and debate were cultural or psychological as well as institutional, and they affected all the tendencies of thought (for those creating imbalance *between* the tendencies see below).

First, some long standing prejudices discouraged the very idea of expressing deep beliefs. Previous non-interventions in the public arena over a long period appeared to leave business disadvantaged against the more professional and familiar efforts of political parties, trade unions or pressure groups. There were fears as to whether the requisite communication skills existed or how assertive voices from business would be received. It was widely felt that the best approach, optimising business's knowledge and experience, would be to 'speak out' in a severely 'practical' tone of voice. Such an approach was empirical; language unadorned, proposals feasible or 'hard-headed', deflationary of both 'dogma' and dilettante oratory. The mentality was bred not surprisingly from the 'output' imperatives of corporate and boardroom strategy. Though not purely 'technocratic', the emphasis on 'concreteness' would emphasise 'problem-solving', 'getting things done'. In discussion with other groups, business leaders would frequently stress that the 'gut' issue for them was the 'practicable' rather than overall direction, emotion or basic values. Indeed, they felt such an outloook exemplified business responsibility and restraint.

Yet while 'practicality' could nearly always command some sort of hearing, it also contained severe limitations. Ideas could be under-developed, concepts poorly related to each other, global visions short-changed. Issues of principle would become disguised with an over-emphasis on the strategy or tactics. Business would often concentrate on 'wars of position': implementation seemed to be the aim even before an issue had been fully explored. Of course, this stance had some plausible arguments on its side, particularly in relation to public policy where the pressures were on for speed and where many business leaders understood their role to be the gaining of immediate concessions. Even in hard practical terms, though, there was neglect of the notion of how other elites could ultimately be 'persuaded': even the mechanics of persuasion, evident in different ways to governments and trade unions, were under-conceptualised. Important messages would come out mutedly or sideways, if at all. Even with unsympathetic governments, for example, criticism was typically given 'more in sorrow than in anger'. Assumptions that business viewpoints would always be 'pragmatic' were encouraged. Responses could be correspondingly limited and business influence less effective than otherwise.

Secondly, various prejudices existed in favour of 'a united voice'. The idea that 'internal' disagreements might be deliberately conveyed to the outside world was generally rejected. This partly reflected deeper cultural factors of business self-perception. Disagreements could take lesser prominence to habits of affability towards business associates (often called 'friends' and greeted by first names) whom one had met repeatedly (and anticipated meeting in future) in clubs, board-rooms or peak bodies and across negotiating tables. The 'club' or 'clan' factor, although generally restricted for each individual at most to a few hundred others, enjoyed some importance. It flourished in the House of Lords, where business peers would speak with senatorial *gravitas* about 'technical' issues or address wider policy issues in restrained, consensual language. In addition, there were tactical, political reasons for preserving an image of business 'unity', particularly in negotiations with government. For the CBI leaders 'disunity' would weaken their case in Whitehall, although in private tougher lines were often taken, especially when threats of grass-roots revolts seemed feasible. Arguments in favour of 'private diplomacy' tended to work in the same direction. But the attitude spilt over into other areas. A neutral language in CBI official publications repeatedly failed to convey the richness of the underlying discussions, as with the debate on employment participation. Some of the more compelling efforts, such as the original Watkinson report, never saw the light of day after facing internal opposition. There were similar mufflings of internal differences in both the BIM and the IOD.

Thirdly, the available forums for debate contained biasses towards under-expression. As the peak bodies grew more bureaucratic and their diversity of interests increased, a greater premium was put on papering over the cracks: debate about 'fundamentals' became more difficult. This was seen most clearly in the CBI Council, with up to 400 attending, representing very wide interests. Debates would typically start from a platform motion drawing on the work of various committees, it would often be challenged by grass roots malcontents, provoking vigorous and often heated exchanges, until the platform would call on senior business 'loyalists' to swing round the doubters. Though this process appeared to offer a safety valve while getting policies through without much alteration, it restricted debate: counter-motions were not allowed, shows of hands rare, the platform could not reasonably appear divided. In the CBI Council and the equivalent BIM and IOD forums the (often vocal) presence of small grass roots interests could deter or irritate weightier participants from the 'blue chip' companies, though partially successful efforts were made to address this problem, notably the CBI's PAC. Other impediments to debate, however, reflected on external institutions. The NEDC and EDCs, for example, produced disappointment even for revisionists in this respect. Their emphasis on policy 'outputs' short-changed urges to 'get things done'; their 'closed' nature confined discussion to tiny elites; and their technocratic emphasis was unhelpful.

Fourthly, even the channels for more open articulation by individuals seldom helped debate. Speaking directly to the public through the media not only contained risks of 'soundbites', stereotyping, trivialisation, or excessive profiling of populists or unrepresentative 'characters', it also meant that differing viewpoints were seldom juxtaposed. Coverage of the peak organisations in the mainstream press, radio and TV also fell short, though this could be a reciprocal of a boring 'united front' blandness on the part of the former. As for books, pamphlets or speeches, both business and its audiences suffered from constraining stereotypes as to what could or should be said. There was an expectation that memoirs would concentrate on corporate experiences: many good memoirs such as those of Edwardes, Harvey Jones and Lazell, did not extend into wider territory. Business high politics was neglected; only Kipping of the peak organisation officials produced a memoir, and that quite secretive. Deeply held beliefs on economic, political and social issues were seldom conveyed: the tone was often bland and did less than justice to the writer. Some misjudged their audiences, either confining their appeal to informed but small and marginal groups or else going indiscriminately for a vague 'public opinion'. Even where such obstacles were overcome, a fragmented, unilateral declaration remained the general rule, with individual and even group opinions passing each other like ships in the night.

This made a formidable array of constraints. It meant that much articulation had to emerge indirectly, unintentionally or tangentially. Repeatedly, communication of belief would have to occur as sub-text or implication, or symbolically through a distinctive style or *persona*. It is all the more striking that so much should still 'get through' at various levels. One thinks of Partridge or Watkinson as organisation leaders; of Plowden, Benson or Robens as 'senior statesmen' in the CBI, Chandos or Erroll in the IOD; of effective communicators with neighbouring elites such as Weeks, Maurice Laing, Campbell Adamson, Ezra or MacFadzean; of gifted carriers of deep social convictions to wider audiences such as Partridge or Walter Goldsmith, Goyder or Parker. One also thinks of the occasional organisational manifesto from the CBI, BIM or IOD or other bodies which, despite all the bureaucratic problems or cultural inhibitions, could be highly effective as rhetoric and communication of business ideas. None the less, by far the biggest part of our story relates to things secreted within narrow channels or only one-half or one-quarter said.

Contributions to public policy

Business leaders tended to be relatively optimistic about the chances for national economic revival. Others might be downcast by some familiar explanations of UK decline, ranging from the penalties of pioneer status or poor industrial relations through to the lack of a post-war rebuilding phase as experienced by the defeated industrial powers after World War II. Such thoughts could induce ideas of 'orderly decline' or outright gloom among economists or civil servants. But the natural disposition and professional self-respect of business leaders tended to generate a 'can do' spirit, a 'get up and go' ethos. Although this attitude could display naïveté, merely extrapolating business 'animal spirits' onto the frailer ground of national economic policy, it was displayed by all the groupings of business thinking. Revisionist optimism invested in ideas of growth and rational consensus, liberationist optimism in concepts of unleashed markets and commercial energies, reconstructionist optimism in social prescriptions for cultural and institutional transformation.

Optimism was usually tempered, however, by a sense of how long reversing decline would take. Seldom, if ever, did the time scales envisaged resemble those of electoral cycles or political manifestos. As might be expected, they were closer to investment, technological or corporate strategy time perspectives, or to expectations as to corporate tenures or personal careers. The revisionists' ideas for 'indicative national planning' looked five or ten years ahead. Most elite business opinion was critical of 'rush' over industrial relations legislation in 1969 and 1971, and it showed successive distrust of 'quick fix' panaceas relating to selective subsidy, siege economy control, devaluation, floating exchange rates, and, later, quantitative monetary targets. A typical *cri de coeur* was for public policy to be more 'continuous', notably on corporate taxation. The liberationists' radical prospectus implied a cumulative process, with trade union laws, privatisation and deregulation carefully paced and systematic. The reconstructionists' calls for democratic or community values to inspire radical changes were also essentially medium to long term. It was both a weakness and a strength that such time perspectives often took inadequate account of 'political realities', leading to repeated misunderstandings or tensions between business leaders and the politicians. From the former, allegations of opportunism, demagogy, excessive or specious promises; from the latter, irritations at slow responses.

Among shortfalls in business thinking about public policy, the more obvious related to European and international relationships. The early period brought few references to the EEC. Even in the years following UK entry few business leaders gave a high profile to discussion of European economic or monetary integration, let alone their political implications: responses here were typically reactive, marginal or 'technical'. Most enthusiasts for the EEC saw it in largely trading or 'technocratic' terms, while the Euro-scepticism that developed later was similarly naively 'economistic' either on the EEC itself or in relation to (usually nebulously conceived) alternatives. There were also persistent shortfalls in coherent or innovative thinking about the inter-related issues of sterling, exchange rate policy, devaluation, and the UK's overseas commitments. Business public thinking showed no great disposition to wrestle with the destabilising, fast-accelerating problems of 'globalising' financial markets, of international movements of capital and still more of foreign exchange. All three ideological tendencies tended to assume a national context for their visions.

Other gaps lay closer to home. If some excuses of technical complexity or remoteness applied to trans-national issues, the same was not true of conduct over industrial relations, employee training, boardroom governance or top rewards. Though corporate failings in these fields were widely recognised as economically and socially damaging, the problem of how to bring 'bad' practices into line with 'good' ones was never fully tackled. This applied even where 'internal' criticism was severe. Business leaders might lambast bad employers, training laggards or 'poachers', boardroom sloppiness or secrecy, top managerial 'short-termism' or 'greed'. But proposals for remedies nearly always fell short. Revisionists would go on relying on ideas of education or persuasion, liberationists on market forces and competition, both groups on notions of 'self-regulation' or, sometimes, a vague 'public opinion'. An extreme case of 'close to home' ambiguity was top management rewards. Despite persistent emphases on their 'incentive' or performance-boosting role, there was inadequate research and discussion on both the appropriate levels of top management pay and their most effective or equitable forms. Overall, this chapter of business social thinking tends to confirm the generalisation that no elite group could be expected to tackle fully its own backsliders.

Some of the shortfalls were organisational. The CBI's expansion, despite vaunting hopes, did not remedy various representational defects. Two in particular stood out, relating to small firms and finance. Business leaders featuring in this study, usually from large firms, said little about the small firm sector. From this viewpoint elite business as well as political concern was typically remote or 'top-down' in spirit. Even after public policy started to remedy the neglect, a milestone being the Bolton Report in 1972, small firms' representation remained confused. Both the CBI and IOD sought to accommodate them. In the CBI there were some resulting policy strains, not always to the benefit of large firm pursuits or revisionist 'progressivism'; in the IOD some small firm echelons were enlisted largely under the free market banner. A tail of small and often competitive would-be representational bodies further confused the field. Overall, it is probable that conservative family firms and militant elements, neither necessarily representative, possessed undue clout relative to newer, less articulate or less organisable entrepreneurial interests.

The gaps over financial institutions were more subtle since these did not necessarily lack weight either in economic affairs or (at least indirectly) in public policy: indeed, some would regard their weight as excessive. They could be criticised as too secret or aloof, however, too little stimulated to engage openly with other parts of business or to explain themselves to public opinion. Leaders in the finance sectors made fewer public policy contributions, and there was a relative lack of debate between industry and 'the City'. The reticence of merchant banks, investing institutions or pension funds, stock exchange and forex markets (though not so much of retail banking) was marked. Yet the shortfalls in both public explanation and policy debate were not compensated either by the Bank of England's formal representation/supervision or the CBI's partial representation, let alone by the processes of 'self-regulation' or legal regulation. The system failed to overcome suspicions of parts of 'the City' or to provide proper discussion of issues such as take-over practices, currency speculation or market pressures on companies towards excessive dividend pay-outs or 'short-termism'.

Nonetheless, despite this long list of deficiencies, the evidence of this study also contains much that is positive. It can be demonstrated, we think, that all three tendencies of business thinking made distinctive and substantial inputs to public policy. From the revisionists, first, came a tradition of civil discourse. Here were arch-exponents of negotiation and courteous dealing with ministers, opposition parties, civil servants, trade unions. Although the Kipping ethos of 'responsible' intermediation between business and public interests may have idealised FBI or CBI practice, it edged nearest to a normative code for relationships in an advanced economy and pluralist democracy. For all their exaggerations of the potentials of 'getting together round tables', the revisionists promoted useful practices of ordered consultation and negotiation. They kept the CBI officially away from a stance which could otherwise have seemed separatist, militant or 'too right-wing'. They played a major part in non-party, non-confrontational national institutions. They helped to avert constitutionally improper and civically hazardous mass collisions with Labour in 1964–66, and again in 1974–76. Even after tripartism fell apart in the 1980s habits of reasoned dialogue persisted with the TUC, the opposition parties and, to some degree, other sectional interests. That such processes were useful in a 'crisis', in terms of 'all hands to the pump' or 'patching things up', spoke of deep commitments to civic involvement, despite their tendency to deflect from formulation of a coherent vision.

The revisionists' commitment to investment-led growth also stands out. Their original turn to 'growth' in 1959–60 played a distinctive formative role. Though others would dispute its merits, their deep aversion to crude deflationism helped to fortify similar governmental beliefs up to the mid-1970s. They persistently put down markers for 'seedcorn' investment in the market place of ideas. Neglected by public opinion, vulnerable to fire-fighting crises or pressures for private and public consumption, investment badly needed articulate championship. This the revisionist-led CBI fairly consistently provided, with an additional voice from the BIM between 1976 and the mid-1980s, notably over public infrastructure. In this area neither the liberationists nor the reconstructionists showed comparable vigour. Although the likely gains to investment from tax concessions or increased company liquidity were nearly always overstated, it was a strength to criticise repeated about-turns in tax and other policies and to argue for greater macro-policy continuity. The broad priority was consistent and, it seems, economically well founded.

The liberationist contributions are harder to assess since more of these came in the 1980s and 1990s where so much is still unclear. Their main inputs did not relate to supply side economics or privatisation where no special forethought or innovation came from business liberationists, as distinct from free market ideologues or politicians. Nor were they in the vanguard over ideas for the social sectors to be subjected to market-competitive approaches. On 'monetarism', as we have seen, they tended to be sceptics. Where the business liberationists seemed to excel was in an ethos of 'enterprise'. They went furthest in extending this from large corporate boardrooms, through new small firms, across to self-employment and popular financial stakes. The revisionists had tended to relate 'enterprise' to established companies, nationalised industries or industrial bodies. Their bias had been more professional, elitist or 'educationalist', while even the UK free market economists had tended to see 'enterprise' within conventional criteria of strictly 'business' risk-taking or decision making. Whereas liberationists at least of the 1970s and 1980s vintages were distinguished by a confident and, it seems, infectious faith in the elasticity of supply of enterprise in wider terms. For all its excesses, misjudgements or neglects of the macro-social dimensions, this emphasis is likely to be accorded considerable importance when the full history of the post-1979 policy shifts comes to be written.

Similarly with the liberationists' contribution to 'hawkish' public policies towards trade unionism after 1979. The support given to governmental toughness towards strikes in 1980–81 was probably of some importance to the Thatcher government, while liberationist advocacy of radical trade union legislation seems to have been invaluable to Conservative opponents of James Prior's more cautious approach. Detailed initiatives over union reforms, as sponsored by the IOD and by business influences at the CPS, presented a credible gradualist approach which avoided the one-off, legalistic approach of the 1971 Industrial Relations Act. By skil-fully exploiting a public mood and a widespread business reaction, liber-ationists drew much broader strands of opinion into supporting such positions, and their 'comprehensive', if one-sided approach to the issue led to real political influence.

For their part the reconstructionists stood out as social missionaries. It fell to them partly to link up more than the others with social ideas long familiar in political thought; partly to provide detailed recipes on which others might draw selectively; partly to envisage the widest array of change instruments. Where others fell back on moral exhortation, per-suasion, 'finer tuning' or market-competitive remedies, the reconstruc-tionists also emphasised legislation, taxation, new institutions or, more vaguely, 'structural' or 'cultural' sorts of shifts. Their policy influence was not negligible, though impeded by shoestring resources as well as massive cultural obstacles. Yet the dilemma over who they were mostly trying to reach was never resolved: whether to seek converts among business peers in piecemeal, Fabian fashion or to follow the logic of their argument by reaching out to a wider audience with their case for complementary radical changes in both business and its social surrounds.

Orthodoxies, muffled conflict and 'might-have-beens'

Beyond the issues of articulation, content and contribution lie more com-plex questions, as suggested at the start of this chapter. In particular, the thesis of orthodoxy and muffled dissent requires consideration. This thesis does not refer to a general under-expression of ideologies as dis-cussed earlier in this chapter. It suggests there is a typical asymmetry between a dominant ideology and other tendencies which are 'under-stated', first as to the extent of their business support, secondly as to their substance or intensity. Thus in chapters 2–4 we observed a revisionist ascendancy, with liberationism relatively 'in exile'; in chapter 6 persistent reconstructionist marginalisation was a feature; in chapters 8–9 partial evidence emerged of a liberationist primacy, with other tendencies much secreted or overlaid. It is worth considering what might have happened if these historical imbalances had been less marked, and what scope may exist for redressing asymmetries of this sort in the future.

A first alternative history or 'might-have-been' applies to the recon-structionists. Suppose the Labour government 1945–51 had adopted a programme for the private sector on Courtauld-Goyder lines: statutory works councils, recast company boards, and wider objectives and accountability for public companies, with national business representa-tion rationalised, parts of equity profits secured for national dividends or worker pensions, and the finance sectors' power and secrecy reduced? Or suppose this agenda had been taken up by socialist revisionists in the 1950s, even becoming a centre-piece of Labour programmes in the 1960s? For reconstructionists, a better outcome might have been expected than the mixtures of Clause 4 traditionalism, trade union conservatism and relatively timid, market adjusting revisionism that actually prevailed in the development of Labour thinking through to the 1980s or beyond.

A second counter-history pertains to the revisionists' version of a 'middle way'. To start with, this would have drawn the Macmillan and Home governments faster towards expansionism, indicative planning and trade union involvement. The Wilson governments of 1964–70 would have been more tempered in their approaches to 'national planning', tax changes and initial public expenditures. Modifications to Conservative policies in the late 1960s would have helped to produce a different sort of Heath government in 1970–72, one less prone to right-wing gestures at the start and less driven to dizzying U-turns later. It would have retained Labour's NBPI and IRC, avoided the anomalies of the Industrial Relations Act 1971, and stood a better chance of success in the 1972 'Downing Street talks' aimed at a voluntary prices and incomes policy. The 'middle way' would have reduced Labour's 'swings to the left' by the mid-1970s and in the early 1980s. For some the same vision led to hopes of a new, 'mould-breaking' political alignment; for most it led to hopes for a less extreme Conservative government by 1979 than actually emerged.

It is no less illuminating to reflect, in the same counter-factual manner, on the implications if liberationism had got off to an earlier and better start. Liberationist ideas first met with incomprehension or suspicion from old-guard business rightwingers. The IOD was discouraging up to 1974–75, while lofty obstruction came from ascendant revisionists in the FBI and CBI. When senior business leaders pursued quite vigorous liberationist ideas within the Industrial Policy Group between 1967 and 1973, not only did they show internal inhibitions but key revisionists vetoed or watered down their proposals. There were also major shortfalls *vis-à-vis* Conservative Party rethinking between 1974 and 1979. Ironically, though Thatcherite measures were to be enacted later in the name of business, these were not pre-developed through much consultation with business. The Conservatives' 'think tank' approach to policy formation after 1975 paralleled some of the criticisms that liberationists had made earlier about tripartism or 'planning'. Stronger policy inputs from business liberationists through the decade to 1979 might have assisted the 1980's free market project in various ways. Additional voices would have contested the scope for hard-line, narrow-based monetarism. The indifference to industry signalled by extreme market doctrine would almost certainly have been questioned earlier. Help might have come in other areas, notably the priorities and methods for privatisation, the administration of privatised concerns, and related issues of utility regulation.

As for the muffling of anti-orthodox opinion in the 1980s and 1990s (chapter 9) judgement has to be even more tentative. It is possible that anti-liberationist currents have been dispersed or suppressed to greater degrees than were anti-revisionist currents before. The business 'counter-culture' has shown little coherence. No manifestos have emerged to parallel those of the IPG, Paul Chambers or Frank McFadzean in their time; nor any sustained rhetorics to match those of, say, Walter Goldsmith in the 1980s. Private dislikes for free market extremism, social division, labour market brutalism or top management 'greed' appear to have been publicly muted. Yet this was at a time when parts of the private sector were coming under wide public criticism in these fields. It is possible that in the future public opinion could turn more sharply against similar excesses, even identifying business *en bloc* with such phenomena; the more so in default of contrary business voices. Ironically, the greatest eventual losses could relate not so much to wider public policy but to business's standing and repute.

Possible improvements

It is not easy to see what could be done to enhance business articulacy and debate, and more particularly to remedy the biases just considered. Inhibiting factors in the wider environment must be reckoned with. Here, as we have seen, the party system has had much to answer for. Though its influence can be exaggerated, it often served to muffle, to confuse, or to load the dice. Exponents of all main tendencies expressed disappointment and frustration with party politics. In business eyes governments of all stripes unfairly associated business views with narrow interest politics. 'Confrontation politics' was considered to have reduced the options for business to promote bi-partisan policies. The traditional identification of business with the Conservatives, though accurately portraying the feelings of many of the grassroots, was felt as a constraint even by many sympathisers. Disagreements over Conservative policies could not be expressed in 'political' terms or, when criticisms were made, they provoked shrill accusations of 'disloyalty'. This applied through successive ideological dominances in the Conservative Party, whether 'one nation' or 'Thatcherite'. Conservative-sympathising liberationists suffered under the latter, Conservative-sympathising revisionists under the former. Particular difficulties arose for representative organisations, not least the CBI.

Ideological differences with Labour, in turn, were often exaggerated even when actual differences were narrowing. This, though, was a two-sided process for Labour continued to be culturally distant from business. Through most of the period it was still sufficiently wrapped up with traditional 'socialism', if only symbolically or theoretically, to make all save a very few business leaders suspicious or ill disposed. Yet Labour's own revisionists did not embrace the more adventurous projects of the business reconstructionists. It was difficult enough to get others to abandon old shibboleths, without adopting new radical critiques. At the same time hopes for a revitalised third force or even coalitionism, desired by many business leaders, did not come to fruition, reducing the enthusiasm and imagination with which many approached the political process.

All this was on top of the wide cultural and psychological factors inhibiting fuller expression (see above). At first sight, then, the chances slim for improving articulacy and debate in the future. Yet to regard the situation as irredeemable would be too negative, and several possible lines of improvement can be envisaged if fuller expression, discussion and public openness are agreed as desirable aims. Filling the organisational gaps already identified would be of some help. Contrary to earlier hopes invested in the CBI, a single 'pan-business' body appears neither feasible nor desirable. Instead, several main representational focusses would ideally develop, each one extensive enough to facilitate 'encompassing-ness', intermediation, relationships with government and public visibility, but also differentiated so as to do justice to deep sectoral contrasts and to discourage an over-concentration of business influence. One priority is a distinctive and comprehensive national representation of small business. Another is new institutions to ensure that representatives of financial institutions and markets discuss both their own interests and public policy issues more collectively. These bodies would incorporate dialogue with, and openness to, the rest of business and the public.

Within the existing peak bodies there should be a readier response to issues which arouse public interest or disquiet. A more open business politics is surely desirable, with internal controversy seen as a public virtue or source of pride, not as embarrassment or disgrace. Improvements might include the publication of minority reports of working parties, and more participatory annual conferences. The peak bodies' negotiating and representational roles, however, would still limit their debating or innovative potentials. Perhaps a new agency might encourage open debate and publish symposia of radically different business viewpoints. Another useful innovation would be a 'think-tank' for the least resourced body of opinion, the business reconstructionists. The media could become more sophisticated *vis-à-vis* business opinion as well as behaviour, learning from the phenomena discussed in this book. The trade unions also have much work to do to improve their role as challengers or interrogators of business. New vehicles for mutual or civic learning may be needed as substitutes for disused or vanished ones: perhaps a 'college' for business leaders to discuss public policy issues and to bring them in touch not only with other elites but with wider interests in society, including those less advantaged.

Whether new public bodies are desirable, perhaps along the lines advocated by reconstructionists, is more controversial. For purposes of business articulacy, it should be clear that revived NEDC-type institutions would be far from sufficient, while formal 'tripartism' would again shortchange other interests. Open accountability to public interrogators could feature more prominently, also dialogue with other social interests. The idea of a national forum may reappear, with some form of parliamentary scrutiny and accountability as an alternative or complement. If so, this would defy the realities of corporate power unless mainstream business leaders themselves were somehow included as well as peak organisation officials. Such ideas could take off if, as seems possible, a tendency develops to countervail or question business influence as it has grown over recent years in the British system.

The prospects for business ideology and ideologies

As we approach the twenty-first century, controversies over 'capitalism' persist. The term may be applied to any system where a business class deploys extensive resources in profit-seeking firms which it initiates, owns or manages, operating through markets more or less swayed by competitive forces. Such an elastic definition of 'capitalism' again suggests the absurdity of a unitary concept. It is, of course, no more than an envelope for widely diverse contents through time and space, even a cloak for conflicting versions.

One forecast would be of an end to business ideology. Perhaps the processes of technocracy, civic segregation and global market convergence will conspire to such effect. Perhaps the educational, political or religious influences which have encouraged rival business ideologies will become less important. But although such a scenario cannot be ruled out, it seems doubtful. The ill-starred history of 'end of ideology' predictions does not support it. The mentality of expressive parts of the business elite is likely to continue to impede it. The sources of ideological conflict inherent in politics, nation, religion or differential socialisation may decrease but are unlikely to disappear. Similarly with 'shifting involvements' within individuals' life spans. Perhaps most important, as long as an overall constellation persists featuring business, significant interests which interact with it, and more or less ubiquitous (national or multi-national) governments, questions will arise as to the desirable positioning of business *vis-à-vis* the rest. Business itself will ask these questions or find itself challenged by them. Pulls of intuition, intellect or gut preference will still be felt towards concepts of emancipated primacy, mutual accommodation or joint social reformation. On the other hand, there are likely to be changes in the forms of such allegiances.

At first sight the prospects for liberationism appear cloudy. The difficulty is partly over the scope for continued gains in the UK. By the mid-1990s top people were enjoying low taxes and high differentials, virtually all the utilities and industrial holdings of the state were back in private hands, inflation was low by any standards, and trade unionism a shadow of its former self. The remaining giant in the liberationists' path remained an obstinately high public spending ratio of national resources. But to attack this would imply a systematic attack either on public and welfare services, or on large-scale unemployment (involving more state activism, rather higher inflation and less 'flexible' labour markets, all abhorrent to them). In addition, by the mid-1990s the issue of European monetary union was posing a dilemma for liberationism as both market and national credo. Moreover, there were doubts as to how far the more romantic or populist aspects of liberationism were being realised. The income, property or psychic gains appeared less secure or satisfying, and much more concentrated on sections of new entrepreneurs, self-employed, management or financial interests than the more inclusive visions of liberationism had suggested.

None the less liberationism was still the chief occupier of ideological space, with little sign of a major counter-force. It was nowhere near the situation which had faced revisionist defenders of the post-war settlement by the 1970s. By then a majority could not recall Britain before that settlement. But by the 1990s a large majority of business top people still clearly remembered the situation of the 1970s as a highly formative experience. It would take several generations of top tenure to pass for that memory to fade. Meantime, there would be vital positions to consolidate. The role of guardian or protector would not be difficult to sustain as the relevant generation themselves grew older. Like the earlier revisionist defenders, their hold on power would take much time to disappear. The new fortresses of semi-regulated privatisation, low income tax, labour force fragmentation, small-time entrepreneurship and capital ownership might not prove as impregnable as earlier enthusiasts had thought, but they still had huge resources on their side. Liberationism, at least in this more preservative sense, would still have a lot going for it.

The scope for revisionism partly hinges on continued pressures for negotiation or bargaining among large-scale interests and with government. Although formal 'tripartism' appears unlikely to reappear, neighbouring forces should still exist with which mutual accommodation is sought. Advantages arise from being a 'moderate' voice of business with which other interests find it easier to treat. Criticisms of business by employee, environmental or consumer interests may argue for some organised response. It is likely that a left-centre government would seek consensus with business over wages, training or employment policies, and that increased EEC integration will lead to further trans-national linkages or negotiating processes. The conceptual challenges for a renewed revisionism, however, are more demanding. Economic pluralism would have to be rethought in terms of macro-goals, institutions and policy instruments. The idea of social balance poses more awkward issues when it is your own interest group, in whole or part, which is thought to be a major (if not necessarily deliberate) contributor to an existing imbalance. Some realignments of revisionism may well emerge, either converging with moderate liberationism or lining up with more radical reconstructionist ideas, probably mainly the former.

As for reconstructionist ideas, some continuity seems assured from values which are inescapable in much political and civic discussion. Reconstructionists could benefit from the relative disarray of revisionism. They could be more widely heeded in the event of a larger-scale 'anti-business' reaction in public opinion. Their best strategy might well be 'prophetic' or 'counter-cultural' rather than piecemeal. A dialectical ally could be Joseph Schumpeter, with his warning that a thrustful 'capitalism', whatever its economic merits, tends to be self-destructive both in setting up hostile forces and in undermining the social frameworks on which it (and other more important values) depends. A strong card for reconstructionists could be to point to more primitive, brutal forces which might take over unless their sorts of changes were carried out: fundamentalist revivalism, racial, ethnic or religious conflict, xenophobia, environmental disasters. But again much rethinking, notably on a social fabric for 'embedding' business and on transnational factors, would be needed in such a 'reconstruction of reconstructionism'.

Perhaps the strongest case for forecasting a persistence or recrudescence of business ideologies relates to their role in a situation where business touches public issues at so many sensitive points. The normative case for them is quite simple. It rests on the need for all sides to be able to make sense of the complex interactions between business, other interests and the organs of a modern state in any society where an important business class remains.

Business freedom, market competition, regulation and the law, all require not only definition but also continuous interpretation, calling in turn for contact, consultation and negotiation between government and business. Government–business linkages may shrink in some ways only to grow in others. Public bodies may directly organise much less only to discover augmented roles as final umpires, lessors or purchasers of services. The myriad ramifications of government for company affairs mean that business interests maintain or intensify their lobbying activities *vis-à-vis* MPs and ministers, with lobbying further provoked by counter-pressures from other groups. The budget continues as a vortex for business representation. Government continues as source of honours and large-scale recruiter of business individuals for quangoes or regulatory bodies. Political parties seek business funding; politicians or civil servants see themselves as future migrants to boardrooms; a host of formal or *ad hoc* opportunities arise for business, civil service and political elites to weave in and out of each others' offices or to consort socially. Amongst new trends, an information society requires increased flows of data, assumptions or predictions between public administrators and those with leverage or insight into advanced technology, economic trends or financial markets.

To imagine that business can operate in this situation without collective public rationales verges on imputing to it both innocence and lack of principle, an uneasy mixture of naïveté and opportunism. Yet it is remarkable how much influential doctrine still encourages such a belief. The most obvious culprit is the classical liberal postulate of a *cordon sanitaire* between an autonomous, 'apolitical' business system and a clinically detached government. The companion traditions of conventional economics foster an absorption in price systems, regulation, macro-economic variables or distributional issues, to the detriment of all that lies between. At the same time, theories of management have neglected the real-life interactions between business and politics, business and public policy, business and ideology, and their normative goals for business have been narrowly circumscribed. This applies not only to the fixation of management studies on 'the firm' but also to 'socially' interpreted 'responsibilities' to 'stakeholders' still conceived in micro- and unilateralist forms. For its part, the mainstream 'business ethics' of the last few decades has neglected collective business interests and formations, and the political power exercised by business individuals, firms, trades or peak bodies. It has preserved a distance from both public policy and civic philosophy. Indeed, the scope of (conventionally conceived) 'business ethics' has been far exceeded by the concerns of publicly involved and articulate business leaders.

The analysis of this book suggests that there are basically three ways in which business can make sense of its complex roles and seek to explain or validate these in an interdependent political economy. Its public philosophy can rest on a 'high' view of business's necessities, virtues and potentials. Unique contributions to collective standards of living, democratic freedoms, social innovation or personal development can be offered as justifications for a highly powerful or expansionist position. Alternatively, more incrementally and cautiously, business can win respect and understanding as well as material concessions through a quasi-senatorial concept of its role, featuring sage economic advice, civil dialogue and prudent self-reform. Or again, there is the view that merit for business points to a reordering of society geared to perennial social values, with joint action to reorientate both business and its surrounds.

For business to play a major part without either a sweeping proposal as its own value or a concept of incremental contribution or an urge towards mutual social reconstruction is inadequate. In default of normative social images of itself, it becomes visionless and maladroit in the public domain, its role tending to lapse in substance or appearance towards the *farouche*, the shadowy or anomic, or the merely pushful. The result is not immunisation from ideology but covert, reactive, derivative permeation by other ideologies. Less than justice is done both to business's intellectual capacities and its deeply held beliefs, and there is vulnerability to impressions of sectionalism, opportunism or manipulation. The business contribution to public policy and debate is impaired in both vitality and legitimacy. There is a lack of norms and criteria of judgement for possibly overmighty business subjects, a further gap in business accountability, and an impression, deserved or otherwise, of excessive business infiltration.

Conclusion

We started this book by commenting on an irony of recent and contemporary history or historiography, a near contradiction between contribution and interpretation. Even where business and its ideas have impacted significantly, it is interpreters from outside business who have shaped our views. The influential narratives or perspectives have been overwhelmingly those of economists, politicians or social theorists, or historians influenced by the latter. The paradox is all the greater in view of the sweeping generalisations made by the outsiders as to business's macro-attitudes or values. Business itself has also been partly responsible by promoting overwhelmingly operational or strategic self-understandings bounded by 'the firm'. To help to redress these imbalances has been an underlying aim of this study. It is to be hoped that, in the future, general and business historians will pay greater attention to the public policy and social ideas of business elites.

However the viewpoints examined in this study develop within business itself, they are still useful in our wider thinking about the direction of contemporary 'capitalism'. The choices they pose are likely to be inescapable. Should business be pivot and *Zeitgeist*, companion to other forces or social tributary? Is our main vision of a centrifugal process with indefinite numbers of independent centres of energy, one which relies on autopiloting by the market's 'spontaneous order' or 'invisible hand'? Do we seek a co-equal pluralism alongside markets, where parallel spheres bargain, collude or compact? Or a graduated order where business is enfolded within more 'socially' orientated structures and cultures? The established theories of political economy have not fully clarified these choices. In varying ways they have perceived business in largely mechanistic terms. They have largely avoided issues relating to business's overall positioning, its power, status and influence in society. Yet if business is to continue as a useful, indispensable or desirable part of advanced systems, such issues have to be faced, and the business viewpoints explored in this book have performed a useful service in helping to illuminate them.

The business leaders not only produced rivalrous visions of the system in which they were key insiders, they also illustrated how 'ideology' is not always explicit, self-conscious or 'political', and how 'public debate' can exist away from designated public sites or processes. They, too, were largely unaware of the highly ramified fund of perceptions, prognoses and prescriptions that was building up. Fragmentation, indirectness and undervaluation were seeing to that, also the sheer confusion of events. By the mid-1990s, had a full picture of their inputs over the previous thirty five years been available, the business leaders would have been surprised by the range of public issues covered, still more by the diversity of operative beliefs and values. Their ideas had made distinctive contributions to public policy, the British political economy and 'capitalism' through a period of dramatic and accelerated change, constituting an inseparable part of the history of our times.

Appendix

This appendix includes (1) a brief outline of the categories of sources used for this study; (2) our definition of 'social articulacy', with detail on border territories, what was included and what was left out; (3) our methods of deriving the core and secondary samples of business leaders who demonstrated social articulacy; (4) comparisons of these samples with 'control' samples of 'silent' business leaders; (5) characteristics of the different ideological tendencies within the core sample; and (6) a list of business leaders in the core sample.

(1) Categories of sources

1. Books, usually memoirs, sometimes general polemics
2. Articles; authored pieces in the press or in specialised business journals (*The Director, Management Today,* banking journals) or in public affairs journals
3. Contributions to collections of essays or symposia, often alongside non-business contributions, in 'think-tank' type publications.
4. Speeches and lectures.
5. House of Lords speeches and evidence to HOL select committees (except where business peers were official front-bench spokesmen)
6. Business representative organisations; the BEC, NABM, FBI/CBI, BIM, and IOD. Minutes of their governing Councils, principal committees or working parties, and, in some cases discussions with government. Also staff papers, correspondence, and in some cases papers of presidents, chairmen or director generals. Annual reports and principal publications.
7. Minutes or papers pertaining to more specialised bodies like the Industrial Policy Group and St.George's House, Windsor.
8. Personal papers of individuals in a few cases.
9. Press sources: reports of statements; solicited quotes; letters to the editor; profiles and interviews in business journals (see 2 above) or the quality press. A survey of *The Times* was conducted for the whole

period, whilst other newspapers, especially the *Financial Times* were examined selectively.

10. Interviews as listed at the beginning of the book.

Radio and TV reports were not included because of special difficulties of access to this source. However, such material was often repeated in the press and, in any case, radio and TV do not appear to have been a significant outlet for business social articulacy.

(2) Definition of social articulacy

We were concerned with statements on major issues of public affairs relating to economic policy and performance, economic organisation or political economy, relationships between business and government or between business and society, politics, and social ethics.

For individuals, a statement had to be attributable and 'personalised'. This excluded 'compulsory' statements: the type of standardised remarks made where a legal obligation was involved, as in the chairman's annual statement to shareholders, unless remarks made therein had been quoted elsewhere (usually in the press) and fulfilled the detailed criteria given below. Also excluded were a few cases where business peers were official party spokespersons in the House of Lords, in which case their articulacy would be determined by other factors.

Our definition of public articulacy excluded (a) statements relating to managerial issues (corporate strategy, finance, marketing, production, research, personnel and other aspects internal to firms); (b) industry and sector-focussed issues of trade policy, exports, productivity, investment etc; (c) technical aspects of interest and exchange rate policies; and (d) highly specific issues of state-industry relationships such as export credits. Statements on 'technical' issues of technology or science policy, often self-consciously 'non-political' in character and separated from wider social articulacy, were excluded from our survey because of the difficulty in extrapolating opinions on broader industrial policy.

Some areas of articulacy were excluded unless a high degree of policy generality was present. For example, 'protectionism' was nearly always invoked in aid of particular industry interests, and hence excluded. But when treated as a general issue of principle of trade policy, as 'protectionism' versus 'free trade', it did enter our frame. Similarly, although statements on issues of competition policy or price control were generally highly industry-specific, for example questioning decisions of the Monopolies and Mergers Commission or the NBPI, they were included when general issues of principle or policy were addressed. Statements on education and training would be included only if, going beyond a typically pious, broad comment, they related to issues of international competitiveness (e.g. Finniston on engineering) or broad policy proposals (e.g. for a national training levy). Thus a plea for more vocationally-trained graduates would not merit inclusion unless related to a socio-economic overview.

Macro-economic comment formed a large segment of articulacy, mostly within the peak business bodies, often in stylised or capsulated form, and this was critical in 'positioning' individuals. Statements about the Budget nearly always entered our material unless the issues were highly technical or, again, restricted to particular industries or sectors (e.g. comments on petroleum revenue tax in the early 1980s). Proposals for general tax changes or new taxes were often important indicators of general positions on political economy or economic policy; also comments on public expenditure and on interest rates despite their frequently ritual character.

The EEC/Common Market issue attracted little comment throughout the period in the above sources. We included general statements for or against entry up to 1973, and for or against closer integration thereafter. The tapering-off of our material by the 1990s will, however, have excluded much comment about monetary union. Narrower industrial, financial and trade issues were not included, in line with the above criteria. Issues of EEC social policy, e.g. on employment participation, received a considerable airing at this level and were fully covered.

Statements on 'local' issues were not included in the survey. Even where business leaders made statements of a general character to the local press, as part of their firms' relationship to a locality, the problems of access to this source, its potentially huge size, and overall bias to internal issues of the firm were considered to demand exclusion.

(3) Articulate business leaders: core and secondary samples

On the basis of the above criteria, several thousands of statements were extracted and analysed. From this survey, we identified a sample of 170 business leaders who qualified in two ways as *socially articulate:*

(a) by being 'business leaders', i.e. chairmen or chief executives of the 'top 100' companies in industry and commerce, the leading banks and financial institutions or nationalised concerns, or leading individuals in the FBI, BEC, CBI, BIM or IOD, or key opinion formers in the business community, regardless of sector or size of company, *and* (b) by crossing an *articulacy threshold* based on range, volume and sophistication of statements on the basis of the criteria in (1) and (2) above.

Some of these articulators had published a single book or pamphlet outlining a wide-ranging viewpoint or had made a large number of shorter comments over a period of time. Most fell between these poles, tending to make several qualifying interventions within a peak organisation, usually over a short period, or to produce one or two relevant speeches or articles. Reflecting our definitions and methods, and the nature of the sources, there was some sample bias towards people who had largely completed their careers by the early 1990s.

However, the large sample of 170 articulators proved no more than a starting point. A more significant 'core' sample of 68 soon emerged. These stood out from the rest by producing considerably larger numbers of statements on more issues over longer periods of time, and with greater sophistication. Most of them were chairmen or chief executives of the largest concerns. Some also held leading roles as president of the CBI or IOD, chairman of the BIM, or chairman of a leading committee in one of these bodies. A few were director generals of these bodies, usually achieving core sample status on this basis alone. Some were included on account of influential, well known or passionate advocacy of relevant causes or viewpoints, usually through the medium of books.

Most members of the core sample employed several channels: typically, one of the peak bodies (producing the largest number of interventions overall), one or two other forums, and press reports of speeches or interviews. Some delivered speeches as members of the House of Lords. Fair numbers also wrote books, pamphlets or articles, put their names to collective statements, or delivered the occasional set-piece published lecture. Occasionally it was clear that books or pamphlets had been 'ghosted'. However, we did not consider this issue significant, could not pursue it in detail and, for practical purposes, regarded the decision to make the statement as sufficient proof of conviction and belief.

(4) Comparison of articulates with 'silent' business leaders

In the interests of testing for representativeness, we extracted a much larger sample of chairmen and chief executives of the 'top 100' industrial and commercial companies, largest banks and financial institutions, and nationalised industries, using *The Times Top 100* series for the years 1965, 1971, 1976, 1981, 1986 and 1991. The number qualifying on this basis was 480. 120 fell into the sample of 'articulators', leaving 360 'silents'. This ratio is not very significant, partly because of the elastic outer definition of 'articulacy', partly in view of definitional problems over, for example, the definition of 'chief executive' in the case of several managing directors, or changes of company identity or ownership during the period. A more significant ratio relates to those 'top company leaders' who qualified for the core sample: forty-seven or roughly 10 per cent of the total of big company chiefs.

We were doubtful about comparisons of industrial sector or company size. In many cases the industrial classifications in *The Times* series were not very reliable or meaningful. Other sources could have been drawn on to make industry comparisons, but very time consumingly, and we decided against this in view of more pressing research priorities. Measures of company size in the series were sometimes missing or also of doubtful value. A comparison between the 120 'articulators' and a 'control' of 250 'silents' where measures were available suggested no significant differences in composition relating to broad economic-industrial sector and, as expected, a slight bias towards the larger end of the big company scale on the part of the 'articulators'.

An analysis of companies in terms of articulate or 'silent' chief executives proved rather more interesting. A small number of large firms, as readers will have noticed, produced several core sample articulators during the period, sometimes also a few lesser ones: ICI, Unilever, Shell, Courtaulds, Cadbury-Schweppes, Vickers, Dunlop, GKN. At the other extreme were some with no articulators: Distillers, Whitbread, Rank Hovis McDougall, Thomas Tilling, Metal Box, Wimpey, Tesco, Great Universal Stores, P&O. Our definitions, of course, were not orientated towards such activities as 'silent' membership of councils of national business organisations, support for think tanks or party political contacts, doubtless involving some of these firms.

A more qualitative 'control' employed *The Dictionary of 20th Century British Business Leaders* (D. Jeremy and G. Tweedale, London: Bowker Saur, 1994). For this the authors had selected individuals whom they judged as significant in business or wider social terms, though not using social articulacy in our sense as a criterion. The *Dictionary* yielded 130 such people who had been active since 1960. This allowed for comparisons of education, role function as founder-entrepreneur, family firm inheritor or professional corporate manager, and public appointments, which suggested that

(a) type of schooling had no relevance to articulacy, though a university education appeared to have some relevance (70 per cent of 107 top company articulators had been to university as compared with 50 per cent of 130 DBL top company heads);

(b) founder-entrepreneurs tended to be less articulate (3 per cent of 107 top company articulators compared with 21 per cent of DBL top company heads), an unsurprising result which probably reflected typically single-minded concentrations on the firm;

(c) public appointments had a strong correlation with articulacy (59 per cent serving on quangoes, EDCs, local government etc, against 19 per cent), even more predictable given the elements of circularity, for example with public offices being held as a result of existing articulacy or memberships of NEDC, quangoes or public inquiries having obvious connections to articulacy in the peak organisations.

(5) Characteristics of core sample and ideological groupings

The following table shows some key characteristics of the core sample of 68 particularly articulate business leaders, also differentiated by main ideological tendency. The latter should be interpreted with care, bearing in mind the broad definitions used for our ideological categories, and in the light of the many qualifications and nuances on 'ideology' provided in the text of this book. For the revisionists the biggest linkages were with significant periods of work outside business (41 per cent), and status as CBI president or director general (51 per cent). There is a slight bias

Some characteristics of the core sample and its main ideological tendencies

	Total	Revision-ists	Liberation-ists	Reconstruc-tionists	Independ-ents
Totals	68	29	20	9	10
Managerial-corporate	58	29	16	7	6
Entrepreneurial	10	–	4	2	4
Small firm involvement	9	2	3	2	2
Heavy industry, capital goods	24	12	6	3	3
Consumer goods, distribution	24	10	7	3	4
Finance	8	1	3	1	3
Peak body major involvement					
– CBI	17	17	–	–	–
– BIM	4	3	–	1	
– IOD	9	–	7	–	2
Part outside business career	20	12	4	2	2
Significant activities in					
– politics	12	3	3	4	2
– religion	11	6	1	3	1
Wrote book/s	22	6	3	9	4

towards heavy industry, though the samples are too small for any statistical significance here, nor does the industry variable appear likely to be very important. For the liberationists the obvious linkage is with status as president or director general of the I O D (35 per cent), though it is worth noticing their rather greater sprinkling of people with links to small firms, entrepreneurship and finance. The small band of reconstructionists are distinguished both by non-involvement in the peak bodies and authorship of books, also with a hint of greater frequency of political or religious activity.

(6) Membership of core sample

Campbell Adamson	Nicholas Goodison
Hugh Beaver	George Goyder
Terence Beckett	Ronald Grierson
Lord (Henry) Benson	Lord (James) Hanson
Austin Bide	John Harvey-Jones
George Bolton	Jan Hildreth
Nigel Broackes	John Hoskyns
Lord (Ray) Brookes	Alex Jarratt
Stephen Brown	Lord (Frank) Kearton
Wilfred Brown	Lord (John) King
Adrian Cadbury	Norman Kipping
Lord Caldecote	Arthur Knight
Fred Catherwood	Lord (Hector) Laing
Paul Chambers	Maurice Laing
Lord Chandos	Leslie Lazell
Michael Clapham	Lord (Frank) MacFadzean
Roy Close	Ian MacGregor
Kenneth Corfield	John Methven
Nicholas Davenport	Jeremy Morse
John Davies	Richard O'Brien
Michael Edwardes	Peter Parker
Ronald Edwards	John Partridge
Lord (Frederick) Erroll	Lord (Ray)Pennock
Campbell Fraser	Lord (Edwin) Plowden
Lord (Derek) Ezra	George Pollock
Monty Finniston	Richard Powell
John Garnett	Denys Randolph
Reay Geddes	Lord (Alfred) Robens
James Goldsmith	Peter Runge
Walter Goldsmith	Basil Smallpiece

Peter Thompson   Siegmund Warburg
Charles Villiers   Viscount (Harold) Watkinson
Lord (Nigel) Vinson   Hugh Weeks
Peter Walters   Lord (Arnold) Weinstock

Endnotes

1 BUSINESS SOCIAL IDEAS IN THE MAKING

1 See appendix for details of sources, definitions and samples.
2 A unitary interpretation in Francis Sutton, Seymour Harris, K. Kaysen and James Tobin, *The American Business Creed*, Cambridge MA: Harvard University Press, 1962, related to the predominantly negative attitudes of US business towards the New Deal in the 1930s. But the phenomena of 'corporate liberalism' in the US from the late nineteenth century onwards have also been extensively discussed.
3 See Albert O. Hirschman, *Shifting Involvements, Private Interest and Public Action*, Oxford: Robertson, 1982.
4 For the concept of 'encompassingness', see Mancur Olson, *The Rise and Decline of Nations*, New Haven and London: Yale University Press, 1982.
5 For the idea of 'core concepts' in ideologies, see: M. Freeden, 'The Stranger at the Feast: Ideology and Public Policy in Twentieth Century Britain', *Twentieth Century British History*, 1,1 (1990) 9–34, and William Connolly, *The Terms of Political Discourse*, Princeton NJ: Princeton University Press 1984. For a more general view of ideology, see Martin Seliger, *Ideology and Politics*, London: Allen and Unwin, 1976. For *political* ideologies in modern Britain, see W. H. Greenleaf, *The British Political Tradition, II: The Ideological Heritage*, London: Routledge, 1983.
6 See John Child, *British Management Thought*, London: Allen and Unwin, 1969.
7 Oliver Marriott, *The Property Boom*, London: Hamish Hamilton, 1967; Jim Slater, *Return to Go, My Autobiography*, London: Weidenfeld & Nicolson, 1977; Ivan Fallon, *Billionaire, The Life and Times of Sir James Goldsmith*, London: Hutchinson, 1991; Tom Bower, *Tiny Rowland, A Rebel Tycoon*, London: Mandarin, 1993.
8 Leslie Lazell, *From Pills to Penicillin: The Beecham Story*, London: Heinemann, 1975; Maurice Corina, *Pile it High, Sell it Cheap, The Authorised Biography of Sir John Cohen, Founder of Tesco*, London: Weidenfeld & Nicolson, 1971; Nigel Broackes, *A Growing Concern*, London: Weidenfeld & Nicolson, 1979.
9 F. C. Hooper, *Management Survey*, London: Pitman & Son, 1948 and 2nd edn 1961; Ernest Bader, *From Profit Sharing to Common Ownership*, Wellingborough: Scott Bader Commonwealth, 1956.
10 'A Code of Business Ethics', Christian Association of Business Executives, 1972. St George's House, Windsor, Consultations on 'Business Ethics', 1967–74: SGW papers.

11 *The British Manufacturer* Oct. 1964, p. 5.
12 Lord (Oliver) Chandos,1893–1972: Conservative politician; Chair, AEI 1945–51, 1954–63, Pres. IOD 1948–51, 1954–1963; cr.1954. *Times* 27.1.72, and Chandos papers, Churchill College Cambridge, Boxes 4/17–20.
13 See Eric Wigham, *The Power to Manage: A History of the Engineering Employers' Federation*, London and Basingstoke: Macmillan, 1973.
14 'Conference on Industrial Relations', 1958: BEC archive. IWS annual reports. Report of Duke of Edinburgh's Study Conference on Human Relations in Industry, 1957. H. A. Clegg, *The System of Industrial Relations in Britain*, Oxford: Oxford University Press, 1970, pp. 163–8.
15 Norman Kipping, *Summing Up*, London: Hutchinson, 1972, pp. 89–90.
16 These economists are discussed in T. W. Hutchison, *Economics and Economic Policy 1946–66*, London: Allen and Unwin, 1968.
17 FBI *Annual Report 1959*.
18 *Scope*, Feb. 1955, p. 39.

2 AN ADAPTED, MODERATED CAPITALISM

1 Inaugural address to CBI 15.9.55; CBI London and SE Reg. Cl 18.11.65; Timber Trade Federation 2.3.66: CBI archive, Laing PP. *Times Review of Industry*, Dec. 1964.
2 This term is more useful than the narrower 'tripartism', since it can cover situations of business–labour bipartism, or more parties to the process (industry/ finance, consumer interests, professional groups etc); also more consistent with a frequent revisionist desideratum, a lesser degree of direct presence by government.
3 See P. C. Schmitter and G. Lehmbruch (eds.), *Trends towards Corporate Intermediation*, London: Sage, 1979, and *Patterns of Corporate Policy Making*, London: Sage, 1982.
4 G. Hodgson, *The Democratic Economy*, Harmondsworth: Penguin, 1984, p. 84. Jonathan Boswell, *Community and the Economy*, paperback edn, London: Routledge, 1994, pp. 65–70.
5 P. Devine, *Democracy and Economic Planning*, 1988. K. Nielsen, 'The Mixed Economy, the Neoliberal Challenge, and the Negotiated Economy', *Journal of Social Economics*, April 1992.
6 G. Lichtheim, *A Short History of Socialism*, London: Weidenfeld & Nicolson, 1970, pp. 184–5, 246, 253. D. Miller (ed.), *The Blackwell Encylopaedia of Political Thought*, Oxford: Blackwell Reference, 1991, pp. 436, 482.
7 Conventional business history's blind spots on both politics and social ideas are evident in the *Dictionary of Business Biography* entries for most of the leaders covered in this chapter.
8 Keynes' fleeting vision of a publicly orientated firm in 'The End of Laissez-faire' was left hanging in the air. The abstract moral values he invoked were aimed at reformist political rulers and a future 'post-economic society', not at current economic operators or changes in economic organisation.
9 Jean Monnet, *Memoirs*, London: Collins, 1978, and see R. Kuisel, *Capitalism and the State in Modern France*, Cambridge: Cambridge University Press, 1981. But some revisionists admired Monnet and his ideas.

10 P. Drucker, *The Practice of Management,* London: Heinemann, 1955. Alfred Mond, *Industry and Politics,* London: Macmillan, 1928.

11 The following material compares twenty-one revisionist-orientated business leaders with twenty-four from other tendencies in the 1960s and 1970s. See appendix for samples and their characteristics.

12 Beaver: Director General, Ministry of Works 1940–45. Kipping: Ministry of Production and Board of Trade 1942–46. Weeks: Ministries of Supply 1939–42 and Production 1942–45, and deputy to Chief Planning Officer, Economic Planning Board, 1947–48. Plowden: Chief Planning Officer, Economic Planning Board, 1947–53. Shone: Ministry of Supply 1940–45.

13 S. Blank, *Industry and Government in Britain: The FBI in Politics 1945–66,* Farnborough, Hants: Dordrecht Publications 1973, pp. 48, 70. Kipping, *Summing Up,* 1972, pp. 10–11, 14. E. Plowden, *An Industrialist in the Treasury,* London: André Deutsch, 1989. Interview with John Whitehorn.

14 Beaver: Pres. FBI 1957–9. Kipping: Director General FBI 1946–65. Weeks: Chair, FBI/CBI Economic Committees 1957–72. Geddes: long active in FBI and CBI. Pollock: Director General BEC 1955–65. Laing: Pres. BEC 1963–65 and CBI 1965–66. Runge: EC Industrial Welfare Society 1950–56 Chair, FBI London and SE Reg. Cl 1958–60, Pres. FBI 1963–65. Shone: Director British Iron and Steel Federation 1950–1961.

15 Kipping, *Summing Up,* p. 58.

16 Blank, *Industry and Government in Britain,* provides a very useful (though sometimes rather uncritical) narrative background on the FBI. Wyn Grant and David Marsh, *The CBI,* London: Hodder & Stoughton, 1977, based mainly on secondary sources, gives less emphasis than Blank to business ideas and ideology, while providing a helpful general account of the CBI's membership, administrative structure and representational role up to 1976.

17 For revisionist views at this time, independently of the peak bodies, see for example HOL debs: Lord Baillieu, 25.10.60, and Lord Melchett, 14.6.61.

18 Kipping, *Summing Up,* pp. 19, 20, 29–30, 49. Once asked about a suitable 'platform' for a policy idea, Kipping advised: ' it would make a good speech . . . unless you're serious, in which case I'll tell you who to see'. Interview with Sir Reay Geddes.

19 Kipping, *Summing Up,* pp. 19, 20, 21, 29, 30, 41, 48.

20 *Summing Up,* pp. 106–7. Theses of over-taxation or excessive welfare were discounted in PEP, *Growth in the British Economy,* 1960. Free market arguments on these fronts would find few echoes at the NIESR or the Department of Applied Economics at Cambridge, with which some revisionists had contact.

21 FBI/CBI Cl minutes include annual discussions of budget representations, both before and after. Minutes of Economics and Budget committees, though patchier, are often helpful.

22 Alfred Robens (NCB) and Richard Beeching (BR) were widely admired. Correspondence Mar. 1963, K. Johnson, C. Howe and N. Kipping, FBI archive. Director General to CBI Cl 17.11.65, and Cl 15.12.65. *Summing Up,* p. 17. Cl 16.2.66, 21.6.66. Report to Cl on Transport Policy, May 1967.

23 CBI Evidence to Fulton Committee, paper to Cl, Nov. 1966, and discussion 16.11.66.

24 Committee on Economic Programmes and Targets (CEPT), 13.6.61, and

report to Grand Cl: FBI archive. Report of EcC on Public Expenditure to CBI Cl, May 1967, and on Public Expenditure on Education, June 1969.

25 Group 1 included leading financiers and the economists Graham Hutton, Alan Peacock, Arthur Seldon and Harold Wincott. Group 3 included economists R. J. Brech, Duncan Burn and Colin Clark. Other groups produced little of note. No overall report emerged.

26 Report to Delegates on 'The Next 5 Years Conference', Brighton, Dec. 1960: FBI archive. Henceforth 'Brighton Conference 1960'.

27 J. C. R. Dow, *The Management of the British Economy, 1945–60*, Cambridge: Cambridge University Press, 1964. PEP, *Growth in the British Economy*, London: Allen and Unwin, 1960. S. Brittan, *The Treasury under the Tories 1951–1964*, Harmondsworth: Pelican, 1964. A. Shonfield, *British Economic Policy since the War*, Harmondsworth: Penguin, 1958. M. Shanks, *The Stagnant Society*, Harmondsworth: Pelican, 1961. *The Robert Hall Diaries*, ed. Alec Cairncross, vol. 2 1954–61, London: Unwin-Hyman, 1991, pp. 256–7.

28 FBI, 'Britain's Economic Performance and Problems', 1957, see ch 1. P. Mathias, 'Unpublished History of the FBI', CBI archive. Brittan *The Treasury under the Tories*, pp. 215–22. Blank, *Industry and Government*, pp. 148, 152. Kipping, *Summing Up*, pp. 85, 95–6. H. Weeks in Economic Studies Committee (ESC) 29.7.63, FBI archive.

29 Brittan, *The Treasury under the Tories*, p. 216. An admirer of Keynes, Monnet and Franks, Weeks developed the FBI/CBI Industrial Trends surveys, enlisted a wide circle of (mostly corporate) economists, and held strong beliefs behind a front of urbane pragmatism. Later, he vigorously contested 'monetarism' in *Economic Comments 1979–85*, London: Leopold Joseph and Sons Ltd, n.d.

30 Reay Geddes, 1912– , Pres. SMMT 1958–59; NEDC 1962–65; Chair Dunlop 1968–78. Address to Inst. of Transport, 2.2.60. Pre-consulted about this 'balloon', Rowan was encouraging and later Geddes was 'grilled' on it by Frank Lee and Denis Robertson of the Treasury. Interview with Sir Reay Geddes.

31 Hugh Beaver, 1890–1967, Managing Director Guinness 1946–60; Pres. FBI 1957–59. His public activities had included work on power stations, air pollution and new towns: *Dictionary of Business Biography*. Brittan *The Treasury under the Tories*, p. 218. Blank, *Industry and Government*, p. 153.

32 Kipping had a reputation for spotting 'promising younger progressives' and, less infallibly, for 'getting the FBI Presidents he wanted'. Interviews with Sir Maurice Laing and Sir Reay Geddes.

33 CEPT, 20.2.61, 8.3.61, 14.3.61, 27.3.61, 19.4.61, 26.5.61, 13.6.61; Rowan to Beaver 24.3.61; 'Draft proposals, Long-term Planning': FBI archive. Themes included feasible growth rates (*c.* 3 per cent), trade-offs (mostly viewed favourably) with anti-inflation and the balance of payments, and national tripartite organisation (anticipating the NEDC). Government views at this time were regarded as 'less progressive'.

34 Discussions on the Labour government's import surcharge, for example, suggest a lack of background analysis: CEAC 9.11.64, FBI archive.

35 Lord (Edwin) Plowden, 1907– , Chair, AEA 1953–59; Chair, TI 1963–76; cr. 1959. HOL debs, 3.8.61. He felt business was politically unaware on the

EEC, over-emphasising the 'free trade' aspect: interview with Lord Plowden. A pragmatic revisionist and classic 'insider', he would be cautious on 'indicative planning' (CBI Eastbourne Conference, 'The Next 5 Years', Jan. 1965) and would later become a key adviser at critical points in the CBI's affairs.

36 The FBI ESC's discussions on RPM were inconclusive: 6.4.64 and 30.7.64, FBI archive. Discussions on tax policy: CEPT, 19.4.61, and Report to Cl, 'Balance of Fiscal System', June 1961. Report of Working Party on Indirect Taxation, Sept. 1963, and Cl, 11.9.63.

37 Adoption came, unenthusiastically, after Brighton: CEPT 26.5.61. Anglo-French planning discussions, Jouy-en-Josas, 27–29 April 1962 (including Kipping, Geddes, Shone, Laing) included emphasis on the limited applicability of French-type planning to the more internationally orientated UK. Laing expressed the political fears to Ernest Harrison, 24.11.61: Harrison PP.

38 Harrison to FBI members, 20.9.61: Harrison PP. He was as upbeat about 'planning' in private correspondence as in his public speeches. Shenfield: CEPT 19.4.61.

39 Geddes, Institute of Transport, 2.2.60. Kipping at Anglo-French discussions, see note 37 above.

40 K. Middlemas, *Power, Competition and the State*, vol. 1 1940–61, Basingstoke: Macmillan, 1986, provides an indispensable overview.

41 *Power, Competition and the State*, II. F. Blackaby (ed.), *British Economic Policy 1960–1974*, Cambridge: Cambridge University Press, 1978. Also K. Hawkins, *British Industrial Relations 1945–75*, London: Barrie and Jenkins, 1976.

42 Industrial Welfare Society, annual reports. Hugh Clegg, *The System of Industrial Relations in Britain*, Oxford: Oxford University Press, 1972, and Howard Gospel, *Markets, Firms and the Management of Labour in Modern Britain*, Cambridge: Cambridge University Press, 1992. Interviews with Sir Maurice Laing and Sir Richard O'Brien. See also ch 5.

43 Conservative attitudes repeatedly emerge in BEC General Purposes Committee (GPC) minutes 1955–60: BEC archive. In 1955 Pollock had sought talks with the TUC on dividends and prices alongside wages but came unstuck partly because of FBI suspicions that he was invading their ground: Blank, *Industry and Government*, p. 131.

44 Wigham, *The Power to Manage*, 1973, pp. 190–2, 208–9. Interview with Sir Stephen Brown.

45 Hunter, Chair of Swan Hunter, previously Pres. of the Shipbuilding Employers' Federation, countered conservative influences in the BEC and was later on the NEDC and the BR board and first Chairman of the Central Training Council. BEC archive: *Dictionary of Business Biography.*

46 BEC Working Party on Employer–TU Relationships, 1959–61; Reports to BEC Cl, 'Prices, Productivity and Incomes', June 1961, and 'Conference on Collective Bargaining', July 1961; Cl 26.7.61, 27.10.62, 23.1.63; GPC 12.5.61, 14.11.62: BEC archive.

47 BEC Cl 25.7.62, 23.1.63, 22.4.64; GPC 12.7.62, 2.10.62, 31.1.63, 25.9.63, 18.10.63, 2.4.64: BEC archive.

48 Lord Sanderson and E. M. Amphett to Pollock 11.4.61; M. Laing and some others, BEC Cl 25.7.62; GPC 3.8.61, 19.1.62, 23.2.62; D. Taylor in NEDC Liaison Committee 26.6.63. BEC archive.

49 Kipping was a veteran tripartist; Beaver had proposed some reciprocal restraint on prices in 1957 (*Industry and Government*, p. 150); Weeks had hinted at dividend or price restraint and encouraged discussion, with mixed results: FBI EcC 21.6.61, 16.11.62, 10.9.63, 30.10.63.

50 But the NABM had been sceptical. Meetings FBI, BEC, ABCC and NABM on Incomes Policy 11.12.63, FBI archive. Paper on Incomes Policy 11.12.63, and notes on same meetings, BEC archive.

51 Cockfield's plan, urged as less *dirigiste*, found some BEC support but Weeks and others saw it as too weighted against profits and felt price review would be more acceptable to government and more saleable to the FBI Cl. Further FBI discussions on price review produced no firm proposals to Cl: ESC 20.1.64, 29.1.64, 21.2.64, and Note to Governing Body 11.5.64. The BEC leaders, if anything more ahead of their colleagues, also had to backtrack: M. Laing to P. Runge, 3.4.64 and Runge's reply 8.4.64: 'Incomes Policy', BEC archive.

52 Peter Runge, 1909–1970, Tate and Lyle 1931, Joint Vice Chair 1958; Pres. FBI 1963–65; Chair Industrial Society 1966–69, obit. *Times* 21.8.70. Runge at FBI AGM 15.4.64: FBI archive, Runge PP.

53 Maurice Laing, 1918– , John Laing, Chair, 1976–82; Pres., BEC 1964–65; Pres., CBI 1965–66. Interview with Sir Maurice Laing. BEC archive. Speeches at TUC Summer School 27.7.59, SW Lancs Productivity Association 20.4.61, Clacton 15.11.63, Glass Makers' Federation 30.11.65, and 'Reminiscences on Life', 19.4.94. The one cited was at CBI London and SE Reg. Cl, 18.11.65.

54 *Summing Up*, p. 83.

55 Brighton Conference 1960; Geddes in Anglo-French Planning Discussions 1962 (Harrison PP); Kipping in BEC–FBI Liaison Group, 27.9.63, BEC archive, Laing in *The Director*, April 1964.

56 Brighton Conference 1960; CEPT 20.2.61 and 26.5.61; Harrison to FBI AGM 9.4.63 (Harrison PP); and statements by Laing, see note 53 above.

57 John Davies at CBI Cl 15.2.67; Cl paper, 'Industrial Management and the Next 2 Years', Feb 1968, and Cl 21.2.68: CBI archive.

58 CBI Cl 20.10.65, 16.3.66, 20.4.66, 19.10.66. Acceptance of legislation on industrial training Cl 17.7.68, and industrial health and safety, Cl 21.2.68. Restrictive practices: Economic Studies Committee 6.4.64, 30.7.64.

59 For example, Brighton Conference 1960, Group 3 on good labour relations as primarily a management responsibility.

60 Kipping in FBI PAC, 9.5.63; Harrison on 'too many trade associations and too narrow in their function' (Harrison PP 9.4.63); Davies at CBI Cl 18.12.68 and on 'excessive fragmentation' and 'extraordinary criss-cross tangle' (farewell speech 19.11.69, Cl papers). For opposition to compulsory reorganisation: Cl 15.12.65, and see ch. 5. The organisational background is analysed in Grant and Marsh, *The CBI*, pp. 55–72.

3   BUSINESS AND THE LABOUR GOVERNMENT 1964–1970

1 Austen Albu, 'The Organisation of Industry' in Richard Crossman (ed.), *New Fabian Essays*, London: Turnstile Press, 1952, pp. 138–41. Similar viewpoints were expressed in essays by Anthony Crosland and Roy Jenkins. Anthony Crosland, *The Future of Socialism*, London: Jonathan Cape 1956, p. 64.

2 See ch. 6. For Crosland's scepticism, see *The Future of Socialism*, p. 357.

3 Earlier nationalisation proposals, though remaining theoretical, would have set up resistances in firms like ICI and from men like Peter Runge of Tate and Lyle. The 'Frognal set' around Gaitskell did not extend contacts to mainstream corporate business: relations with Oliver Franks and Plowden were of a different nature. Equally, none of the 'Brighton generation' seems to have had contact with Labour leaders in opposition. Interviews with Sir Reay Geddes, Sir Fred Catherwood, Sir Maurice Laing, Edmund Dell.

4 Aubrey Jones papers, Boxes 4/47, 4/133, include examples of names bandied back and forth in connection with NBPI membership, where there were difficulties in recruiting suitable figures especially from the City. On the recruitment of industrial advisers: Fred Catherwood, *At the Cutting Edge*, London: Stodder & Houghton, 1995, p. 53.

5 Fred Catherwood, 1925– , Managing Director British Aluminium 1960–62; Chief Industrial Adviser, DEA 1964–66, Director General NEDO 1966–71; Chief Executive, J. Laing and Son 1972–74; Chair, BIM 1974–76; MEP 1979–94. *At the Cutting Edge; The Christian in Industrial Society*, London: Tyndale Press, 1964; *Britain with the Brakes Off*, 1965. Donald MacDougall, *Don and Mandarin*, London: Murray, 1987, pp. 150–1.

6 Fallon, *Billionaire, The Life and Times of Sir James Goldsmith*, p. 215. Lord Young, *The Enterprise Years*, London: Headline, 1990, p. 14.

7 For Brown, see ch. 6. Interviews with Aubrey Jones, Edmund Dell, Sir Richard O'Brien, Grigor McClelland. For Warburg see Jacques Attali, *A Man of Influence*, London: Weidenfeld & Nicolson, 1986. Stokes, initially quite favourable to the government, had begun to back off by mid-1966: see *The Director*, Nov. 1964, June 1966. Ben Pimlott, *Harold Wilson*, London: HarperCollins, 1992, pp. 632, 687, 700, 707–8, 725.

8 Lord (Frank) Kearton, 1911–1992, Courtaulds Managing Director 1957, Chair 1964–75; Chair IRC 1966–68; Chair BNOC 1976–79. *Times* 16.10.65, 12.1.66, 27.10.66, 30.11.67. Speech to Bradford Textile Society, 'Size and Efficiency in Business', 10.1.66 (lent by Sir Norman Wooding). Kearton's 'baleful/sweetly considerate' contrast: D. C. Coleman, *Courtaulds*, 3 (1980), 317–19. Douglas Jay, later a Courtaulds director, portrays Kearton in *Change and Fortune*, 1980, pp. 445–9.

9 Melchett was grandson of the industrialist/politician Alfred Mond, a tripartist advocate: HOL debs, 25.10.60, 14.6.61, 5.11.64. Ronald Grierson, *A Truant Disposition*, London: Weidenfeld & Nicolson, 1992. For Villiers, see ch. 6.

10 Wyn Grant and David Marsh, *The CBI*, London: Hodder & Stoughton 1977, pp. 25–27. Herbert Bowden proclaimed the government's view to the first full CBI Cl 15.9.65. Interview with the late Lord Benson.

11 Laing; *The Director*, Nov. 1964; *Times Review of Industry*, Dec. 1964; address to CBI Cl 21.9.66.

12 Wigham, *The Power to Manage,* pp. 113–16. Interviews with Sir Stephen Brown and Sir Gerry Norman.

13 John Davies, 1916–1979, Vice-Chair Shell-Mex 1961–65, Director General CBI 1965–69; MP 1970; Ministry of Technology 1970, Secretary of State, Trade and Industry 1970–72. This view of Davies draws on the CBI archive and numerous interviews.

14 The Statement is reprinted in Brittan, *Steering the Economy,* p. 204. Meetings, business representatives and George Brown, 12.11.64, 1.12.64, Runge PP; Runge and Kipping to FBI Grand Cl 15.12.64; Runge to membership 4.1.65: FBI archive.

15 Runge to Brown 8.4.65 Runge PP, and speech to Cl 9.4.65. Kipping, Beaver, Davies and Runge had all written very positively to Jones. Runge observed: 'There is a great deal of support for what you are trying to do but it is the contrary view which is more vocal': Jones papers, Churchill College, Cambridge: 20.3.65 (4/135), 19.3.65, 17.6.65 (4/47).

16 CBI Cl 20.10.65. Laing to SW Reg. Cl 18.11.65: Laing: PP. Davies to LSAC 27.4.66 for strength of top-level CBI support.

17 CBI Cl 3.8.66, 21.9.66, 19.10.66,1.9.66. Senior critics like Lord Sinclair had been effectively muffled: FBI PAC 12.12.64. Later critics included former NABM stalwarts, Mayer, Luke, Robson.

18 Laing, arguing for support for the 'July measures', had described it as the 'worst financial crisis since the War': Cl 20.7.66.

19 CBI Cl 18.2.67, 19.4.67, 18.10.67; LSAC rept on 'PIP after June 1967', Feb. 1967.

20 CBI EcC 5.11.68, 7.1.69, 1.4.69, 3.6.69 for discussions of monetary policy.

21 Laing to membership 4.8.66: Laing PP. 'Industrial Management and the Next 2 Years', Feb. 1968, Cl papers. Cl 17.1.68, 21.2.68, 20.3.68. 'PIP after 1969', Feb. 1969, Cl papers.

22 Cl 21.1.70. Notes for CBI meeting with Barbara Castle, 16.2.70 (Norman PP).

23 FBI ESC 20.11.64, 29.6.65. Group 2, 'Planning': *Next 5 Years Conference,* Jan. 1965; FBI EcC papers.

24 For CBI's initial rejection, see Middlemas, *Industry, Unions and Government,* Basingstoke: Macmillan, 1983, pp. 50–1. Meeting with George Brown, 12.11.64, and later, CBI, TUC and DEA 1.1.66: Brown PP.

25 Cl 4.8.65, EcC 8.12.65.

26 Meeting CBI, TUC and DEA, 1.1.66: Brown PP.

27 EcC 31.1.67, 12.4.67, 1.8.67, 31.10.67, 2.4.68. Cl 21.2.68. Brown to Advertising Association, 2.4.68, sums up the official line on economic policy at this time: Brown PP.

28 Interviews with Sir Maurice Laing, Sir Stephen Brown, Sir Gerry Norman, Sir Donald MacDougall.

29 Cl 17.1.68. The Industrial Expansion Act's *dirigiste* flavour differed from the government's other industrial measures: Andrew Graham, 'Industry Policy', in W. Beckerman, *The Labour Government's Economic Record,* London: Duckworth, 1972, pp. 195–6.

30 EcC 6.12.66, 3.1.67, 12.4.67. John Davies to Stephen Brown, 26.1.67: Brown PP. 'Industrial Management in the Next 2 Years', Feb. 1968, Cl

16.4.69. F. Blackaby (ed), *Economic Policy 1960–1974*, Cambridge: Cambridge University Press, 1978, for position of corporate profitability in these years.

31 EcC 5.11.68, 7.1.69, discussion of Bracewell Milnes' papers on monetary policy. Similar ideas were being discussed in the Industrial Policy Group, see ch. 4.

32 Cl 18.10.67, Stephen Brown, speech to Scientific Instrument Manufacturers' Association, 16.11.67: Brown PP. EcC 31.10.67, 27.11.67, 5.8.69, 2.9.69, 6.10.69, 31.3.70.

33 *Industry and Government* (George Earle memorial lecture 1967), and CBI paper 'Industrial Management: The Next Two Years'.

34 Davies, memo for meeting with Jenkins 15.12.67; Brown to Manchester Bankers' Institute, 25.3.68: Brown PP. Reactions to Budgets: Cl 20.3.68, 16.4.69.

35 EcC 3.1.67, 31.1.67, 2.5.67 4.7.67; Cl 17.5.67, 6.12.67: see also ch. 5.

36 See ch. 1.

37 Howard Gospel, *Markets, Firms and the Management of Labour in Modern Britain*, Cambridge: Cambridge Univerity Press, 1992. Alfred Robens, *Ten Year Stint*, London: Cassell, 1972.

38 Eric Wigham, *Strikes and the Government*, London: Macmillan, 1976; Kevin Hawkins, *British Industrial Relations 1945–1975*, London: Barrie and Jenkins, 1976.

39 Cl 15.9.65, 20.10.65, 15.12.65 for discussions of the LSAC's work.

40 CBI's written and oral evidence to Royal Commission on Trades Unions and Employers' Associations, *Minutes of Evidence*, henceforth Donovan Commission; 23.11.65, 7.12.65 8.2.66.

41 Cl 15.12.65. The evidence was given by Laing, Davies, Norman Sloan and Kenneth Allen: opening statement to the Commission Q.s 980–981.

42 *Minutes of Evidence*, esp Q.s 3232, 3243, 3307, 3345.

43 *Minutes of Evidence*, Q.s 3307, 3390 for differences with the EEF.

44 See ch. 4 for liberationist views in the Industrial Policy Group. Cl 15.11.67.

45 LEPAS: legally enforceable procedure agreements, supported as a key union reform by militants and by the old BEC element. For CBI's shifting position: Stephen Brown, *Minutes of Evidence*, Q.11243.

46 The Final Report of the Donovan Commission said little about industrial unions or reforming employers' associations. For the criticisms of Donovan at the time, see Denis Barnes and Eileen Reid, *Government and Trade Unions*, London: Heinemann, 1980.

47 Reaction to the Final Report was muted, Cl 16.4.69, 18.9.69. Meeting CBI and Barbara Castle, 12.12.69: Norman PP. For Samuel Beer's analysis, see *Britain Against Itself*, London: Faber & Faber, 1982.

48 Cl 19.2.69 16.4.69, 18.2.70, memo on Industrial Relations 11.7.69; meeting CBI and Castle 10.11.69; 12.12.69, notes for meeting with Castle 16.2.70; Norman to Castle 3.3.69: Norman PP.

49 Cl 15.9.65, 20.10.65, 17.11.65, 20.7.66, 3.8.66, 21.9.66, 19.10.66, 1.11.66, 15.2.67, 15.11.67, 17.1.68. The criticisms came from a small number on Council. Most of the weightier exponents of free market viewpoints were to be found elsewhere: see ch. 4.

50 Cl 15.9.65, 20.10.65, 1.11.66, 20.7.66, 3.8.66, 19.10.66, 15.2.67, 17.1.68.

4 LIBERATIONIST CAPITALISM IN THE WILDERNESS 1960–1975

1 Lazell: *Growth Through Industry*, IEA, 1967. Bolton: *Times*, 4.5.67.
2 Paul Chambers, 1904–1981, Inland Revenue; Indian Civil Service; Control Commission in Germany; ICI 1948, Chair, 1960–1968; Pres., IOD 1964–68. *Business, Economists and Government*, IEA, 1965, p. 15.
3 George Bolton, 1900–1982, Bank of England head of international dealings; IMF; Chair, Bank of London and South America 1957–1970; H. G. 'Leslie' Lazell, 1903–1982, Chair Beechams 1958–68, author of *From Pills to Penicillin*, London: Heinemann, 1975; Halford Reddish, 1898–1978, Chair, Rugby Cement 1939–1976: 'his passionate defence of free enterprise made the IOD ... look like the Left Book Club', obit. *Times* 14.10.78.
4 Lord (Frank) MacFadzean, 1915–1992, Colonial Development Corporation; Shell 1952, Chair, 1972–76, Chair, British Airways 1976–79, Rolls-Royce 1979–83; cr. 1980; obit. *Daily Telegraph* 27.5.92. *Galbraith and the Planners*, Glasgow: University of Strathclyde, 1968; *The Economics of J. K. Galbraith*, London: Centre for Policy Studies, 1977; and essay in Israel Kirzner *et al.*, *The Prime Mover of Progress*, IEA, 1980.
5 Lord (Nigel) Vinson 1931– , Founder and Chair, Plastic Coatings 1952–72; Chair, Industrial Participation Association 1971–78; Deputy Chair, CBI SFC 1979–84; cr. 1985. (Co-author) *Why Britain Needs a Social Market Economy*, London: Centre for Policy Studies 1975; *Industrial Participation*, summer 1978.
6 The phrase is Ronald Grierson's, *A Truant Disposition*, p. 53.
7 Cited in R. Lewis and R. Stewart, *The Boss*, London: J. M. Dent and Sons, 1958, p. 168.
8 IOD Cl 2.12.70: IOD archive.
9 *Times* 27.6.68.
10 Lazell, *Growth Through Industry*, 1967. MacFadzean, 'Foreword' to John Jewkes, *A Return to Free Market Economics*, London: Macmillan 1978, p. ix.
11 Grierson, *A Truant Disposition*, p. 33.
12 Lord Drogheda, *Double Harness*, London: Weidenfeld & Nicolson, 1978, p. 184. Institute of Directors, *Nationalisation*, London, 1958, p. 14.
13 *A Truant Disposition*, pp. 7–9, 10.
14 Harry Miller, *The Way of Enterprise*, London: André Deutsch, 1963, p. 232.
15 *A Truant Disposition*, p. 107.
16 *A Truant Disposition*, p. 97, 109: he was as scathing of the performance of business leaders in the IRC as he was of the government's role.
17 Denys Randolph, speech to IOD annual convention 1978: Randolph file.
18 Edward Lewis (Chair of Decca), *Growth through Industry*, p. 144; Ray Brookes, *The Director*, Oct. 1968.
19 Graham Hutton, *Politics and Economic Growth*, London: Institute of Economic Affairs, 1968, pp. 2–3.
20 For example, the IEA collections, *Growth through Industry*, *The Prime Mover of Progress*.
21 MacFadzean, 'Market Forces and Those who Foretell the Future', *World Economy*, 4.1 (1981).

22 Chambers, *Economics, Business and Governments*: 'It is utterly wrong to . . . persuade people to do something in the national interest which by inference you say is against their own interest.'

23 IOD *Annual Report* 1962.

24 Chambers, MacFadzean and Edwards had been educated at the LSE when anti-Keynesian influences were strong there, and Chambers remained close to Robbins and his views.

25 *Britain's Economic Problems and Policies*, FBI, 1957. Group 1, FBI Brighton Conference 1960. *Scope*, Oct. 1959. *Times* 25.1.60, IOD convention 1961, *Times* 5.2.63, 8.3.67. Chambers had chaired an internal Conservative Party committee on economic growth in 1961/2 whose report appears to have been cautious and non-innovative on macro-economic policy: Jim Tomlinson, 'The British Economy in the Postwar Years', *Review of Economic History*, November 1966.

26 CBI EcC 5.12.67, 5.11.68: CBI archive.

27 IOD, *Denationalisation*, 1958.

28 Spears, an Edenite anti-appeaser during the 1930s, had acted as Churchill's main contact with de Gaulle and the Free French.

29 Drogheda, *Double Harness*, p. 183. IOD annual reports. This view of Powell owes much to interviews with people who knew him.

30 For Chandos, see Ch. 1. PEC and Council members in the 1950s and 1960s included Ian Lyle of Tate and Lyle and AOI, Lord Boyd (ex-Conservative Cabinet Minister), Lord Drogheda of the *Financial Times*, one of the Institute's few 'liberals', Col. W. H. Whitbread, Nicholas Cayzer, John Baring, David Wolfson of Great Universal Stores, and Charles Wheeler of AEI.

31 By 1974, out of 44,457 members, those overseas were declared as 8,466, including 3,159 in Australia: IOD Cl 4.6.74. There had been *c.* 600 members in Rhodesia in 1969: Cl. 9.9.69. Mr Vorster, PM of the Republic of South Africa, was made a Life Honorary Fellow: IOD Cl 1.3.72.

32 Interview with Alan Davies. In *Annual Report 1970*, the Taxation Committee proposed income tax be reduced long term to a two-tier 50/25 per cent rate.

33 Cl 3.10.61 and PEC 16.10.61: although hostile to 'socialist forms of planning', the IOD decided to remain publicly neutral on the new NEDC. IOD archive.

34 IOD Cl 28.7.64. Drogheda, *Double Harness*, p. 182.

35 The only account is John Jewkes' partisan post-mortem, 'Entrepreneurs on the Defensive: The Industrial Policy Group', in *A Return to Free Market Economics*, pp. 170–91.

36 The *Times* 12.10.67 saw its formation as indicating discontent with the CBI Economic Committee.

37 Papers 1–3, on macro-economic policy, taxation and public expenditure, owed much to the IPG steering group which, apart from Chambers, included Lazell, Joseph Lockwood, David Barran and Lord Boyd – all of basically similar outlook.

38 The similarities were unsurprising since the IPG and FBI documents were all originally drafted by Shenfield.

39 For example, John Partridge to Chambers 6.7.67; Steering Committee 3.7.68, 6.1.69 for revisionist attempts to modify liberationist proposals in draft papers: CBI DG's papers. *Britain's Economic Performance*, pp. 7, 14–15, 18.

40 The draft paper on taxation had gone even further in attacking the principle of progressive taxation. Revisionist members insisted on its dilution as well as cutting proposals to abandon investment incentives. IPG meetings 3.7.68, 6.1.69: CBI DG's papers.

41 This aroused early CBI suspicions: John Davies to Paul Chambers, 22.12.67: CBI DG's papers.

42 The IPG chairman Arnold Hall concluded that 'no compromise was possible' on the paper, IPG meeting 9.3.72. IPG papers: Boleat.

43 Meeting 6.2.73. Monetarist sympathisers included Arnold Hall and Ralph Bateman, a future CBI President, but Plowden, Woodroofe (Unilever) and Page (Metal Box) were critics of 'monetarist' policies. Jewkes, 'Achievements and Failures of the IPG 29.10.73', suggesting reasons for non-publication of the inflation paper, on which Alan Walters had advised. IPG papers: Boleat.

44 Davies to Chambers, 27.12.67; John Partridge at IPG meeting 15.2.68. CBI DG's papers.

45 Members disliked the idea of appearing on TV to criticise the unions 'for fear of upsetting the workers and aggravating the situation', meeting 26.2.73: IPG papers: Boleat.

46 Letters to Shenfield from Runge, 29.5.69, Laing, 29.5.69, Partridge, 29.4.68, Geddes, 29.5.69: CBI DG's papers.

47 Discussions on inflation, Jan.–Feb. 1973. IPG papers: Boleat.

48 Discussions on inflation with individual industrialists, Jan.–Feb. 1973. IPG papers: Boleat.

5   THE PEAKS AND PRECIPICES OF REVISIONISM
    1969–1974

1 Campbell Adamson, 1922– , RTB; DEA 1967–69; Director General CBI 1969–76; Chair, Abbey National 1978–89. His views emerge in CBI Cl, EC and EPC minutes; more freely, sometimes, in the Partridge and Clapham PP, and Swinden Papers 1972–76. *Times* 13.5.71, 25.5.71, 24.9.71, 10.12.71, 23.3.72, 9.6.72, 29.6.72, 22.5.73. Interview with Sir Campbell Adamson.

2 John Partridge, 1908–1982, Imperial Tobacco 1923, Chair, 1964–75; Pres., CBI 1970–72. *The Director*, July 1966; *Times* 24.2.71, 18.5.72. Speeches: 'The Moral Problems of Our Industrial Society', 14. 4.51; William Temple College, 18.5.57; 'Some Problems of the Under-Developed Countries', 25.4.61; 'Management in the Future', 6.6.64; 'Co-partnership and the Industrial Scene', 20.4.66. Also 'British Industry and the New Policy', 9.5.73, and 'Industry and Society', 7.1.74. Partridge papers.

3 Michael Clapham, 1912– , ICI 1938, Chair, Metals Division 1959, Deputy Chair, ICI 1968–74; Pres., CBI 1972–74; Deputy Chair, Lloyds Bank 1974–80. 'Multinational Enterprises and Nation States', Stamp Memorial Lecture 26.11.74. Interview with Sir Michael Clapham.

4 Speeches at CBI London and SE Reg. Cl 1.2.73, and Cardiff Business Club, 'Business and Government: Co-operation or Conflict ?', 19.3.73. Notes for Junior Carlton Society 25.3.74. Speech at CBI annual dinner 14.5.74. CBI archive, Clapham PP.

5 Cardiff Business Club 19.3.73; CBI annual dinner 14.5.74; Industrial

Society conference 5.1.73; CBI S. Reg Cl 7.6.73, including 'prejudices on employee participation'; FPA 28.3.73; Notes for Conservative Finance Committee lunch 1.8.72: CBI annual dinner 15.5.73; and British American Chamber of Committee 13.2.74: Clapham PP. Clapham to Heath 10.10.72 urging 'a direct communication from you to the nation and to every company and trade union leader, supported by CBI and TUC': Swinden papers.

6 Richard O'Brien, 1920– , BMC 1961–66; DEA 1966–68; Delta Metal 1968–76; Chair, CBI EPC 1971–76; Chair, MSC 1976–82. Written evidence to Donovan Commission (ref: WE/303) 1967. 'Social and Economic Policy: A Package', u/d 1972; 'More Thoughts on a Failure', 24.11.72; O'Brien to E. J. Robertson (D 196 misplaced) and A. Swinden 2.7.74 and 4.7.74; and Note on Oral Evidence of CBI to Royal Commission on Distribution of Incomes and Wealth 3.4.75: Swinden papers.

7 For Watkinson, see ch. 7.

8 *The Director*, Dec 1972: 70 per cent of a sample of company chairs agreed the govt 'had abandoned its free market objectives', with some openly critical, though A. W. Pearce of Esso and the banker J. O. Blair-Cunynghame were more benign. Two anonymous chairmen associated too much doctrine at the start with an excessive counter-swing by 1972.

9 The best overall accounts: K. Middlemas, *Power, Competition and the State*, vol. 2, 1961–74, Basingstoke: Macmillan, 1990, and John Campbell, *Edward Heath*, London: Jonathan Cape, 1993. For the Conservative controversies: Martin Holmes, *Political Pressure and Economic Policy: British Government 1970–74*, London: Butterworth, 1982; J. Bruce-Gardyne, *Whatever Happened to the Quiet Revolution?*, London: Charles Knight, 1974; Ralph Harris and Brendon Sewill, *British Economic Policy 1970–74, Two Views*, London: Institute of Economic Affairs, 1975. For the economy: Blackaby (ed.), *British Economic Policy 1960–74*.

10 Eric Silver, *Victor Feather TUC*, London: Victor Gollancz 1973; Jack Jones, *Union Man*, London: Collins, 1986. Allan Flanders, *Management and the Unions*, London: Faber & Faber, 1970; Eric Wigham, *Strikes and the Government*, London: Macmillan, 1976; Kevin Hawkins, *The Management of Industrial Relations*, Harmondsworth: Penguin, 1978; Henry Phelps Brown, 'A Non-Monetarist View of the Pay Explosion', *Three Banks Review* March 1975.

11 Adamson, confidential note, 'The Structure of Government', 4.8.70; Partridge PP. Office note, 'Meeting Director General and Sir K. Joseph', 30.6.69, Director General, Papers 1970–77. Note, 'Prices and Incomes', 6.7.70, PP. Director General on 'The Structure of Government', Sept. 1970, Cl Papers. EcC 2.11.70.

12 CBI EcC 1.9.70, 30.11.70, 4.1.71; Taxation Panel and EcC (early 1971, u/d); EcC 5.4.71. Adamson, note, 'Meeting with Chancellor of Exchequer' 5.8.70, Partridge PP.

13 Cl 20.1.71. Director General on 'The Budget', April 1971, Cl Papers. Cl 21.4.71. J. Partridge to A. Barber 31.4.71, PP. CBI Annual Report 1971.

14 *British Economic Policy*, pp. 58–62, CBI EcC 4.8.70, 1.9.70, 30.11.70, 4.1.71, 1.2.71, 1.3.71, 5.4.71, 3.5.71. Director General, 'Prices and Incomes Policy under the New Government', July 1970, Cl Papers. Cl 15.7.70, 18.11.70.

Unsigned note, 'Prices and Incomes', 6.7.70, and Director General file note, 'Meeting with Chancellor', 5.8.70: Partridge PP.

15 Director General to Cl, July and Oct. 1970; Cl 15.7.70, 18.11.70, 20.1.71; EcC 30.11.70, 4.1.71.

16 L. Johnman, 'The Conservative Party in Opposition 1964–70', in R. Coopey, S. Fielding and N. Tiratsoo (eds.), *The Wilson Governments 1964–70*, London and New York: Pinter, 1993. D. Barnes and C. Heron in 'The Trade Unions and the Fall of the Heath Government', *Contemporary Record*, Spring 1988.

17 CBI EPC 1.7.70, 9.10.70; Memorandum to Cl 11.11.70; Cl 15.7.70, 21.10.70, 18.11.70, 16.12.70.

18 *Industrial Society*, July and Nov. 1970, Jan. and March 1971. Robens: 'Industry and Government', Sir George Earle Memorial Lecture, 30.11.70. Watkinson, HOL debs 5.4.71. Pearce, *The Director*, Dec. 1972. For other critics, see George Bull, *Industrial Relations: The Boardroom Viewpoint*, London: The Bodley Head, 1972.

19 'The Legal Framework of Industrial Relations', July 1970, CBI EPC. 'Industrial Relations Legislation', Oct. 1970, Cl Papers. Cl 15.7.70, 21.10.70, 18.11.70, 17.2.71. Meetings with R. Carr 22.10.70 and 11.11.70, EPC papers. Partridge to R. Carr 21.12.70, Partridge PP. CBI Annual Report 1971.

20 For earlier episodes of 'voluntary-ism', see Blank, *British Industry and Politics 1945–65*.

21 'Secret Note by President and Director General, The Inflationary Situation', July 1971, Cl Papers. Cl 15.7.71, 15.9.71. Partridge to Barber, 18.7.71 and 20.7.71, and Barber to Partridge 23.7.71: 'I am extremely grateful to you and Campbell for all you have done. You have helped to provide a real opportunity for a breakthrough.'

22 Interviews, Sir Campbell Adamson, Alan Swinden, John Whitehorn. Blackaby (ed.), *British Economic Policy*, p. 61. Confidential letter Pres. and Director General to Cl, 'Price Restraint', 12.4.71, 'General Budget Representations', Jan. 1972, and Director General's Supplementary Report, April 1972: Cl Papers. Cl 20.10.71, 19.4.72. EcPolC 29.11. 71, 31.1.72, 28.2.72. Notes, Visit of Pres. and Director General to US and President's appeal for renewed price restraint, early 1972; Correspondence Partridge/Barber, April 1972: Partridge PP.

23 Cl, 21.4.71, 20.10.71, 19.1.72, 16.2.72, 15.3.72, 19.4.72. Conclusions Committee on Public and Private Sector Relationships, April 1971; Confidential note, 'Unemployment', Oct. 1971, Director General's Supplementary Reports, Nov. 1971, April 1972, 'Regional Policy', Feb. 1972: Cl Papers. EcPolC 4.10.71, 29.11.71, 31.1.72, 28.5.72. *Times*, 24.9.72, 21.10.71, 10.12.71.

24 Partridge on business's concern for 'the national interest . . . social justice . . . compassionate treatment of those who fall behind in the race' (IOD West of England Branch 3.3.72), and a 'joint will between management and unions' to crack inflation (CBI Eastern Reg. Cl 20.4.72).

25 Memdoranm on Industry Bill, June 1972, Cl Papers. Cl 21.6.72. EcC 5.6.72. Clapham to J. Davies 23.6.72, who apparently thought his criticism of the Bill's powers 'immoderate and unrealistic': Clapham PP.

26 This view relies mainly on the Swinden and Clapham papers, CBI archive, and papers kindly made available by Sir Richard O'Brien.

27 CBI Brief for meeting with Govt and TUC, 18.7.72, and R. O'Brien, 'Social and Economic Policy', 31.7.72: Clapham PP. Notes, 'Chequers 16.10.72', 'CBI Position Paper for Downing Street 26 Oct.' 4.10.72, and Briefing for Downing St 25.5.73.

28 Notes of Downing St meetings 18.9.73 and 16.10.73: Swinden papers.

29 Clapham to Heath 10.10.72, Swinden to Adamson 6.9.72 and 15.9.72, O'Brien to Swinden 3.10.72; CBI Position Paper 2.11.72, Memdorandum CBI Meeting with PM 30.5.73, and 'Points to be covered' for Downing St Team 24.7.73: Swinden papers. Meeting on Pay and Prices after the Freeze 8.12.72, Clapham PP.

30 Some were less resistant to dividend control, seeing advantages to investment from higher profit retentions; others preferred capital market allocation processes *via* high distributions: but there was virtual unanimity that dividend control was a lesser evil to control of profit margins.

31 Cl 19.7.72, 18.10.72, 20.12.72, 17.1.73, 21.2.73. There were worries over investment, interest rates, 'poaching', and indefinite curtailment of competitive forces. Meetings with 'Top Ten' 14.6.72, top retailers 10.7.72, and leading industrialists 13.7.72: Clapham PP.

32 A paper stating that export and investment-led growth, restrained consumption and lower inflation would require more attention to monetary policy *and* continued pay controls, with price and (probably) dividend controls 'as a balance', raised no major objections on Cl 18.7.73. EcC 31.7.72, Spec. EcC 13.11.72, Econ. Pol C, 12.4.73, 5.6.73, 3.12.73, Fin. Pol. C 31.7.73.

33 Letters to Adamson from J. Reiss 28.6.72, H. Laing 29.6.72, and T. Pearce 3.7.72, and to Clapham from M. Laing 17.7.72, J. P. Engels 29.6.72, Lord Kearton 7.6.72 ('strictly p and c'), and Lord Pilkington 22.6.72 and 28.6.72. Hand-written note on meeting with clearing bank chairmen 10.7.72. All in Clapham PP.

34 C. Bell to Clapham 11.6.73: Swinden papers. Cl 18.4.73. Hand-written note on 'meeting with 100'; R.W. Evans of the Rank Organisation, to Clapham 23.3.73, where the citation of Edwards occurs; Kearton to Partridge 28.3.73: Clapham PP.

35 B. Bracewell Milnes to Taxation Committee, 29.1.73, Note on 'General Budget Representations' 30.1.73, and Taxation Committee, 14.3.73: EcC papers.

36 Director General's Report to Cl, Feb 1973, Cl papers. Cl 17.1.73 and 21.2.73. Interviews with Alan Davies, Barry Bracewell Milnes, and Sir Campbell Adamson.

37 Notes for meeting on industrial representation 24.6.70, meetings with industrialists 25.6.70 and trade and employers' associations 26.6.70, and Heath to Partridge, welcoming the inquiry 4.1.71: Partridge PP. Director General, 'Industrial Representation in GB', Sept 1970, and reports to Cl, Dec. 1970, and July and Sept 1973, Memoranda on Commission's Report, Dec. 1972, and Inquiry, March 1973: Cl papers. Cl 16.9.70, 20.9.72, 20.12.72, 18.4.73. For a helpful discussion, see Wyn Grant and David Marsh, *The CBI*, London: Hodder & Stoughton, 1977, pp. 72–8.

38 Paper, 'Policy Options on Pay' 9.1.74: 'to allow unemployment to rise . . . relying on orthodox monetary and fiscal measures' would be economically, industrially and politically 'unviable' or 'unacceptable': Swinden Papers. Ec PolC 3.12.73. NEDC Liaison Committee 3.12.73. Director General to Cl and paper, 'Europe: what Progress?', Oct. 1973. Cl 21.11.73, 19.12.73, 16.1.74, 4.2.74 (emergency meeting), 20.2.74. CBI Annual Report 1973. There was also much work in this period on European monetary integration and wider economic and industrial objectives *vis-à-vis* the EEC: see Grant and Marsh, *The CBI*, pp. 180–4.

39 Clapham: *Wolverhampton Express* 14.1.74, and speech in New York 1.3.74: Clapham PP. Adamson: *Times* 29.11.73, *FT* 14.12.73, and CBI file, 'Adamson Resignation', on property speculation or some 'non-industrial manifestations of wealth' as opposed to wider profit imperatives, and that 'we employers should add our views strongly on the side of the fairer society'.

40 'Party Political Contacts 1969–75' (Adamson file) and 'Shadow Cabinet Dinners (Labour Party) 1970–72' (PP) outline exchanges with successive Opposition leaders. In one, 21.1.72, Tony Benn records Harold Wilson saying it was a scandal the CBI offered price restraint, with the government offering nothing in return: *Diaries 1968–72*, p. 407. A Benn initiative in April 1972 for CBI contact with Labour policy thinking does not appear to have got far.

41 Cl 16.1.74, 4.2.74 (emergency meeting), 20.2.74. Meetings 28.1.74 and 5.2.74, Heath, Barber, Whitelaw, Carrington, Walker, Armstrong: Clapham, Adamson, Partridge, O'Brien, Swinden: Clapham PP. Interviews with Sir Michael Clapham, Sir Campbell Adamson, and Lord Ezra.

42 Adamson to CBI Cl, 'Explanation of Comments on Repeal of the IRA', 26.2.74.

43 Letters to M. Clapham from Sir Tatton Brinton 27.2.74, T. Beckett 27.2.74, T. Hudson 17.4.74, R. Martin 25.4.74: Clapham PP.

6 SYSTEMIC CHANGE IN CAPITALISM?

1 George Goyder, *The Responsible Company*, Oxford: Blackwell, 1961.

2 Charles Villiers: *Start Again, Britain*, London: Quartet, 1984.

3 Among those mentioned in this chapter three were family firm inheritors (Samuel Courtauld, Jock Campbell, Grigor McClelland); three were freeranging small/medium firm CEs (George Goyder, Wilfred Brown, Thomas Heron); three chose firms tolerant or attuned to their ideas (Peter Parker, Richard O'Brien, Fred Catherwood).

4 Samuel Courtauld 1876–1947, Chair Courtaulds 1921–46, philanthropist, art collector. His essay, 'Government and Industry: their future relations', first prepared for a Conservative Party committee, taken up by J. M. Keynes and published in the *Economic Journal*, April 1942, was followed by a series of wartime addresses, later published as *Ideals and Industry*, Cambridge: Cambridge University Press, 1948.

5 *Ideals and Industry*, pp. 2, 3, 6, 8, 26, 30, 32, 37.

6 *Ideals and Industry*, pp. 2–10, 13–15, 17–18, 19, 22, 27, 29, 32, 39, 67–8, 76–9, 102, 123–4.

7 George Goyder, *Signs of Grace*, London: Cygnet Press, 1993, p. 10. Peter

Parker, *For Starters: the Business of Life*, London: Jonathan Cape, 1989, pp. 44–5, and interview with Sir Peter Parker. Villiers, *Beyond the Sunset*, Stoke Abbott: Thos. Harmsworth Publishing Company, 1992, pp. 39–40, 41, 43, 53, 70. John S. Peart-Binns, *Maurice B. Reckitt, A Life*, Basingstoke: Boderdean Press, Marshall Pickering, 1988, pp. 56–7. Peter Thompson, *Sharing the Success*, 1990, p. 23.

8 *Signs of Grace*, p. 11. Wilfred Brown, 'Luck and the Route to the Top', Brown Papers. Parker, *For Starters*, p. 9. Nicholas Davenport, *Memoirs of a City Radical*, London: Weidenfeld & Nicolson, 1974, pp. ix, 42–3. Interview with Sir Peter Thompson. Jock Campbell, 'Private Enterprise and Public Morality', *New Statesman*, 27.5.66.

9 George Goyder 1908– , Managing Director, British International Paper Company 1935–71, Member, General Synod of Church of England 1948–75.

10 Lord (Wilfred) Brown 1906–1985, Chair Glacier Metal Company 1934–65, Minister of State, Board of Trade 1965–70.

11 Goyder, *The Responsible Company*, London: Hutchinson, 1961, p. 81. His principal ideas in *The Future of Private Enterprise*, Oxford: Blackwell, 1951, interested Herbert Morrison and Tom Williamson of the GMWU in 1950, with disappointing results, and later Alexander Fleck, chair of ICI: *Signs of Grace*, pp. 78–83, 105.

12 *The Future of Private Enterprise*, and *The Responsible Company*.

13 Nicholas Davenport, for many years a director of the Natural Mutual Life Assurance Society and financial columnist of *The Spectator*, was friendly with Dalton, Gaitskell, Jay, Callaghan etc: *Memoirs of a City Radical*, p. ix. *The Split Society*, London: Victor Gollancz, 1964.

14 *The Split Society*, pp. 62–3, 160–2, 168–9, 171–3, 183–4. For his discussions with Labour leaders on a State Participation Unit Trust: *Memoirs of a City Radical*, pp. 190, 202–7.

15 Wilfred Brown and Eliot Jacques, *Exploration in Management*, London: Heinemann, 1960, and John Child, *British Management Thought*, London: Allen and Unwin, 1969, pp. 147–50, 195–203. Wilfred Brown, *The Earnings Conflict*, London: Heinemann, 1973, pp. 9–10, 34, 39, 64–6, 77, 83. Brown to Lord Trenchard, u/d July 1979: Brown Papers.

16 *The Earnings Conflict*, pp. 10, 13, 27, 30, 33–4, 42, 58–9. 'Employee Participation and the Labour Party Green Paper', June 1974, and 'Employee Participation in Industrial Management', u/d: both in Brown Papers.

17 Brown, *Piecework Abandoned*, London: Heinemann, 1971. He told Barbara Castle, April (u/d) 1968, such schemes made people 'selfish and un-co-operative', and Brown to Wilson 22.12.75: Brown papers. For the NCRD idea: 'Inflation and a Possible Solution', 1972, and 'Proposals for a Flexible National Wage Policy', 1979 (both privately published), and HOL debs 30.7.75, 3.3.76, 10.4.78, 17.6.79.

18 Professor (William) Grigor McClelland, 1922– , Managing Director Laws Stores Ltd 1949, Chair 1965–78; Director, Manchester Business School 1965–77; Member IRC 1966–71; Chair Joseph Rowntree Charitable Trust 1965–78. *And a New Earth*, London: Friends House Service Committee, 1976.

19 Fred Catherwood, *The Christian in Industrial Society*, London: Tyndale Press, 1964, pp. 8, 17, 25, 36, 64–7, 87, 91. *A Better Way: The Case for a Christian Social Order*, Leicester: Inter-Varsity Press, 1975, pp. 29, 76–9, 119, 122–4, 149. See also chs 3 and 7.

20 Lord (Jock) Campbell of Eskan, 1912–1994, Chair Bookers 1952–66; Chair Statesman and Nation Publishing Co. 1964–77; cr. 1966. 'The Role of Big Business in the New Nations', *Optima*, Dec. 1963, and HOL debs 7.7.66, 1.8.66.

21 Thomas Heron had been founder and Chief Executive of Cresta Silks Ltd. 'The Idea of Equality in Industry', Church Union Summer School of Sociology, 1961. Also 'Man at Work' in M. B. Reckitt (ed.), *Prospect for Christendom, Essays in Catholic Social Reconstruction*, London: Faber & Faber, 1945.

22 'Participation in the Enterprise', report by CABE UK to Uniapac World Congress 1968. CABE (Christian Association of Business Executives) had been formed in 1964 out of two small Catholic groups with interests in ideas of management 'trusteeship', 'just wage', 'fair price', worker participation and 'economic co-operation'. CABE included revisionist and other currents as well as reconstructionists, and had become inter-denominational by the 1970s. Askonas Papers.

23 Peter Parker, 1924– , Organising Secretary, Director of Edinburgh's Study Conference 1955–56, Managing Director, Engineering Group, Bookers 1956–66; Chair Rockware 1971–76; Chair British Rail 1976–83; Chair BIM 1984–86. 'The Social Dimension of Management', *Co-Partnership*, April 1970; '1994', Lubbock Lecture on Management, 1980; *For Starters,* London: Jonathan Cape, 1989.

24 Peter Parker, *A New Industrial Polity*, Stamp Memorial Lecture, 1977. Also *Missing our Connections*, Richard Dimbleby Lecture, London: BBC 1983.

25 *A New Industrial Polity*.

26 *A New Industrial Polity*. Parker cited Churchill. He went well beyond the BIM's proposal for a national economic forum, see ch. 7.

27 Charles Villiers, 1912–1992, Chair Henry Schroder Wagg 1960–68; Managing Director, IRC 1968–71; Chair, Guinness Mahon 1971–76, Chair, BSC 1976–80, and BSC Industry 1980–89. 'Notes on Industrial Policy' 1969; 'Government and Industry', *FT* 1971; 'Tomorrow's Management', Lubbock Lecture 14.5.71; 'Britain in the '70s', Anglo-Netherlands Assocn 26.3.74; 'Industry and Government', London Round Table 1975; 'We All Live Here', BSC 1976: Villiers papers.

28 Villiers, *Start Again Britain*, 1984, and evidence to Select Committee on Overseas Trade, 1985. *FT* 18.10.89. 'How much industrial change ?', Feb. 1988; Speech to Satro Conference 30.6.88; *Small Business*, no. 117, Nov. 1988; 'Introduction to Comparative Business Cultures', Templeton College, 1.2.89; and speech to American Chamber of Commerce 3.3.89: Villiers papers.

29 *Start Again Britain*.

30 *Start Again Britain*. See *Beyond the Sunset*, for a retrospect.

31 John Marsh, 1913–1992, Director, IWS 1950–61; Director, later Director General, BIM 1961–73. *People at Work*, London: Industrial Welfare Society, 1957; *Ethics in Business*, London: Industrial Society, 1970.

32 John Garnett, 1922– , ICI 1947–62, Director Industrial Society 1962–86. Articles in *Industrial Society People at Work*, 1978/85. IS Annual Reports 1962–86. Garnett initiated behind-the scenes employer/TU approaches to improved national industrial relations in 1973 and 1979–80: IS archive, Warwick.

33 Discussions on a 'code' at St George's House, Windsor: 30 May–1 June 1969, 7–9 May 1971, 12–14 Nov. 1971, 21–23 and 27–29 April 1972, 6–8 Oct. 1972. S G W papers.

34 D. Hunter-Johnston 4.8.72, and P. Cannon to H. J. Gray 29.6.72: CBI Company Affairs Committee, henceforward CBI CAC.

35 P. S. Wright, Chair Quotations Committee, Stock Exchange July 1972; Roger Bardell of British Insurance Association to H. J. Gray 10.7.72; and W. Godfrey Morley to Gray 6.7.72: CBI CAC.

36 Ralph Bateman, July 1972, and H. D. Husbands, Director Legal Affairs, Ford Motor Co., to H. J. Gray 4.7.72: CBI CAC.

37 They appear to have included David Orr (Unilever), Reay Geddes, E. J. Gibbons (BICC), A. R. Harvey (Shell), Lord Shawcross, R. Verdon Smith (Lloyds Bank), and Lord Watkinson.

38 CAC Interim Report, Jan. 1973.

39 Criticisms came from CBI regional councils (SE, Western, Midlands, E. and W. Ridings) and the SFC, variously alleging an over-critical tone towards business, potential misuse by government, and damage to competitiveness. Doubts increased within the CAC whose Final Report offered only a very broad 'set of principles'.

40 Summary of Comments on Interim Report to end-March 1973. Letters to Watkinson from Benson 4.4.73, Shawcross, 4.4.73; Leslie O'Brien, 16.4.73; Orr 3.8.73. CAC 17.4.73. Watkinson to Adamson 10.5.73 and Gordon Richardson 9.8.73; John Clay to E. S. McNair 30.7.73. CBI CAC.

41 David Orr expressed doubts regarding the availability of suitable NEDs, their means of influence, and conflicts between 'sharing profit responsibility' and 'expecting them to . . . sit in judgement on their [full-time colleagues'] performance': 'The Public Company', July 1972; Orr to R. Bateman 6.11.72 and to Watkinson 3.9.73: CBI CAC.

42 P. Cannon to H. J. Gray 29.6.72; A. R. Harvey to Watkinson 7.7.72; David Orr, 'The Public Company' (though he favoured a continued primary responsibility to shareholders); and D. Hunter-Johnston, memorandum 4.8.72.

43 The Interim Report proposed industrial relations as an important board function, company joint councils, and full information to employees in CJCs.

44 Parallel proposals from the EPC (under Richard O'Brien) for plant, works and company councils, except in very small firms, were to be rejected by CBI Cl after criticisms in the SFC and many regions which angered relevant HQ staff. Papers to Cl, July and Sept. 1973; Cl 18.7.73, 19.9.73. Watkinson and others persisted, as did the BIM with its more advanced proposals, including worker directors.

45 *The Responsible Worker*, 1975, pp. 88–89.

46 P. Cannon to H. J. Gray 29.6.72; D. Hunter-Johnston, memorandum 4.8.72.

47 Orr, 'The Public Company', July 1972; E. J. Gibbons, memorandum 18.7.72; Lord Shawcross, memorandum July 1972; Benson to Watkinson 4.4.73;

N. Vinson to Watkinson 1.6.73; Comments on Interim Report by Imperial Group: CBI CAC. G. Gilbertson of ICI to Clapham, 31.5.73: Clapham PP.

48 Report on Northern Reg. Cl 19.3.73; Summaries of Comments on Interim Report suggesting no widespread feeling either way in the CBI regions: CBI CAC.

49 Views on CAC were mostly adverse: 11.6.73, 17.7.73, with the BIM not in support either (J. Arkell to Adamson 3.7.73): CBI CAC. The government's White Paper on Company Law Reform, July 1973, was agnostic, as on much else, though backing the NED proposals.

50 Beer, *Britain Against Itself*; Ralf Dahrendorf, *On Britain*, London: BBC, 1982.

51 O'Brien was disappointed by the participation debacle in the CBI (note 44 above): interview with Sir Richard O'Brien. Later, as Chair of a CBI working party, Peter Thompson would be similarly disappointed: *Sharing the Success*, London: Collins, 1990, p. 205, and interview with Sir Peter Thompson.

52 *Signs of Grace*, pp. 109–10. Catherwood, *At the Cutting Edge*, 1995, but see *Pro-Europe?*, 1991, for his criticisms of right-wing, free market views. *Beyond the Sunset*, pp. 48, 71, 206.

53 M. I. Lipman, *Memoirs of a Socialist Business Man*, London: Lipmew Trust, 1980. Anti-Clause 4 efforts and themes of market adaptation held centre stage for revisionists: see Tudor Jones, *Remaking the Labour Party: From Gaitskell to Blair*, London: Routledge, 1996.

7 TURMOIL, REALIGNMENT AND RECOVERY

1 Relevant papers of Sir Donald MacDougall, made available for this study, include several instances of such admissions in CBI-government discussions.

2 Interviews with Sir Michael Edwardes, Sir Terry Beckett, Sir Peter Walters.

3 Note of lunch meeting 31.1.75: SGW papers. Others present included Catherwood and Geddes. *Daily Telegraph* 12.2.75 and *Industrial Society*, Sept./Oct. 1976 on the need for management power to be strongly boosted. Interviews: Sir Maurice Laing, Lord Caldecote, Sir Michael Clapham, Sir Alex Jarratt.

4 BIM ESAC 19.4.78, 23.8.78, 23.1.79, and Catherwood to Chief Executives of forty-six companies, 21.12.78, and note on 'Balance of Bargaining Power', 9.4.79: ESAC papers. C. Smith, J. Child and M. Rowlinson, *Reshaping Work, The Cadbury Experience*, Cambridge: Cambridge University Press, 1990, pp 178, 327.

5 E.g. Plowden, *Times* 22.4.76, attacking the fall in real profitability and public sector denigraton of management; Caldecote, *Times* 21.5.76, claiming insufficient funds for new investments, and Jarratt, *FT* 12.2.77, on resources squandered in an 'unrelenting equalisation of rewards and benefits for all irrespective of individual contribution'.

6 E.g. a previously understated business leader, Marcus Sieff, in accepting these awards; *Times* 7.12.76, 4.7.78.

7 Weinstock, *Times* 26.9.76; Robens, 'Managing Great Britain Ltd', Ashridge Lecture, Ashridge Management College, 1976; Goldsmith, *Times* 2.8.77.

8 Goodison, *Times* 22.10.76, 14.2.78. Vinson (jointly), *Why Britain Needs a*

Social Market Economy, CPS 1975; CBI Conference 1977, and *Industrial Participation*, Summer 1978. Hoskyns laid out his argument in detail in 1976–77 in the MS for a book. Though still a political independent, he would soon move to a position on the intellectual 'New Right' in the Conservative Party. Interview with Sir John Hoskyns.

9 Sir Arthur Knight, papers. Interview with Sir Nigel Broackes. Reports to CBI Cl of Working Parties on Aid to Political Parties (Oct. 1975) and Electoral Reform (Sept. 1976): among their advisers was David Butler of Nuffield College, Oxford. CBI archive.

10 For a brief account of these relations in these years see K. Middlemas, 'The Party, Industry, and the City', in A.Seldon and S.Ball (eds.), *Conservative Century: The Conservative Party since 1900*, Oxford: Oxford University Press, 1994, pp. 484–87.

11 Operating with faulty Treasury figures on company, Healey appeared to disregard warnings by Clapham and Adamson on company liquidity: Edmund Dell, *A Hard Pounding*, Oxford: Oxford University Press, 1991 p. 39. Benn described the CBI representations as 'just one long moan', *Benn Diaries*, London: Hutchinson, 1989, p. 130.

12 Eleven meetings between CBI and Healey were necessary before he conceded stock appreciation relief in the November 1974 budget: MacDougall, *Don and Mandarin*, London: Murray, p. 212.

13 The 1972 Group (of Labour supporters from business) was contacted in the hope that they could influence the Cabinet: 1972 Group, Executive Committee 25.11.75. Wilfred Brown papers. The Group, much supported by Wilson and, later, Callaghan, was in fact predominantly moderate and anti-Bennite: Brown papers, and interview with Lord Gregson.

14 Meeting CBI and Benn, 17.5.74: Clapham CBI PP. See also *Benn Diaries*, 28.11.74 and 12.2.75, where Adamson attacks the Industry Act as 'a charter for workers control'.

15 Meeting CBI and large manufacturing firms, 3.5.74: Clapham PP.

16 Though the CBI failed to prevent the NEB taking shares in profitable firms, its scope for compulsory acquisition was greatly weakened by the requirement for shareholdings above 30 per cent to obtain parliamentary approval. Adamson, *Times*, 16.5.75.

17 Moderates attacking the Industry Act included David Orr (Unilever), *Times* 17.2.75, Robens, *Times* 3.10.74 for Benn as an 'academic revolutionary', and Lord Seebohm (Barclays), *Times* 31.10.75, attacking 'planned egalitarianism'.

18 CBI Cl 21.1.76.

19 SFC, advocating no CBI involvement in pay control 1.5.74, criticising response to Benn's policy 5.6.74, and urging a more partisan political stance, 3.7.74.

20 Clapham PP, including R.Holder to Clapham, 15.3.74, attacking 'industrial bureaucrats'.

21 EPC 4.12.74 and 7.1.75, after a paper advocating a definite income guideline had been rejected by Council. The EPC's Pay Group, which researched the question, remained firmly opposed to a voluntary policy: EPC 4.12.74.

22 CBI Cl. 18.12.74, 15.1.75, 19.2.75. Leading moderates were Cadbury, Caldecote, Kipping, Maurice Laing, O'Brien, Plowden. Hawkish (often City-based) views were stronger in the Financial Policy Committee. A State of

Sterling meeting 15.1.75, under Lord Seebohm, concluded that full austerity measures might soon be needed.

23 Cl 1.5.75. MacDougall, *Don and Mandarin*, p. 221. The policy introduced in 1975 was voluntary but with sanctions on guideline-breaking employers, using government purchasing, investment allowances, regional aid and the Price Code.

24 John Methven, 1926–1980, ICI Legal Department; Director, Office of Fair Trading 1973–76; Director General CBI 1976–80. For Methven's harder-edged revisionism; *Management Today*, March 1976: 'My own belief is that industry and government should work closer as in France and Japan . . . while emphasising . . . the over-riding importance of profit'. A self-description as 'non-political': *Times* 10.4.78.

25 MacDougall, *Don and Mandarin*, p. 228 thought Methven could be 'abrasive and even rude'.

26 Lord (Harold) Watkinson, 1910–1995, family firm; Conservative MP 1950–64, Minister of Transport 1955–59, Minister of Defence 1959–62; Managing Director Schweppes 1963–68; Chair, Cadbury-Schweppes 1969–74; Chair, BIM 1968–70; Chair, CBI CAC 1972–73; Pres. CBI 1976–77. *Blueprint for Industrial Survival*, London: Allen & Unwin 1976; *Turning Points* Salisbury: Michael Russell, 1986. Watkinson had declined Mrs Thatcher's offer of the Conservative Party chairmanship in 1975: Middlemas, *Power, Competition and the State*, vol. 2, p. 195. His political skills were widely admired: see MacDougall, *Don and Mandarin*, p. 228.

27 His 1974 paper to Council, 'Industry and Government', had defended a conventional relationship between government and industry while caustically attacking the Labour government in this area: CBI Cl 17.7.74.

28 It is hard to imagine Adamson publicly promising action *versus* the Bullock Report which would make the Industrial Relations Act debate 'look like a vicarage tea-party': *Times* 18.3.77. *Blueprint for Industrial Survival*, p. 147; CBI Cl paper Nov. 1976, CBI *Annual Report*, 1977; *Turning Points*, p. 201. Interview with the late Lord Watkinson.

29 MacDougall, *Don and Mandarin*, pp. 230–1.

30 *Turning Points*, p. 208. P. Taylor to Alan Swinden, Employment participation file, 3.10.75: '[Watkinson] would rather take the chance of bull-dozing a clear policy document through Council than give a weak document to the Commission.'

31 'Participation agreements' for firms with over 2000 employees were to be backed by permissive legislation and guaranteed by independent arbitration. They allowed for board/workforce agreement on any type of participation system, with all employees involved. The CBI strongly urged priority for below-board measures rather than worker directors. Cl 16.7.76, Evidence to Bullock Committee.

32 The Bullock majority report proposed trade union directors on a unitary board, with virtual parity with other interests: non-TU members within the firm would have no say in the process. The (business member) minority advocated a supervisory board with 1/3 each of worker, shareholder and independent representatives.

33 Meeting CBI and PM and ministers, 15.2.77: CBI employment particip-

ation files. Callaghan was told industry was united as never before on this issue and no compromise was possible.

34 The White Paper proposed joint representation councils within plants to discuss company policy, and a supervisory board with up to 1/3 trade union directors, selected by the JRCs.

35 EPC 19.10.78: the EPC, as in 1974, was left to draw up a Code of Practice for participation.

36 EPC 17.3.77. Enthusiasts retained mutualist language to describe RPD: James Barker, Chair, EPC, to Alan Swinden, 19.10.76, on 'three parties to the new Social Contract': Swinden papers.

37 EPC 4.7.77.

38 Cl 17.5.78, EPC 1.11.78, and Cl 6.12.78 where members call for greater emphasis on productivity and flexibility. Anxieties focussed on evidence that Labour was considering more sophisticated price control if re-elected, without making commitments on incomes policy.

39 D. C. Cross (Hambros) SFC 4.5.77, 7.1.77, 4.5.77. 'Pay policy', Report of the SFC Working Party, 30.6.78 (responding to the EPC's RPD proposals). According to one SFC member: 'it has been produced by the owner-manager who wanted to be successful in the market-place and it was time that his voice was heard': SFC 5.7.78.

40 Methven's pessimistic comments to Cl 17.1.79. The EPC had noted demands for greater pay freeedom in the Economic Policy Committee and Cl, as well as the SFC, as early as Feb. 1978, 1.2.78.

41 *Don and Mandarin*, p. 223. EPC 3.1.79.

42 EPC 4.4.79. Some members wanted a stronger *legislative* commitment on secret ballots, as strongly backed by the SFC. The commitments against picketing and closed shop did, however, move a step away from the EPC's previous agnosticism.

43 Cadbury to CBI Cl 20.10.76 showed a limited acceptance of monetarist means of controlling inflation, with clear targets for monetary growth, though not so tight as to restrict industry's access to credit and to be used alongside incomes restraint and reduced public spending.

44 Adrian Cadbury, 1929– , Cadbury-Schweppes, Deputy Chair/Managing Director 1969–74, Chair, 1975–89; Chair, CBI EcC 1974–80. *The Company Chairman*, London: Director Books 1990. An advocate of 'social responsibility', he would play a leading role in corporate governance debates: see *The Cadbury Committee Report: Financial Aspects of Corporate Governance*, 1992.

45 Walter Eltis and Robert Bacon, *Britain's Economic Problem: Too Few Producers*, London: Macmallan, 1976.

46 Cl 20.10.76 for the reception, though EPC 2.8.76 included fears that the CBI might appear too 'politicised'. IOD support: PEC 15.11.76.

47 Lord Drogheda, *Double Harness*, pp. 184–5: he notes that the IOD suffered badly from the inflation of 1973–5.

48 Lord (Frederick) Erroll, 1914– , Conservative MP 1945–64; Board of Trade, Minister of State 1959–61, President 1961–63; Minister of Power 1963–64; President Lond Chamber of Commerce 1966–69; Chair, Whessoe 1970–87; Bowater 1973–84, Consolidated Gold 1976–83; IOD Chair, Cl 1973–76, President 1976–84.

49 Interview with Lord Erroll. He had been an IOD Council member since 1948.
50 Jan Hildreth, 1932– , NEDO 1965–68; London Transport 1968–72; John Laing 1972–74; Director General IOD 1975–78. Profile: *The Director*, Dec. 1974. On appointment Hildreth promised to speak dispassionately on such issues as the comparative importance of the private and public sectors.
51 IOD Cl 25.9.74.
52 PEC 20.1.75. IOD *Annual Reports* 1976–79 for details of its relationship with the media. Interview with Jan Hildreth.
53 The IOD's evidence to the Royal Commission on Wealth, was closely argued by Davies and Bracewell Milnes. Abolition of closed shop, PEC 17.1.77 seeking firm commitment from the Conservatives. Taxation policy, Cl 8.3.78, confirming goal of a two-tier income tax structure of 50 and 25 per cent, funded by increases in indirect taxation.
54 For Vinson and CPS, see Richard Cockett, *Thinking the Unthinkable*, London: HarperCollins, 1994, Chs 6 and 7.
55 IOD *Annual Report* 1975.
56 *The Director*, Nov. 1977, and Nov. 1978.
57 For an explication of the idea, see *Times* 2.3.78.
58 The entrepreneur would be allowed to 'reap the rewards commensurate with the risks he has taken and the efforts he has made': *Business Leaders' Manifesto*, p. 5.
59 Roy Close, 1920– , NEDO 1966, Industrial Director 1969–73; Chair, University of Aston Management Centre; Director General BIM 1976–85.
60 Lord (Derek) Ezra, 1919– , NCB 1947, Deputy Chair, 1967–71, Chair 1971–82; cr. 1983; HOL Liberal front bench spokesman. He had spearheaded pro-EEC discussion in the CBI in the late 1960s.
61 A considerable overlap of CBI/BIM roles existed in this period: e.g. Catherwood and Ezra (both speaking at CBI Cl in a semi-official BIM capacity), L. Tolley, M. Edwardes, Lord Caldecote, A. Bide, R. Halstead.
62 Interview with Roy Close.
63 BIM Chairman's Committee 10.9.75. This meeting also agreed to do nothing conflicting with the CBI.
64 Roy Close, *Power, Responsibility and Management*, British Institute of Management, p. 31. Papers to Chairman's Committee 14.12.76 and 9.5.78, noting most middle and senior management (the bulk of BIM membership) were 'moderate in their views and attitudes'.
65 On direct tax cuts, the Manifesto quite boldly urged a basic rate below 30 per cent and a top rate of 60 per cent, then 50 per cent, funded through shifts in indirect taxation, but incomes policy was commended. The BIM had generally endorsed *Road to Recovery*; BIM Chairman's Committee paper 2.12.76.
66 Ch.C 16.4.74. Ch. C 16.9.76, and Cl 13.12.77, where Close's budget proposals for major tax cuts divided Council for an alleged 'irresponsibility'.
67 In the 1976 *Annual Report* Catherwood claimed managers had been treated as 'non-persons' in the debates over Industrial Strategy and counter-inflation policy.
68 BIM *Annual Report 1977*.
69 ESAC 22.9.77 paper advocating some form of central machinery, and a

relativities board, no price controls, and importance of educating through economic forecasts.
70 BIM Ch.C 24.8.78 discussing paper Ch.C (78)22.
71 Ch. C 24.8.78.
72 Replies to Catherwood on 'balance of bargaining power', 9.5.79, ESAC papers, included calls from some managers for controls on the TUs and more localised bargaining.

8   BUSINESS AND EARLY THATCHERISM

1 *Report of 1979 CBI Conference.*
2 Interview with Lord Vinson. Similar views were stated by the Thatcherite sympathiser Lord (Hector) Laing.
3 Director General's file on 1980 Conference speech, CBI papers: the resigners included John King (Babcock and Wilcox), Nicholas Cayzer (British and Commonwealth Shipping) and James Goldsmith (Cavenham Foods). Beckett always insisted that he was urging a 'bare knuckle' fight on behalf of industry against foreign competitors, not against the government.
4 Lord (Raymond) Pennock, 1920–1993, ICI 1947– , Deputy Chair, 1975–80; Chair BICC 1980–84; President CBI 1980–82; cr. 1982.
5 By the late 1980s Pennock, now President of UNICE (the confederation of European employers), became reconciled to many of the government's policies.
6 Campbell Fraser, 1923– , EIU 1952–57; Dunlop Rubber Co. 1957, Managing Director, 1972, Chair, Dunlop Holdings 1978–83; President, CBI 1982–84.
7 Terence Beckett, 1923– , Ford Motor Co., Chair, Ford UK 1974–80; CBI PAC 1976–78; Director General CBI 1980–87; Governor NIESR 1978– .
8 Interview with Sir Terence Beckett.
9 MacDougall's notes, meetings with Labour front bench spokesmen, 7.2.80, 8.7.80, 16.9.80: MacDougall papers.
10 For example, Director General's report to CBI Cl, Feb. 1981.
11 The BIM was influenced by James Ball as ESAC chairman: ESAC 8.8.79, 30.10.80, 7.5.81.
12 Arguments mooted at meetings CBI and Chancellor 23.5.79, and CBI and PM and economic ministers, 9.7.79: MacDougall's notes, MacDougall papers. The CBI dissociated itself from William Reddaway, an external economic adviser, when he produced a very critical report of government policies in August 1980.
13 CBI staff paper, 'Fiscal and Monetary Policy', May 1979; *Don and Mandarin.* pp. 250–1.
14 MacDougall and Methven 7.3.81 MacDougall papers; interview with Sir Donald MacDougall.
15 Notes of meeting CBI and Howe and Prior 13.6.80; MacDougall papers and CBI Cl Sept. 1980.
16 Beckett had already told Council that the 'squeeze on industry had gone far enough': CBI Cl 15.10.80.
17 CBI 1981 budget representations.
18 PAC 2.4.81: some wanted 'a less adversarial approach'. The SFC did not support the PSBR overshoots: SFC 7.4.81.

19 MacDougall's notes of govt/CBI meeting 17.12.81: MacDougall papers.
20 CBI Cl 16.9.81; Beckett to Howe 31.7.81: CBI meeting with Chancellor
     10.6.82; Close to Howe 27.4.82. Doubts about recovery: EcC 25.11.82,
     27.7.83, 29.9.83, 22.3.84, 6.9.84; and BIM ESAC 31.10.83, 16.1.84.
21 BIM Cl 14.11.85.
22 CBI Cl 29.7.81.
23 CBI officials allegedly described Keith Joseph as a 'fundamentalist' and 'anar-
     chist' on the issue: M. Holmes, *The First Thatcher Government*, London:
     Macmillan, 1985, p. 155. Staff paper 'CBI involvement in the NEDC', Jan.
     1982. Note of meeting CBI and Howe and Prior 13.6.80: MacDougall
     papers.
24 G. Chandler, 'The Need for Neddy', *MT* Nov. 1983 see also Lord Watkinson,
     Are Business and Politics Compatible?, Ashridge Management College, 1980.
     BIM Chair C 16.2.82. Knight papers. Beckett's wariness: Stockton Lecture,
     Times 15.1.82.
25 Conference could be even more difficult for the leadership, as in 1979 when
     Taylor Woodrow's motion on abolishing the closed shop easily passed despite
     opposition from the platform. These events were important straws in the
     wind.
26 EPC 7.1.81, 6.5.81. This controverts Middlemas's view of the EPC as a power-
     ful supporter of the Thatcherite TU reforms: *Power, Competition and the State*,
     vol. 3. pp. 554–5 n.43.
27 Cl 17.6.81, also PAC 7.3.83 discussing the Green Paper 'Democracy in
     Trade Unions'. CBI Cl 15.6.81, 16.3.83. BIM ESAC 8.8.79.
28 'Guidelines For Action on Employee Involvement', July 1979, Cl 18.7.79.
29 IOD PEC 16.2.81.
30 *Times* 11.12.81. MacGregor, *The Director*, Dec. 1980. Walter Goldsmith to
     Howe 23.10.79, IOD Cl papers.
31 Alex Brummer and Roger Cowe, *Hanson, A Biography*, London: Fourth
     Estate, 1994, pp. 12–13, 172, 179–181, 189–94. Nigel Vinson, *Owners All*,
     CPS, 1985, Nicholas Goodison, *Shares for All*, CPS, 1986.
32 Walter Goldsmith, 1938– , Black and Decker 1966, Managing Director 1974,
     Chief Executive and European Director, 1975; Director General IOD
     1979–84. *The Winning Streak* (with David Clutterbuck), London: Weidenfeld
     & Nicolson, 1984. *The New Elite* (with Berry Ritchie), London: Weidenfeld &
     Nicolson, 1987.
33 Interview with Walter Goldsmith.
34 Internal policy brief for Director General 30.1.81: file on IOD/CBI rela-
     tions, CBI PAC papers.
35 *Inv. Chron.* 5.10.79; PEC 15.9.82; speech to RHA 12.5.81 referring to
     unnamed business critics as voicing opinions 'straight from the Labour party
     HQ or Congress House'.
36 Interview with Walter Goldsmith.
37 Goldsmith to Howe 11.1.83; also PEC 24.1.82; Cl 23.11.83. The IOD
     argued that UK business was not over-taxed through employers' national
     insurance charges compared to Europe, and that the priority was not cuts
     in corporation tax but tax reduction geared towards individuals, who were
     over-taxed by comparison to other countries.
38 *FT* 26.2.82: signatories included Hanson, Basil Collins (Cadbury Schweppes),

Arnold Hall, R. Halstead, McAlpine. IOD Cl 22.3.83. The same argument meant that corporation tax reductions did not have priority, IOD Cl 22.11.83.

39 Walter Goldsmith, draft budget submission Nov. 1981 (Cl paper C81/15).
40 PEC 2.12.84. PEC 12.12.84.
41 Goldsmith to Howe 11.1.83: IOD Cl papers.
42 But this argument was not used during the height of the recession: IOD Cl 24.7.85, paper by Bracewell-Milnes: this was similar to Milton Friedman's evidence to the Treasury Select Committee in 1980.
43 The Tax Committee Chair Bruce Sutherland (also Chair of the ABCC and Deputy Chair of the CBI Taxation Committee) described it 'as all in all ... an excellent budget', 11.3.81, a view Council welcomed 'with acclamation'. Goldsmith warned Howe privately that they would not repeat this gesture.
44 For the former view: 18.1.84 De Zulueta *versus* Goldsmith and Bracewell-Milnes. Kenneth Corfield, an untypical IOD President, urged the infrastructure with a nice twist on Victorian values: 'We owed much to our Victorian forebears for their expenditure on the national infrastructure ... and we should emulate them'.
45 IOD Cl 30.1.85; CBI SFC 7.4.81, IOD PEC 17.3.82 warning against 'siren voices calling for reflationary measures' which would end up creating more unemployment.
46 IOD Cl 16.7.80; 30.9.80; CBI SFC 1.7.80, 2.9.80, 4.5.82.
47 *Daily Telegraph* 11.5.79.
48 CBI SFC 'Policy Priorities' June 1979; IOD PEC 18.2.81, 18.11.81.
49 Cl 26.9.79; PEC 20.2.80; Cl 16.7.80.
50 Cl 21.1.80; 21.5.80; PEC 17.3.82. Goldsmith's outspoken anti-unionism caused the resignation of two members of the Institute's Industrial Relations Committee.
51 E.g. Eddie Shah during the Messenger dispute: PEC 20.12.83.
52 Cf. the views of Leonard Neal and TURC in *Liberties and Liabilities,* CPS 1980. However, the IOD remained neutral on the issue of contracting-in to the political levy: Cl 14.7.82 and 20.6.84.
53 Goldsmith to Howe 15.11.81: IOD Cl papers, calling for radical surgery of the state sector, rather than making the industries themselves more 'efficient' under existing ownership.
54 CBI SFC, 'Policy Priorities', June 1979. IOD, *Business Leaders' Manifesto,* 1979.
55 A classic statement is the SFC's 'Capital-Owning Democracy', March 1984. Within two years a number of its ideas had become official CBI policy.

9 NEW ORTHODOXY? MUFFLED DISSENT?

1 For theses of a basic ideological continuity under John Major see Dennis Kavanagh and Hugo Young, Nicholas Crafts on industry policy, and Robert Taylor on industrial relations and employment, in Denis Kavanagh and Anthony Seldon, (eds.), *The Major Effect,* London: Macmillan, 1994.

2 Middlemas, *Power, Competition and the State*, vol. 3, 1991, pp. 373, 392. D. Willis and W. Grant, 'The UK: Still a Company State ?', in M. C. P. M. Van Schendelen and R. J. Jackson, *The Politicisation of Business in Western Europe*, London: Croom Helen 1987. Paul Heelas and Paul Morris (eds.), *The Values of the Enterprise Culture*, 1992.

3 CBI, *A Europe for Business*, 1985; *Change to Succeed*, 1986; *EMU, A Business perspective*, 1989; *Economic Priorities*, 1990; *Business Agenda for the '90s*, 1991; *Times* 14.11. 93, 15.11.93. IOD Annual Reports 1990, 1992.T. Melville Ross in *The Director*, Feb., April and June 1995.

4 IOD, *Forward to Prosperity: A Business Leaders' Manifesto*, 1992, p. 4.

5 IOD Annual Reports 1986, 1990; *Business Leaders' Manifestos* 1987, 1992; *The Direction of Tax Reform*, 1986; *Reform in Difficult Times*, 1991; *Public Spending: a Programme for Action*, 1993.

6 This view relies on the following main CBI sources: Cl 20.1.82, 21.7.82, Standing Committee Report Sept. 1983, 21.9.83. *Change to Succeed*, 1986. *Business Agenda for the 1990s*, 1991; *Maintaining the Momentum of Economic Recovery*, 1988; *Economic Priorities for 1989: Building on Business Success*,1989; *Economic Priorities for 1990*, 1990; *The Way to Balanced Growth*, 1994.

7 CBI, *Building Stronger Partnership between Business and Secondary Education*, 1988; *Making Labour Markets Work: A Review of TECs and LECs*, 1993; *Thinking Ahead: Ensuring the Expansion of Higher Education into the 21st Century*, 1994. *Flexible Labour Markets: Who Pays for Training*, 1994, temporised on a training levy and found little support for it among the 400 firms surveyed. Graham Day advocated levies and penalties: *Times* 8.11.93.

8 *Business Agenda for the 1990s*, 1991; CBI Cl paper June 1984. *People: The Cutting Edge*, 1988, found improvements in 'downward' communication but much less in 'upward'. *Employee Involvement*, 1990, showed limitations of existing formal schemes. Employee share ownership was emphasised in *Nation of Shareholders*, 1990. *A Europe for Business*, 1986, and *The European Community and Social Engineering*, 1986.

9 CBI, *Change to Succeed*,1986; *Business Agenda for the 1990s*,1991.

10 Financial crisis and reorganisation in 1985–7 were followed by pre-occupations with a Management Charter and formation of the Institute of Management (1992). ESAC lapsed in 1988, then revived uncertainly; budget and other representations were reported cursorily; and successive chairmen avoided comments on major public policy. BIM Annual Reports 1987–1992.

11 Parochial attitudes often emerge in National Life Story Collection: 'City Lives'. City memoirs were rare: Nicholas Davenport, Lionel Fraser, Ronald Grierson, John Kinross, Jim Slater (see bibliography). For a long historical view of this 'dualism', see G. Ingham, *Capitalism Divided*, Basingstoke: Macmillan, 1984. Some relevant City attitudes in the 1980s: Margaret Reid, *All Change in the City*, Basingstoke: Macmillan, 1988.

12 Report of Select Committee on Overseas Trade, Nov. 1985. HOL debs: Aldington, 1.4.86; Benson, 22.1.92; Brookes, 3.12.85 and 24.4.91; Caldecote, 11.3.87; Ezra, 14.11.85; Kearton 3.12. 85; Laing, 9.6.91 and 22.1.92; Pennock, 22.1.92;Weinstock on 'national self immolation', 3.12.85.

13 HOL debs: Young, 3.12.85; Harris, 3.12.85; Hanson, 3.12.85, and 9.11.87; O'Cathain, 15.1.92. Castleman, *Bankers' Magazine* Nov. 1987; Leigh Pemberton, *Bankers Magazine*, Aug. 1987, ; Cuckney, in Derek Ezra and David Oates, *Advice from the Top*, Newton Abbott: David and Charles 1989, p. 56, 58; *Bankers' Magazine*, Nov. 1986 lamenting City's bad image and offering an economic rationale for 'greed and aggressiveness'.

14 *Investing for Britain's Future: Report of the CBI City/Industry Task Force*, 1987. The CBI had not criticised financial institutions in its first evidence to the Aldington Cttee. Later it focused mainly on pro-industry generalities, see *Business Agenda*, 1991, and *Partners for Success*, 1993, while sponsoring a semi-detached National Manufacturing Council in 1992.

15 Howard Davies, CBI DG, claimed most of the Cabinet now recognised the importance of industry: *Times*, 13.1.93. For industry policy by the early 1990s, Crafts in *The Major Effect*.

16 James Goldsmith, 1933– , Chief Executive successively Mothercare, Cavenham Foods, Bovril Group, Allied Supplies. *Counter Culture*, (1) 1985, (2) 1987, (3) 1990, (4) 1991. *Vision, Identity and Environment*, ASI, 1990.

17 Michael Edwardes, 1930– , Chair/Chief Executive Chloride 1968–77; Member, NEB 1975; Chair/Chief Executive British Leyland 1977–82; Chair, Charter Consolidated 1987– . *RSA Journal*, Aug. 1976; *The Dir*, Oct. 1980. *Back from the Brink*, London: Pan, 1984. Interview with Sir Michael Edwardes, May 1995.

18 Jeremy Morse, 1928– Executive Director of Bank of England 1965–72; Lloyds Bank Deputy Chair, 1975–77, Chair 1977–93; Chair, Committee of London Clearing Bankers 1980–82. *Bankers Magazine*, Jan. 1980, Nov. 1985, Jan. 1986; *FT* 19.3.82. Repeats call for a 'new system' of international co-operation for monetary stability, *FT* 14.4.83. Per Jacobssen Lecture 1985, Cardiff Business Club 23.3.87, Chartered Institute of Bankers 16.12.92, CABE 23.6.93. Interview with Sir Jeremy Morse.

19 Benson: evidence to Select Cttee 1985 and HOL debs 7.2.90; Eric Roll, *Crowded Hours*, London: Faber & Faber, 1985, HOL debs 23.1.85, 7.2.90; and Caldecote, HOL 28.11.91. A tripartite note was struck by Neil Johnson of the EEF: *Times* 21.10.93. Letter to Editor, *Times*, see 29 below.

20 Arthur Knight: 1917– Courtaulds, FinD 1961, Chair 1975–79; Chair, NEB 1979–80. *Private Enterprise and Public Intervention: the Courtaulds Experience*, 1974. Speeches: Long Range Planning Study 3.12.74; BIM 17.1.78. *FT* 12, 13 and 28.11, and 2 and 3.12. 1980. *Fiscal Studies*, March 1982; *Wilson Revisited: Industrialists and Financiers*, 1982; *Policy Studies*, April 1983. 'Proposals for an Industrial Policy Group', Nov. 1981, and 'Policy Issues for Industrialists', 1982: Knight Papers. Interview with Sir Arthur Knight.

21 E.g. Bryan Nicholson on 'too many companies' reinstating 'overbearing autocratic attitudes to their workforces' (*Involvement and Participation*, November 1983); Lord Sieff on too few leaders emphasising human relations (BIM Workshop, 1986); Lord Alexander of Weedon on the risk and limitations of small shareholding (Gilbart Lecture, 1991); Owen Green on defiance of 'feel-fair factor' over top rewards and 'free market disciples scoring own-goals' (*Times*, 27.2.95).

22 Lord (Hector) Laing: 1923– , United Biscuits, Managing Director 1964,

Chair 1972–90; Joint Treasurer, Conservative Party 1988–93; cr. 1991. *MT*, July 1972; *Industrial Participation*, autumn 1973; Evidence to Select Committee on Trade, April 1985. Ezra and Oates, *Advice from the Top*, 1989 Interview with Lord Laing.

23 HOL debs 5.5.93, 25.11.93. Cockett, *Thinking the Unthinkable*, pp. 276, 301. Interview with Lord Vinson.

24 *MT* March 1994. Alex Brummer and Roger Cowe, *Hanson, A Biography*, London: 1994, pp. 124–5, 189, 195, 210. Lord Young, *The Enterprise Years*, 1990. Also *The Director*, May 1987; 'Business is finally achieving the importance and status in the public eye that it deserves'. John Hoskyns: 'an economic miracle' and 'Britain's long debate on the future of capitalism is nearly over': *The Director*, May and July 1987.

25 Richard Giordano, IOD annual report 1982, report on 1983 convention.

26 Peter Walters, 1931– , BP from 1950, Managing Director 1973–90 and Chair 1981–90; Chair Midland Bank 1991–94; CBI PAC 1982–90; President, IOD 1986–92. IOD Annual Report 1982. *The Director*, May 1986. Interview with Sir Peter Walters.

27 CPS Annual Report 1994; AOI, '40 Years of Fighting for Free Enterprise'; ASI, 'Making Ideas Change the World'; Cockett, *Thinking the Unthinkable*, pp. 279, 285.

28 David Thomas, *Alan Sugar, The Amstrad Story*, London: Pan books, 1990.

29 *Times*, 1.3.92. Signatories included John Cuckney, Rocco Forte, Richard Giordano, Stanley Kalms, David Lees, Ian MacLaurin, Patrick Meaney, Nigel Mobbs, Geoffrey Mulcahy, Robert Scholey, Alan Sugar, Clive Thompson, Peter Walters.

30 Of thirty-six respondents, twelve were currently Chairman/Chief Executives of large companies; fourteen had held such positions, mostly in the recent past; while ten, generally overlapping with the last category, were currently Chm/C Es of medium or small concerns. Nineteen had held top roles in peak business bodies. Four fell into other core sample categories. Only nine had retired, though there was some bias to the older generation. Where possible responses were discussed in relation to public statements during the period or earlier. Ideology and opinion were not necessarily representative, though a wide spectrum was included.

31 Goyder re-edited his message in *The Just Enterprise*, 1987; Parker maintained his views but became a less prominent public figure; Villiers worked on regional job creation, dying in 1991; O'Brien was active on wide social issues; Catherwood became a leading MEP. Wilfred Brown had died in 1981.

32 John Harvey Jones, 1924– , ICI 1956. *Making it Happen*, 1988; *Getting it Together*, 1991; Dimbleby Lecture 1986; *RSA Journal*, May 1984 and May 1986.

33 Anita Roddick, 1942– , Founder and Managing Director Body Shop 1976– . *Body and Soul*, London: Ebury, 1991. Ezra and Oates, *Advice from the Top*, pp. 12–13.

34 Peter Thompson, 1928– , Unilever 1952–62; GKN 1962–4; Rank Organisation 1964–7; BSC 1967–75; Chair, NFC 1976–84. *Sharing the Success*, 1990. Interview with Sir Peter Thompson.

35 *MT*, May 1994.

36 *MT*, Jan. 1986; *The Dir*, Apr 1987; Ezra and Oates, *Advice from the Top*, pp. 124–37; Ian MacGregor, *The Enemies Within*, London: Collins, 1986; Thomas, *Alan Sugar*, p 258.

37 Cadbury, *The Company Chairman*, 1990. The Cadbury Committee Report: Financial Aspects of Corporate Governance, 1992.

38 RSA Inquiry, *Tomorrow's Company*, 1995. Programme for conference 29.1.96.

39 For example, Stephen O'Brien, Director of Business in the Community, 'I spend my time spreading the message that it is in the company's commercial interests to get involved in their communities': *Management Today*, August 1986.

40 IPA, *Towards Industrial Partnership*, 1993, endorsed *inter alia* by Anthony Cleaver, Harvey Jones, Bryan Nicholson, Bob Reid, David Sainsbury.

41 It is hard to see a major body sponsoring language like 'the cosy, self-adulating myth of a 'company image'' and 'too often an image of self-interest rather than service and duty' (John Garnett, *Industrial Society* May/June 1962), or implying wide justification of 'criticisms of the separation of ownership and control, directors not being supervised, alienation of the employee and interests of workers ignored' (CBI CAC Interim Report 1973), or exhorting business 'to foresee, relate and respond to changing perspectives of society, which question the economic results of business performance, the basis of managerial authority and the very purpose of business itself' (BIM, *Management in a Changing Society*, 1973).

42 *Bankers Magazine*, June 1987 and July 1988.

43 SGW Papers.

44 IBE Annual Report 1994. Current publications were on 'Company Philosophies', 'Codes of Ethics', 'Ethical Considerations in Take-Overs', and 'Environmental Issues'.

45 CBI, 'Vision 2010', 1987 (views of below-35 business leaders); BIM, 'Profile of British Industry – the Manager's View', Dec. 1987, BIM papers.

Bibliography

PRINCIPAL ARCHIVAL SOURCES

'Warwick' indicates Modern Records Centre, University of Warwick

FEDERATION OF BRITISH INDUSTRIES ARCHIVE (WARWICK)

Minutes of Grand Council 1960–65
Minutes of Economic Policy Committee 1960–65
Minutes of Economic Studies Committee 1960–65
Presidents' Papers: William MacFadzean 1959–61, Ernest Harrison 1961–63,
    Peter Runge 1963–65
Minutes of Committee on Economic Programmes and Targets 1961
Mathias, Peter, 'Industry and Government: The History of the Federation of
    British Industries, part 3, 1946–1966' (unpublished)

BRITISH EMPLOYERS' CONFEDERATION ARCHIVE (WARWICK)

Minutes of General Purposes Committee 1960–65
Minutes of Council 1961–65
Miscellaneous papers on industrial relations and incomes policy 1958–64

NATIONAL ASSOCIATION OF BRITISH MANUFACTURERS (WARWICK)

Minutes of Executive Committee 1960–65

CONFEDERATION OF BRITISH INDUSTRY ARCHIVE (WARWICK)

Minutes of Council 1965–1985
Minutes of Economic Policy Committee 1965–85
Minutes of Employment Policy Committee 1969–85
Minutes of Company Affairs Committee 1972–73
Minutes of Smaller Firms Council 1974–85
Minutes of President's Advisory Committee, 1976–85
Presidents' Papers: Sir Maurice Laing 1965–66; Sir Stephen Brown 1966–68;
    Sir Gerry Norman, 1968–1970, Sir John Partridge 1970–72, Sir Michael
    Clapham 1972–74
Director-General's Papers: John Davies 1965–69, Sir Campbell Adamson 1969–74
Social Affairs Directorate: Swinden Papers

INDUSTRIAL SOCIETY ARCHIVE (WARWICK)

INSTITUTE OF DIRECTORS ARCHIVE (INSTITUTE OF DIRECTORS, LONDON)

Minutes of Council 1960–1985
Minutes of Policy and Executive Committee 1960–1985
Minutes of Company Affairs Committee (various periods)
Miscellaneous policy papers 1979–86

BRITISH INSTITUTE OF MANAGEMENT ARCHIVES (INSTITUTE OF MANAGEMENT, LONDON)

Minutes of Council 1976–85
Minutes of Chairman's Committee 1976–85
Minutes of Economic and Social Affairs Committee 1976–85

CHURCHILL ARCHIVES CENTRE, CHURCHILL COLLEGE, CAMBRIDGE

Papers of Viscount Chandos
Papers of Rt Hon Aubrey Jones

THE NATIONAL LIFE STORY COLLECTION: CITY LIVES (LONDON)

Selected interviews

ST GEORGE'S HOUSE, WINDSOR

Consultations on 'Business Ethics' and 'Attitudes to Industry', 1967–92

PRIVATELY HELD PAPERS

Peter Askonas (Christian Association of Business Executives)
Mark Boleat (Industrial Policy Group)
Lord (Wilfred) Brown (courtesy of Lady Brown and Angus Brown)
Sir Arthur Knight
Sir Donald MacDougall
Sir Richard O'Brien
Sir John Partridge (courtesy of David and James Partridge)
Sir Charles Villiers (courtesy of Lady Villiers)

MAIN OFFICIAL PUBLICATIONS

House of Lords, *Debates* (Fifth Series) 1960–1993
Royal Commission on Trades Unions and Employers Associations (Donovan) 1965–68, *Minutes of Evidence and Report*
Royal Commission on Distribution of Wealth (Diamond) 1974–76, *Minutes of Evidence and Report*

House of Lords Select Committee on Overseas Trade (Aldington) 1984–85, *Minutes of Evidence and Report*

WORKS BY BUSINESS LEADERS

Bader, Ernest, *From Profit Sharing to Common Ownership*, Wellingborough, Scott Bader Commonwealth, 1956–57

Barford, Edward, *A Lance-Corporal of Industry*, London: Elm Tree Books, 1972

Beeching, Lord (Richard), 'Government and Management', Oration at the London School of Economics, 8 Dec. 1966

Benson, Henry, *Accounting for Life*, London: Kogan Page, 1989

Bloom, John, *It's no Sin to Make a Profit*, London: W. H. Allen, 1971

Bolton, George, *A Banker's World: The Revival of the City 1957–70, Speeches and Writings of Sir George Bolton*, ed. Richard Fry, London: Hutchinson, 1970

Broackes, Nigel, *A Growing Concern*, London: Weidenfeld & Nicolson, 1979

Brown, Wilfred, *Piecework Abandoned*, London: Heinemann, 1971
  Inflation and a Possible Solution, privately published, London, 1972
  The Earnings Conflict: Proposals for Tackling the Emerging Crisis of Industrial Relations, Unemployment and Wage Inflation, London: Heinemann, 1973

Brown, Wilfred, and Hirsch-Weber, Wolfgang, *Bismarck to Bullock, Conversations about Institutions in Politics and Industry in Britain and Germany*, London, Anglo-German Foundation, 1983

Cadbury, Adrian, *The Company Chairman*, London: Director Books in association with Institute of Directors, 1990.

Campbell of Eskan, Lord (Jock), 'Private Enterprise and Public Morality', *New Statesman*, 27 May 1966

Catherwood, Fred, *The Christian in Industrial Society*, London: Tyndale Press, 1964
  A Better Way: The Case for a Christian Social Order, Leicester: Inter-Varsity Press, 1975
  Pro-Europe?, Leicester: Inter-Varsity Press, 1991
  At the Cutting Edge, London: Hodder & Stoughton, 1995

Chambers, Paul, 'A Business View', in *Businessmen, Economists and Government*, Institute of Economic Affairs, 1965
  'Introduction', in Vera Lutz, *Central Planning for the Market Economy*, London: Institute of Economic Affairs/Longman, 1968

Chandler, Geoffrey, 'The Political Process and the Decline of Industry', *Three Banks Review*, March 1984
  'Britain's Industrial Crisis: Sacred Cows or Real Solutions?', *Royal Society of Arts Journal*, Oct. 1987

Chandos, Lord (Oliver), *Memoirs*, London: Bodley Head, 1962

Clapham, Michael, *Multinational Enterprises and Nation States*, London: Athlone Press, 1975

Corfield, Kenneth, *Business Responsibilities*, Foundation for Business Responsibilities, 1972
  Science, Politics and Industrial Policy, University of Southampton, 1983

Courtauld, Samuel, *Ideals and Industry*, Cambridge: Cambridge University Press, 1949

Davenport, Nicholas, *The Split Society*, London: Victor Gollancz, 1964
  Memoirs of a City Radical, London: Weidenfeld & Nicolson, 1974
Davies, John, *Industry and Government*, Foundation for Business Responsibilities, 1967
Drogheda, Lord, *Double Harness*, London: Weidenfeld & Nicolson, 1978
Duncan, Val, *Is Democracy in its Present Form making the Efficient Working of the Capitalist System Impossible?*, London: Rio Tinto Inc., 1973
Edwardes, Michael, 'Government and Industry: Some Strategic Issues', *RSA Journal*, August 1976
  Back from the Brink: An Apocalyptic Experience, London: Pan, 1984
Federation of British Industry, *Britain's Economic Problems and Policies*, FBI, 1957
Finniston, Montague, *The World an Oyster and Industry the Pearl*, University of Birmingham, 1979
Forte, Lord (Charles), *My Autobiography*, London: Sidgwick & Jackson, 1986
Fraser, Lionel, *All to the Good*, London: Heinemann, 1963
Garnett, John, *The Work Challenge: Leaders at Work*, London: The Industrial Society, 1973
Geddes, Reay, *In Pursuit of Prosperity*, Address to the Institute of Transport, 2 February 1960, privately printed, 1960
Goldsmith, Walter (with D. Clutterbuck), *The Winning Streak*, London: Weidenfeld & Nicolson, 1984
Goldsmith, Walter (with Berry Ritchie), *The New Elite*, London: Weidenfeld & Nicolson, 1987
Gollancz, Victor, *Reminiscences of Affection*, London: Gollancz, 1968
Goodison, Nicholas, 'How City and Industry can Close Ranks', *Management Today*, May 1981
  Shares for All: Steps towards a Share-owning Society, London: Centre for Policy Studies, 1986
Goyder, George, *The Future of Private Enterprise*, Oxford: Blackwell, 1951
  The Responsible Company, Oxford: Blackwell, 1961
  The Responsible Worker, London: Hutchinson, 1975
  The Just Enterprise, London: André Deutsch, 1987
  Signs of Grace, with additional chapters by Rosemary Goyder, London: Cygnet Press, 1993
Heron, Thomas, 'Man at Work', in M. B. Reckitt (ed.), *Prospect for Christendom, Essays in Catholic Social Reconstruction*, London: Faber & Faber, 1945
  'The Idea of Equality in Industry', Church Union Summer School of Sociology, July, 1961
Hooper, F. C., *Management Survey*, 1948; 2nd edn, London: Pitman & Son, 1961
  'The Function of Management in Industry and Commerce', *The Royal Society of Arts Journal*, vol. 108
Jones, John Harvey, *Making it Happen: Reflections on Leadership*, London: Collins, 1988
  Getting it Together, London: Heinemann, 1991
Kearton, Lord (Frank), Size and Efficiency in Business, address to the Bradford Textile Society annual meeting, 10 January 1966, privately printed, n/d
Kinross, John, *Fifty Years in the City: Financing Small Business*, London: John Murray, 1982

Kipping, Norman, *Summing Up,* London: Hutchinson, 1972
Kirzner, Israel *et al., The Prime Mover of Progress: The Entrepreneur in Capitalism and Socialism,* IEA, 1980, essays by Vinson, MacFadzean and Knight
Knight, Arthur, *Private Enterprise and Public Intervention: the Courtaulds Experience,* London: Allen & Unwin, 1974
'UK Industry in the Eighties', *Fiscal Studies,* March 1981
Wilson Revisited: Industrialists and Financiers, London: Policy Studies Institute, 1982
'Ideas and Action: How to Improve Industrial Performance', *Policy Studies,* 1983
Knox, Andrew, *Coming Clean: A Postscript After Retiring from Unilever,* London: Heinemann, 1976
Laing, Hector, *The Balance of Responsibility,* United Biscuits, 1987
A Parting Shot, United Biscuits, 1990
Lazell, Leslie, *From Pills to Penicillin: The Beecham Story,* London: Heinemann, 1975
Lipman, M. I., *Memoirs of a Socialist Business Man,* London: Lipman Trust, 1980
McClelland, W. Grigor, *And a New Earth,* London: Friends Home Service Committee, 1976
MacFadzean, Frank, *Galbraith and the Planners,* Glasgow: University of Strathclyde, 1968
J. K. Galbraith: A Study in Fantasy, London: Centre for Policy Studies, 1978
MacGregor, Ian, *The Enemies Within,* London: Collins, 1986
Marsh, Richard, *Off the Rails: An Autobiography,* London: Weidenfeld & Nicolson, 1978
Neal, Leonard (ed.), *Liberties and Liabilities,* London: Centre for Policy Studies, 1980
O'Brien, Richard, *Education, Industry and People,* University of Birmingham, 1978
Orr, David, 'An Industrial Strategy: Help or Hindrance?' *RSA Journal,* January 1982
Parker, Peter, *A New Industrial Polity,* Stamp Memorial Lecture, 1977
'1994', First Lubbock Lecture on Management, Eglaw, Surrey: Maurice Lubbock Memorial Fund, 1980
Missing our Connections, Richard Dimbleby Lecture, March 1983, London: BBC, 1983
For Starters: The Business of Life, London: Jonathan Cape, 1989
Pasold, Eric, *Ladybird Ladybird: A Story of Private Enterprise,* Manchester: Manchester University Press, 1977
Robens, Alfred, *Human Engineering,* London: Jonathan Cape, 1970
Industry and Government, Foundation for Business Responsibilities, 1970
Ten Year Stint, London: Cassell, 1972
Managing Great Britain Ltd. Ashridge Lecture 1976, Ashridge Management College, 1977
Roddick, Anita, *Body and Soul,* London: Ebury, 1991
Roll, Eric, *Crowded Hours,* London: Faber & Faber, 1985
Schumacher, Ernest F., *Small is Beautiful,* London: Blond and Briggs, 1973
Shone, Robert, *Problems of Investment,* Oxford: Basil Blackwell, 1971
Price and Investment Relationships, London: Paul Elek, 1975

Sieff, Lord (Israel), *Memoirs*, London: Weidenfeld & Nicolson, 1970

Sieff of Brimpton, Lord (Marcus), *Don't Ask the Price*, London: Fontana/Collins, 1987

'The Responsibilities of Business Management', *RSA Journal*, October 1966

Slater, Jim, *Return to Go, My Autobiography*, London: Weidenfeld & Nicolson, 1977

The Zulu Principle, London: Orion, 1992

Smallpeice, Basil, *Of Comets and Queens*, Shrewsbury: Airlife, 1981

Thompson, Peter, *Sharing the Success: The Story of NFC*, London: Collins, 1990

Villiers, Charles, *Start Again, Britain*, London: Quartet, 1984.

Beyond the Sunset, Stoke Abbott: Thos. Harmsworth Publishing Company, 1992

Vinson, Nigel, 'Shifting Power to Working People', *Industrial Participation*, Summer 1978,

Owners All, London: Centre for Policy Studies, 1985

Vinson, Nigel, and Wassall, M., *Why Britain Needs a Social Market Economy*, London: Centre for Policy Studies, 1975

Watkinson, Viscount (Harold), *Blueprint for Industrial Survival: What has Gone Wrong in Industrial Britain since the War*, London: Allen & Unwin, 1976

Are Business and Politics Compatible? Ashridge Management College, 1980

Turning Points: A Record of Our Times, Salisbury, Wilts: Michael Russell (Publishing) Ltd, 1986

Jewels and Old Shoes, privately printed, 1990

Weeks, Hugh, *Economic Comments, 1979–85*, London: Leopold Joseph and Sons Ltd, n/d

Young, David, Lord Young of Graffham, *The Enterprise Years: A Businessman in the Cabinet*, London: Headline, 1990

BOOKS ON BUSINESS LEADERS, FIRMS AND INDUSTRIES

Attali, Jacques, *A Man of Influence: Sir Siegmund Warburg 1902–1982*, London: Weidenfeld & Nicolson, 1986

Bower, Tom, *Tiny Rowland, A Rebel Tycoon*, London: Mandarin, 1993

Bower, Tom, *Maxwell, The Outsider*, London: Mandarin, 1988

Brummer, Alex, and Cowe, Roger, *Hanson, A Biography*, London: Fourth Estate, 1994

Clegg, Hugh, *The Employers' Challenge: A History of the National Shipbuilding and Engineering Disputes of 1957*, Oxford: Oxford University Press, 1957

Coleman, D. C., *Courtaulds, vol. 3: Crisis and Change, 1940–65*, Oxford: Clarendon Press, 1969

Corina, Maurice, *Pile it High, Sell it Cheap, The Authorised Biography of Sir John Cohen, Founder of Tesco*, London: Weidenfeld & Nicolson, 1971

Dudley, Geoffrey F., and Richardson, Jeremy J., *Politics and Steel in Britain 1967–1988: The Life and Times of the BSC*, Aldershot: Dartmouth, 1990

Edwards, Ruth Dudley, *Victor Gollancz*, London: Gollancz, 1987

Evans, Harold, *Vickers, Against the Odds 1956–77*, London: Hodder and Stoughton, 1978

Ezra, Derek, and Oates, David, *Advice from the Top: The Business Strategies of Britain's Corporate Leaders*, Newton Abbott: David and Charles, 1989

Fallon, Ivan, *Billionaire, The Life and Times of Sir James Goldsmith*, London: Hutchinson, 1991

The Brothers,The Rise and Rise of Saatchi and Saatchi, London: Hutchinson, 1988

Gourvish, T. R., *British Railways 1948–1973: A Business History*, Cambridge: Cambridge University Press, 1986

Hall, Richard, *My Life with Tiny,A Biography of Tiny Rowland*, London: Faber & Faber, 1987

Hannah, Leslie, *Engineers, Managers and Politicians:The First 15Years of Nationalised Electricity Supply in Britain*, London: Macmillan, 1982

Jeremy, David, *Capitalists and Christians: Business Leaders and the Churches in Britain 1900–1960*, Oxford: Oxford University Press, 1990

Jeremy, David, and Tweedale, Geoffrey, *Dictionary of Twentieth Century British Business Leaders*, London: Bowker Saur, 1994.

Jones, Robert, and Marriott, Oliver, *Anatomy of a Merger:A History of GEC,AEI and EE*, London: Jonathan Cape, 1976

Lewis, R. and Stewart, R., *The Boss:The Life and Times of the British Business Man*, London: J. M. Dent and Sons Ltd, 1958

Miller, Harry, *The Way of Enterprise*, London: André Deutsch, 1962

O'Sullivan, Timothy, *Julian Hodge, a Biography*, London: Routledge & Kegan Paul, 1981

Ovenden, Keith, *The Politics of Steel*, London: Macmillan, 1978

Raw, Charles, *Slater Walker:An Investigation of a Financial Phenomenon*, London: André Deutsch, 1977

Reader,W. J., *ICI:A History*, vol. 3, London: Oxford University Press, 1976

Rees, Goronwy, *St Michael,A History of Marks and Spencer*, London: Weidenfeld & Nicolson, 1969

Reid, Margaret, *All-Change in the City:The Revolution in Britain's Financial Sector*, Basingstoke: Macmillan, 1988

Smith, Chris, Child, John, and Rowlinson, Michael, *Reshaping Work:The Cadbury Experience*, Cambridge: Cambridge University Press, 1990

Thomas, David, *Alan Sugar,The Amstrad Story*, London: Pan Books, 1991

Tse, K. K. *Marks and Spencer: Anatomy of Britain's Most Efficiently Managed Company*, Oxford: Pergamon, 1985

Turner, Graham, *The Leyland Papers*, London: Eyre & Spottiswoode, 1971

Windle, Ralph, *The Poetry of Business Life:An Anthology*, San Francisco: Berrett-Koehler, 1994

Young, Stephen, and Hood, Neil, *Chrysler UK:A Corporation in Transition*, New York: Praeger, 1977

PRINCIPAL GENERAL SOURCES

Bacon, Robert, and Eltis, Walter, *Britain's Economic Problem: Too Few Producers*, London: Macmillan, 1976

Beckerman, W. (ed.), *The Labour Government's Economic Record 1964–1970*, London: Duckworth, 1972

Beer, Samuel, *Britain Against Itself*, London: Faber & Faber, 1982

Blackaby, F. (ed.), *British Economic Policy 1960–1974*, Cambridge: Cambridge University Press, 1978

Brittan, Samuel, *Steering the Economy,* revised edition, Harmondsworth: Penguin, 1971

Britton, Andrew, *Macro-Economic Policy in Britain 1974–87,* Cambridge: Cambridge University Press, 1991

Brown, Henry Phelps, 'A Non-Monetarist View of the Pay Explosion', *Three Banks Review,* March 1975

Cairncross, Alec, *The British Economy since 1945: Economic Policy and Performance 1945–1990,* Oxford: Blackwell, 1992

Campbell, John, *Edward Heath,* London: Jonathan Cape, 1993

Clegg, Hugh, *The System of Industrial Relations in Britain,* 2nd edn, Oxford: Oxford University Press, 1972

Cockett, Richard, *Thinking the Unthinkable: Think-Tanks and the Economic Counter-Revolution 1931–1983,* London: HarperCollins, 1994

Crouch, Colin, and Dore, Ronald, *Corporatism and Accountability: Organised Interests in British Public Life,* Oxford: Clarendon Press, 1990

Dell, Edmund, *A Hard Pounding: Politics and Economic Crisis 1974–1976,* Oxford: Oxford University Press, 1991

Donoughue, Bernard, *Prime Minister, The Conduct of Policy under Harold Wilson and James Callaghan,* London: Jonathan Cape, 1987

Drucker, Peter, *The Practice of Management,* London: Heinemann, 1955

Gilmour, *Dancing with Dogma: Britain under Thatcherism,* London and New York: Simon & Schuster, 1992

Grant, Wyn, and Marsh, David, *The CBI,* London: Hodder & Stoughton, 1977

Grant, Wyn, and Sargent, Jane, *Business and Politics in Britain,* Basingstoke and London: Macmillan, 1987

Hanscher, Leigh, and Moran, Michael (eds.), *Capitalism, Culture and Economic Regulation,* Oxford: Clarendon, 1989

Hawkins, K., *British Industrial Relations, 1945–1975,* London: Barrie and Jenkins, 1976

Healey, Denis, *The Time of My Life,* London: Michael Joseph, 1989

Holmes, Martin, *The First Thatcher Government 1979–1983,* London: Macmillan, 1985

Hoover, Kenneth, and Plant, Raymond, *Conservative Capitalism in Britain and the U.S. A Critical Appraisal,* London: Routledge, 1989

Johnman, Lewis, 'The Conservative Party in Opposition 1964–1970 in R. Coopey, S. Fielding and N. Tiratsoo (eds.), *The Wilson Governments 1964–1970,* London: Pinter, 1993

Johnson, Christopher, *The Economy under Mrs Thatcher 1979–1990,* London: Penguin 1991

Jones, Tudor, *Remaking the Labour Party: From Gaitskell to Blair,* London: Routledge, 1996

Kavanagh, Denis, and Seldon, Anthony (eds.), *The Major Effect,* London: Macmillan, 1994

Kessler, Sid, and Bayliss, Fred, *Contemporary British Industrial Relations,* London: Macmillan, 1992

Lawson, Nigel, *The View from No.11: Memoirs of a Tory Radical,* London: Corgi, 1993

Middlemas, Keith, *Politics in Industrial Society: The Experience of the British System since 1911,* London: André Deutsch, 1979

Power, Competition and the State, 3 vols., Basingstoke: Macmillan, 1986–1991

Industry, Unions and Government: Twenty-one years of NEDC, Basingstoke: Macmillan, 1983

Pimlott, Ben, *HaroldWilson,* London: HarperCollins, 1992

Prior, James, *A Balance of Power,* London: Hamish Hamilton, 1986

Riddell, Peter, *The Thatcher Decade: How Britain has Changed during the 1980s,* Oxford: Blackwell, 1989

Shonfield, Andrew, *British Economic Policy Since the War,* Harmondsworth: Penguin, 1958

Modern Capitalism: The Changing Balance of Public and Private Power, London: Oxford University Press, 1965

Skidelsky, Robert (ed.), *Thatcherism,* London: Chatto and Windus, 1988

Stewart, Michael, *Politics and Economic Policy in the UK since 1964: The Jekyll and Hyde Years:* Oxford: Oxford University Press, 1977

Useem, Michael, *The Inner Circle: Large Corporations and the Rise of Business Political Activity in the US and UK,* Oxford: Oxford University Press, 1984

Van Schendelen, M. C. P. M., and Jackson, R. J. (eds.), *The Politicisation of Business in Western Europe,* London: Croom Helm, 1987

Wigham, Eric, *The Power to Manage: A History of the Engineering Employers' Federation,* London and Basingstoke: Macmillan, 1973

Wilson, Graham, *Business and Politics: A Comparative Introduction,* London: Macmillan, 1985

Index